SONS OF PRIVILEGE

SONS OF PRIVILEGE

The Charleston Light Dragoons
in the Civil War

W. ERIC EMERSON

University of South Carolina Press

Published in Columbia, South Carolina,
by the University of South Carolina Press

Manufactured in the United States of America

09 08 07 06 05   5 4 3 2 1

Library of Congress Cataloging-in-Publication Data

Emerson, W. Eric, 1966–
  Sons of privilege : the Charleston Light Dragoons in the Civil War / W. Eric
Emerson.
    p. cm.
  Includes bibliographical references and index.
  ISBN 1-57003-592-X (cloth : alk. paper)
  1. Confederate States of America. Army. South Carolina Cavalry Regiment, 4th.
Company K. 2. Charleston (S.C.)—History—Civil War, 1861–1865—Regimental
histories. 3. South Carolina—History—Civil War, 1861–1865—Regimental
histories. 4. United States—History—Civil War, 1861–1865—Regimental histories.
5. Soldiers—South Carolina—Charleston—History—19th century. 6. Upper class
—South Carolina—Charleston—History—19th century. 7. Charleston (S.C.)—
History—Civil War, 1861–1865—Social aspects. 8. South Carolina—History—
Civil War, 1861–1865—Social aspects. 9. United States—History—Civil War,
1861–1865—Social aspects. 10. United States—History—Civil War, 1861–1865
—Cavalry operations. I. Title.
E577.64th .E44 2005
973.7'457—dc22
                                                                              2005013005

For my parents

CONTENTS

ILLUSTRATIONS

Figures

Maps

Tables

ACKNOWLEDGMENTS

I am deeply indebted to a number of people who assisted me with this project and the dissertation that preceded it. First and foremost, I would like to thank the staff and board of managers of the South Carolina Historical Society, who patiently tolerated my academic pursuits and aided me whenever possible. My thanks also go to the editorial board of the *South Carolina Historical Magazine,* whose collegial discussions provided me with a welcome respite from my editorial responsibilities and with much needed academic insight.

A number of individuals and institutions provided invaluable assistance while I researched this book. In particular, Michael Coker was always quick to provide me with information about the Charleston Light Dragoons while he researched topics of his own interest. His knowledge of available visual materials at the South Carolina Historical Society was indispensable. Nicholas Butler and Karen Stokes both led me to unprocessed and seldom utilized materials in those same collections, which allowed me to incorporate documents that I otherwise might have missed. I also am grateful to longtime historical society member Robert Cuthbert, who patiently and graciously shared his insights regarding his own research on prominent lowcountry families. In addition, Randolph Kirkland was a wonderful source of information concerning the Kirkland family and its rich history. He and his wife, Patricia, were always gracious hosts on my visits to Magnolia Hall, and I rank my time spent there as some of my most enjoyable in South Carolina.

Allen Stokes and the staff of the South Caroliniana Library, Tracy Power and Patrick McCawley at the South Carolina Department of Archives and History, the staff of the University of North Carolina's Southern Historical Collection, the staff of Duke University's Rare Book, Manuscript, and Special Collections Library, Allen Roberson and the South Carolina Confederate Relic Room and Museum, and Sharon Bennett and the Charleston Museum—all provided valuable assistance in locating materials. I also would like to thank Robert Krick, retired chief historian of the Fredericksburg-Spotsylvania National Military Park, Wilber E. Meneray of Special Collections at the Tulane University Library, Weston Adams, Paul Gervais Bell Jr., Russell Case, William H. Chandler, Allen Miles, Benjamin Allston Moore Jr., and Elizabeth Settle for their assistance in finding information that I might otherwise have overlooked. I wish to thank Shanna McGarry, Jessica Stephens, and John B. Waring for their assistance with the maps. My gratitude also goes to Gordon Rhea for his assistance with the chapter involving the Overland Campaign, and to Dr. Alexander Moore, who read the manuscript and provided me with countless suggestions regarding sources and content.

I owe much to Lawrence F. Kohl and the members of my dissertation committee, who read this manuscript in an earlier form. Larry read drafts of my dissertation and always returned them quickly with insightful commentary. Howard Jones, Richard Megraw, and Kari Frederickson took time from their busy schedules to read the dissertation and provided valuable comments and suggestions. Furthermore, I would like to extend my gratitude to the faculty, staff, and graduate students of The University of Alabama's history department, which gave me four years of intellectual stimulation and many fond memories.

My deepest gratitude goes to George C. Rable, who directed my dissertation. He found merit in a topic that many would have disregarded, and he patiently and reassuringly guided me through countless drafts, which he quickly returned for revision. It has been a pleasure and honor to be associated with him.

Finally, I would like to thank my family. My wife, Cathy, patiently provided support during difficult times and gentle prodding when I lost focus. During the course of my work on this project, we had two beautiful daughters, Grace and Claire, who have inspired me to be a better historian and, I hope, a better person. To these women in my life, I owe much. For their smiles, laughter, affection, and love, I am eternally grateful.

INTRODUCTION

> For the ashes of his fathers,
> And the Temples of his Gods.
> *Inscription, Charleston Light*
> *Dragoons Monument*

Magnolia Cemetery is the most prominent Civil War burial site in Charleston, South Carolina. It is situated on the western bank of the Cooper River, an oasis of natural beauty among the tank farms and warehouses that characterize the neck of the Charleston peninsula. Among the cemetery's moss-draped live oaks stands an obelisk of native stone commemorating the wartime deeds of the Charleston Light Dragoons, one of the city's most prominent militia organizations. Most visitors to the cemetery would notice nothing unusual about this Confederate marker. On closer investigation, however, they would see that it is set apart from the majority of Confederate graves and monuments. So, too, did the unit's members set themselves apart from their comrades while they lived, choosing instead to associate with and fight alongside men of their own social background.[1]

This longstanding cavalry troop originated in a city with a large and disparate population, but the unit's members overwhelmingly represented a single group: the city's (and the region's) economic and social elite. Its members carried the surnames of antebellum Charleston's oldest and most prominent families. The sons, nephews, and cousins of the state's largest planters and slave owners filled the company's ranks. Beside them stood the sons of the lowcountry's wealthiest factors and merchants, men who had reaped great profits from their business dealings with planters.

At the outset of the Civil War, Charleston's planters, factors, and merchants, long since mutually dependent, overwhelmingly supported the fledgling Confederacy. As proof of their resolve, they sent their fathers and sons to join the Charleston Light Dragoons. These newest members, like the unit's prewar veterans, stood to gain the most from secession and lose the most should the experiment in Southern nationalism fail. The wartime service of so many men of wealth undercuts notions of the Civil War as a "rich man's war, a poor man's fight."[2]

This is not to argue that those who joined the company during the war did so without considering self-interest. For the dragoons, the Confederacy's survival was closely tied to their privileged existence. Their families had amassed fortunes at the expense of the enslaved men and women who toiled in the rice and cotton fields, along the city's wharves, and in its largest homes. The vast concentration of slaves in the lowcountry was a constant and sometimes frightening reminder of the institution that drove the region's economy.[3] Without slavery the dragoons would have lacked the necessary wealth to maintain their position at the top of the lowcountry's economic and social ladder. Their service, therefore, was a tangible means of protecting a way of life that they and their ancestors had long enjoyed.

Those who filled the ranks of the Charleston Light Dragoons were men of privilege, men who according to the dictionary's definition of privilege were granted both "rights and immunity" as a benefit of their "peculiar positions." Their surnames and their social, political, and financial status afforded them both tangible and intangible benefits. These factors worked to the dragoons' advantage because there were substantial numbers of Charlestonians, South Carolinians, and others willing to acknowledge and facilitate the special treatment of these men and their families.

Historians have argued that the centrality of privilege declined with the end of the American Revolution and the beginnings of the new republic.[4] In South Carolina and especially in the lowcountry, however, concepts of prerogative still resonated on the eve of the Civil War. One historian has argued that privilege survived in South Carolina because slavery created an environment that allowed "every white to assume a minimal class superiority," which "maintained for an unusual length of time the deference of less fortunate whites toward the more privileged planter class."[5] In Charleston and the lowcountry, the social elite or "better sort" modeled their behavior on the example of landed British aristocracy. In New England, the Protestant work ethic that "frowned on conspicuous consumption and paid homage to the dignity of work" was much more prevalent than in the South. The economic gap between rich and poor was greater than in the North, largely due to the high number of slaves that lived on the region's plantations.[6] In 1860, however, few areas of the South had as large a slave population as the lowcountry, meaning that the overwhelming majority of the region's residents played some type of subservient role.[7]

Charleston assumed a major role in transplanting concepts of prerogative to other areas of the state because it set the social and political tone for South Carolina. When cotton cultivation and slavery spread to the backcountry after the Revolution, lowcountry planters owned many of the new plantations.[8] Ideas of deference and privilege therefore traveled with them to the interior.

Privilege was a condition to which the dragoons had been born and had become accustomed. Consumption of fine wine and food, as well as leisure and travel, formed the texture of daily life. But there was also a languor to this existence, a boredom that could be maddening on a warm summer's afternoon. Many who joined the dragoons had crafted lives in which they awaited the next big event, an opportunity to move beyond the routine of the counting house or plantation and beyond the parties of another Charleston social season. Military service for these men allowed them to serve the Confederacy, the government that would protect their wealth and way of life, while simultaneously providing them with an escape from their everyday existence.

For the Charleston Light Dragoons, however, the transition to military life was less dramatic than for the typical Confederate unit. The dragoons were widely reputed to be "a company of gentlemen," and their Civil War service was, like their antebellum existence, "privileged." This military manifestation of prerogative is what set the Charleston Light Dragoons apart. When South Carolinians held important Confederate military positions during the war, they extended to the dragoons the same privileges that these men had enjoyed in their antebellum lives. Commanders from other parts of the Confederacy followed suit, so the antebellum status of unit members dictated the terms of their military service.

The service experiences of the Charleston Light Dragoons, therefore, were an anomaly in the more broadly democratic military experience of the Civil War and, more important, in the egalitarian American military tradition. For the most part, service during the Civil War threw together men from different social and economic experiences in both armies. In these units, men of disparate backgrounds found common cause in the protection of liberty and other values shared by white Southerners.[9] Unlike these other units, however, the dragoons were not a unit constituted from men of all classes and professions. The company was for the most part a socially homogenous unit. Service in the Charleston Light Dragoons allowed members to stand in the ranks with others of their own social and economic position. For much of the war, service in the dragoons was less arduous and dangerous than duty with other Confederate units, but it still qualified as service to the Confederacy. Few other units in the Confederate armies embodied so completely the wealth of the planter class; none were more intimately tied to the birthplace of secession. The dragoons represented the elite of Charleston and the lowcountry and, in their own opinion, the region's most valuable citizens.

Instead of weakening the unit's feelings of self-importance, the dragoons' Civil War service in fact reinforced it. This attitude of superiority was not born of confidence gained in intense training or from acts of bravery and solidarity on the battlefield. Rather, it was the result of a system of prerogatives and patronage so pervasive that it permeated many elements of the Confederate military establishment. Where else in nineteenth-century America could an entire unit be shielded from military rules and the worst hardships of military service because of its members' surnames or their political and social positions?

And yet the dragoons and their families believed in the principle of service to protect the advantages they enjoyed. Noblesse oblige (literally nobility obligates), the concept that those associated with high rank or birth are obligated to behave honorably, was a very tangible principle to company members. It was related to the idea of "gentility," which one historian has called "a more specialized, refined form of honor, in which moral uprightness was coupled with high social position."[10] For these men and those who knew them, there was no question that they were of high social standing, and there was little question that they were obligated to serve the state and the Confederacy. Honor of a more primitive form also dictated that they serve in a martial capacity. As gentlemen, affronts to their honor could and did result in duels. So enraptured were they and others of their class with dueling that it became a consuming interest to some.[11] Therefore, for the city's elite, it was a rich man's war *and* a rich man's fight.[12]

The concept of privilege, more than any other factor, dictated the dragoons' role in the Civil War. Commanders shielded the dragoons from the most distasteful aspects of service for much of the war. They lived an existence far less strenuous or dangerous than the typical Confederate soldier. Their prerogative, however, did not remain intact throughout the war. Military exigencies strained the bonds between the state's most prominent leaders, forcing them to make decisions that would affect the fates of friends, relatives, and associates. They expended men of less illustrious backgrounds until forced to call upon this "company of gentlemen" to do the work of their social inferiors. For the dragoons, the Southern rhetoric that extolled the gentleman cavalier and noblesse oblige forced them to set unrealistic expectations for their actions in combat. Mere service was not sufficient: they were expected to display courage equal to their social stature.[13] The dragoons could logically point to their patriotic motives, especially given their membership in a class of Southerners that had been among the most adamant in defending Southern rights against both the threats of the North and the moderation of the upper South.[14] When combined with their notions of noblesse oblige and combat inexperience, these factors led the dragoons to fight with more bravery than discretion in large battles, thus suffering heavy losses. By 1865, only a handful remained.

At war's end, little was left of the system of privilege that had protected the unit for so long. Those who survived the struggle returned to a city no longer controlled by their families, friends, or closest associates. From this state of affairs, the survivors of the dragoons and other sons of privilege endeavored to once again create a place for themselves. Charleston's former elite revived the organizations that had been arbiters of status and privilege.[15]

For the dragoons and those younger men who served in the company after the war, however, the unit's combat record was the most remarkable aspect of its reputation. The unit's historian, Edward L. Wells, wrote much about its origins in an attempt to extol and preserve the noble virtues of the planter class.[16] His words inspired future generations of dragoons to serve their country in places as far away as Mexico and France. No subsequent conflict, however, defined the public perception of the dragoons like the Civil War. In a brief time its members were transformed from wealthy dilettantes to hardened veterans, from sons of privilege to heirs of a ruined city.

SONS OF PRIVILEGE

Chapter 1

ORIGINS IN PRIVILEGE

To investigate the character and qualifications of such applicants. . . .
Rule 8, Revised Constitution, Charleston Light Dragoons

During the first two centuries of the existence of Charleston, South Carolina, its citizens organized numerous militia companies. One such company was the Charleston Light Dragoons. Founded on July 10, 1792, the dragoons were one of the city's oldest militia companies, though the unit did not adopt a constitution until July 15, 1835.[1] By the beginning of the Civil War, the dragoons had gained a reputation as an elite organization, owing more to its members' social and economic status than to its antebellum service record. Unit members took pride in their honored position in South Carolina's militia and enjoyed numerous advantages over service in less socially prominent units.[2]

Not unlike other volunteers, the men who joined the dragoons before the war had mixed motives. Membership in the unit was often social. Dragoons enjoyed camaraderie, strong drink, and good food. Most men likely coveted the added prestige that accompanied membership in such a renowned organization. Finally, but by no means least important, was the sense of satisfaction that members gained by serving to protect fellow Charlestonians from enemies near and far. Moreover, the dragoons believed that their unique circumstances entitled them to preeminent status among militia companies, an attitude that the unit's members, and many of the wealthiest South Carolinians, helped perpetuate.

The Charleston Light Dragoons also had the obvious advantage of hailing from South Carolina's most important city. English settlers founded Charles Town in 1670, and by the eve of the American Revolution, the city was at the peak of her wealth and prestige as one of the richest in the British Empire.[3] From Charleston, the lowcountry's crops—rice, indigo, and Sea Island cotton —departed, and consumer goods and large numbers of slaves arrived. Rice was the region's most profitable and important export, and the crop's cultivation was labor intensive and required large numbers of slaves. As early as 1708 slaves outnumbered the colony's white inhabitants, and their presence shaped the colony's future.[4]

Rice cultivation not only provided great wealth for planters, but it also generated huge profits for many Charleston merchants and the factors who served them. These men quickly invested their commissions in business. In doing so they invested in Charleston's booming economy and accumulated enough assets to establish themselves as "gentlemen-planters" in the surrounding countryside. Consequently, quick wealth allowed merchants to rise to the status of the planters, their former customers.[5]

This newfound wealth for planters and merchants created an economic and social elite that often solidified its status through intermarriage. By the mid-1700s a series of tightly bound groups were forming along the rivers and in the towns of the lowcountry.[6] Land holdings in four districts of South Carolina —Charleston, Beaufort, Colleton, and Georgetown—were the source of these groups' great wealth.

Charleston District, in addition to being the seat of government for the City of Charleston, was also home to a number of plantations along the Ashley and Cooper rivers and their tributaries. By 1860 many of these plantations were no longer producing large crops of rice but, instead, served as nearby country homes for large planters.

In Colleton District, which was located to the south and west of Charleston, planters established rice plantations throughout the Ashepoo, Combahee, and Edisto rivers basin. The marshlands formed by these and other rivers in the district created an environment perfectly suited for rice cultivation on large plantations. Colleton District was also home to a number of plantations where Sea Island cotton was the most profitable crop.[7]

Farther to the south, in Beaufort District, the numerous rivers and tidal marshes bordered by the Savannah and Combahee rivers also provided an excellent environment for the cultivation of rice and Sea Island cotton. Beginning in the 1820s rice cultivation moved along the eastern bank of the Savannah River into St. Peter's Parish.[8]

To Charleston's north, the rivers of Georgetown District were home to the state's largest rice plantations. Plantations lined the banks of the North Santee River, but farther to the north, the Waccamaw, Peedee, Black, and Sampit rivers, which all fed into Winyah Bay, were at the center of rice cultivation.[9] By the mid-nineteenth century, Georgetown's planters, a small, close-knit group of immensely wealthy men, were producing over 30 percent of the rice grown in the United States.[10]

In the lowcountry districts, social mobility depended upon one's ability to benefit from rice cultivation (and to a lesser degree from Sea Island cotton and indigo), and the state's largest rice planters profited handsomely.[11] Accumulated wealth allowed lowcountry planters to own plantation houses near the rice fields and summer homes in a town, city, or district removed from the heat, insects, and disease of the plantation areas. Many planters chose to spend much of their time away from their plantations, in town homes in Charleston or Newport, Rhode Island, or even Europe.

By the 1830s, however, the trappings of wealth, the plantations, summer homes, and trips abroad, could not hide the lowcountry's steady economic decline. Because of an almost exclusive reliance on rice cultivation, the low-country's population and economy failed to keep pace with the rest of the nation. Between the end of the Revolution and the beginning of the Civil War, Charleston's population grew at a much slower rate than comparably sized northern cities. In 1790 Charleston ranked fourth in the nation in terms of population. By 1860 it ranked twenty-second. As a port, the city fell behind as well. Charleston was the South's largest port in the eighteenth century, and after the Revolution it experienced growth in the number of both port entries and clearances, but its gains were so marginal that by 1860 it ranked as the South's third-largest port, behind New Orleans, Louisiana, and Mobile, Ala-bama. In addition, by 1860 Charleston was no longer on the direct trade route to Europe. It had become a satellite of northern ports.[12]

International events also increasingly threatened lowcountry wealth. For years planters exported most of their rice to Europe. In the early nineteenth century, however, British and Dutch colonial expansion into Asia opened up new sources of rice production, and soon merchants there flooded American and European markets with cheap rice. By 1859 Asian rice had significantly weakened the lowcountry's hold on the European market.[13]

The weakening of the rice market and Charleston's decline as a port city had a dramatic effect on the wealth of the lowcountry's inhabitants. In 1860 the mean per capita wealth for the area was still higher than that in New En-gland and the Middle Atlantic States, but the gap between those areas and the South Carolina lowcountry had narrowed dramatically. All this signaled a sig-nificant deterioration of the lowcountry's economy between the 1780s and 1860.[14]

Although the region's planters and merchants were still quite wealthy by the standards of mid-nineteenth-century America, their declining fortunes became the subject of worried conversation in Charleston. Charlestonians had long considered themselves the guardians of English culture and values in the South. They modeled their homes, dress, and furniture after English exam-ples. They patterned their way of life on that of the English landed aristocracy, partly from necessity, yet partly from choice. The unhealthy environment of lowcountry plantations forced planters to migrate annually to summer homes in healthier environments, where they lived a leisurely lifestyle much like their English forebears. This yearly exile, however, created a taste for life away from the plantation, making the planters even more reliant upon white overseers and black drivers to keep their plantations profitable. Despite declining for-tunes, many planters tried to maintain a sumptuous lifestyle worthy of their revered ancestors.[15]

While the conspicuous consumption of some planters hid their declining fortunes, others still made good money cultivating rice. After all, rice prices were more stable than cotton prices. Rice planters seldom had to be concerned with exhausted soil since periodic flooding replenished necessary nutrients. But the complexities of growing rice, the precision with which the fields had to be flooded, and the need for regular dike maintenance necessitated a competent plantation manager. Those planters who turned their backs on the "English" or leisurely approach to plantation management could expect a profit. Those who continued to spend their time as absentee landlords lost their estates to those more willing to actively manage their holdings, few of whom were from old families.

By the 1820s, planters found their holdings surrounded by land owned by ex-overseers who had learned the economics of rice planting by successfully managing plantations for their employers. Such men quickly took advantage of their former employers' declining fortunes, buying plantations from some of the lowcountry's oldest families.[16] These economic realities eventually meant that the traditional aversion to other professions, including trade, declined markedly. The result was an unusual degree of social mixing. Members of old South Carolina families and nouveau riche planters, merchants, and factors increasingly mingled in organizations such as the Charleston Light Dragoons.

These economic and social changes occurred during a period of mounting sectional strife. The large concentration of slaves in the lowcountry exacerbated the South's anxieties about northern abolitionists and intensified a sense of political crisis. The basis for these anxieties was the large number of slaves inhabiting the lowcountry. Although there had been a black majority in the region as early as 1708, more than one hundred years later, this disparity was much greater.[17] By 1830 blacks (mostly slaves) made up over 75 percent of the lowcountry's population. In Charleston, nearly 58 percent of the population was of African descent.[18]

The large number of slaves in the lowcountry and frequent rumors of slave revolts often made planters apprehensive. Between 1791 and 1793, five hundred refugees arrived in Charleston from Sainte Domingue (now Haiti), bringing with them tales of murder and plunder at the hands of former slaves, and dramatically intensifying planter concerns. Twenty years later, their worst fears were confirmed. In 1822 a slave warned Charleston's city fathers of a forthcoming slave rebellion. After apprehending those involved, the state tried and executed the rebellion's mastermind, Denmark Vesey, and numerous other conspirators. Seven years later, in 1829, an abortive slave insurrection in Georgetown troubled the region's white residents for more than a year. In 1831 William Lloyd Garrison began publication of his abolitionist newspaper, the *Liberator*. That same year Virginia's largest slave rebellion, led by Nat Turner, created a sensation throughout the South. As a result, lowcountry slave owners organized vigilance groups to monitor slave movements and meetings.[19]

The Nullification Crisis of 1832–33 played a vital role in reinforcing the siege mentality of lowcountry whites. Southerners, many among them South

Carolinians, opposed congressional efforts to impose a protective tariff and increasingly found comfort in the theory of nullification as proposed by John C. Calhoun. In October 1832, Nullifiers in the South Carolina legislature won a vote to call a Nullification Convention, and in November 1832 the convention declared the Tariffs of 1828 and 1832 null and void.[20] In response, President Andrew Jackson supported a Force Act to ensure that the tariffs were enforced, which led South Carolina to muster the state militia. Before the two sides could come to blows, the Compromise Tariff of 1833 defused the crisis. Throughout the Nullification controversy, white South Carolinians grew more apprehensive, in part because of sharp political divisions between Nullifiers and Unionists but also because of growing worries about the security of their slave property.[21]

In this increasingly volatile political and social climate, the Charleston Light Dragoons decided to incorporate. At the time of their incorporation, they were a volunteer company in the South Carolina militia. In 1792 Congress had passed "An Act more effectually to provide for the National Defense by establishing an uniform Militia throughout the United States." On May 10, 1794, South Carolina followed suit with "An Act to organize the Militia throughout the state of South Carolina in conformity with the Act of Congress."[22] Together, these two acts established the state's militia forces.

According to the militia's structure, nearly every able-bodied free male between the ages of eighteen and forty-five was required to serve. In the South, militia duties entailed more than registering potential members and training. The militia also served as a police force and an auxiliary slave patrol.[23] In areas such as the South Carolina lowcountry, this last task was particularly important, especially during insurrection panics.

White males in South Carolina joined either the line militia or the volunteer militia. Most chose the former. Line militia units might gather for training only twice a year, although companies in some regions of the state assembled once a month.[24]

The volunteer militia involved more specialized service, including artillery, cavalry, and rifle units. These were voluntary organizations of men who wished to serve in units of their own choosing. Unlike the line militia, volunteer militia companies had a great deal of autonomy and were the elite of the militia system.[25]

For those who did choose such service, volunteer companies were popular for a variety of reasons. First, members could serve with friends and neighbors. Second, volunteer organizations could incorporate, which provided numerous legal benefits. Incorporated companies selected their membership and their officers. They drafted bylaws, assessed dues, controlled their own finances, and held their own courts-martial. By incorporating, they became semi-independent bodies or clubs.[26]

The elite of the volunteer militia was the cavalry. The added expense of a mount and elaborate uniforms closed cavalry outfits to all but the wealthiest citizens. In South Carolina, volunteer cavalry troops were organized into all-volunteer commands, exclusive of the line militia, adding more prestige to these units. And yet, even among the militia elite, there were units that vied for the wealthiest and most prominent citizens to fill their ranks. One of these was the Charleston Light Dragoons.[27]

On July 8, 1835, the dragoons incorporated as a volunteer militia cavalry troop. By resolution, the company appointed a committee to choose a name for the unit, select a uniform and equipment, and draft rules governing the members' behavior, all of which were formalities since the unit had been in existence since 1792. The constitution stated that the unit was formed for the "protection and service of Charleston."[28]

The company incorporated at a time when South Carolinians were bracing for slave insurrections that would supposedly be incited by the increasingly vocal northern abolitionist movement. To Charleston's wealthiest residents, the Nullification Crisis also had revealed how antislavery interests both inside and outside the state threatened slavery, which was the very foundation of the wealth and power of lowcountry planters. The atmosphere of unease among Charleston's white elite, to which the dragoons belonged, was therefore a factor in their decision to incorporate, a not uncommon pattern among volunteer militia companies.[29]

After incorporation, as before it, the dragoons held musters and recruited members to serve on slave patrols. Like those of other militia units, the dragoons' musters were a time for the unit to display its skills and perform for family and friends. Slave patrols, however, were of a more serious nature. In South Carolina, militia units were responsible for slave patrols and, therefore, responsible for the safety of the lowcountry's white residents.[30] The dragoons performed this task with other militia units, but this company soon established itself as one of the most elite of all Charleston's militia units. As such, it held a place of honor at all ceremonial events.

By the standards of the 1850s, the dragoons were a well-equipped and relatively well-trained troop. In 1853 they served as an escort for Governor John L. Manning during his visit to Charleston for a militia inspection. Manning and local militia commanders all were impressed by the dragoons' conduct.[31]

The dragoons were keenly aware of their favored position within the state's militia. Realizing they had made a good impression on the governor the previous year, the dragoons offered their services to Manning again in early 1854. A local judge had condemned two men, one of whom was from a wealthy Charleston family, to be hanged for using a pack of dogs to kill a fugitive slave. At the troop's February 6, 1854, meeting, the dragoons adopted a resolution offering their services to escort the men to their execution, an unusual request because one of the prisoners was of the same class.[32] On February 20, at a special unit meeting, Dragoon Captain S. Simons presented a petition in which unit members pledged to muster under any circumstances (except "severe illness") with Captain Simons in order to escort other units and ensure the safe conduct of the prisoners to Walterboro, located nearly fifty miles west of Charleston.[33] On March 1, 1854, Governor Manning called out the militia to prevent a mob from stopping the unpopular execution. As expected, he sent the dragoons to Walterboro as an escort for infantry and artillery units and to ensure that the execution took place.[34] The dragoons successfully escorted the two men to the gallows, where they were executed.

At the unit's next meeting on March 6, 1854, the company reveled in success as a unit that had earned the governor's confidence. The commander of the escort unit, Captain Arthur Middleton Manigault, paid the dragoons several compliments "in regards to their gentlemanly and soldierly like bearing that had characterized the performance of their duties." The meeting ended with the company adjourning to celebrate their success with champagne and, no doubt, more discussion of their glorious service.[35] That the governor called on the dragoons, a unit of men who could have easily sided with the defendants, demonstrates that the company had developed a reputation for loyalty to the governor, one only enhanced by their efforts on this occasion.

Part of the dragoons' mystique was derived from their selective recruiting methods, which differed from that of other volunteer militia companies only in the social stature of the members and recruits. Like other companies, the Charleston Light Dragoons recruited from family, friends, and acquaintances and through local newspapers, drawing members from the area served by the brigade, roughly Charleston District.[36] Those living outside Charleston District who wished to join the unit simply had to establish a residence in the city. Potential members submitted a letter of application, a document that was read at a company parade, drill, or meeting. The captain then turned the application over to the Committee on Letters, which assessed "the character of the applicant" and reported back to the company with a recommendation. If the recommendation was favorable, the entire company voted on the applicant. Once accepted, the new dragoon had one month to acquire a suitable mount, equipment, and uniform as stipulated in the unit constitution. He also had to pay a fee to the treasurer to receive proof of membership.[37]

The unit's recruitment and selection process and organizational structure was very similar to that of a gentleman's club. The Charleston Light Dragoons, like other volunteer militia units, had a chain of command that included a captain, two lieutenants, a cornet, four sergeants, four corporals, and privates, plus specialists.[38] As an incorporated body, however, the unit had a president (the captain) and a secretary/treasurer. Even more indicative of its status was its annual election of five stewards from the ranks. These men reserved appropriate meeting spaces, coordinated the arrangements necessary for the unit's anniversary parade, and provided refreshments at unit meetings.[39] They essentially served the same purpose as would a club's or fraternity's social committee.

The exclusivity of the dragoons added to their appeal. The unit recruited members from the city's upper strata, men who knew each other through a series of ties that bound them and the rest of their class. Like the vast majority of the lowcountry's elite, most were members of the Episcopal Church.[40] Of wartime members, several attended Charleston's two oldest churches, St. Michael's and St. Philip's. St. Michael's was the place of worship for Joel Roberts Poinsett Pringle, Oliver H. Middleton Jr., Miles Brewton Pringle, Dragoon Captain Benjamin H. Rutledge, and others. Other dragoons, such as Francis K. Middleton, belonged to the congregation of nearby St. Philip's.[41] Most dragoons, when at their plantations, also attended the nearest church or chapel. Dragoon Miles Brewton Pringle's family was also members of St. Andrews, which was near their plantation, Runimede, and they attended All Saints Church, Waccamaw, on occasion when in Georgetown District.[42]

Just as Episcopal Church membership helped establish a planter's place within the moral order of polite society, marital ties bound most of the families whose men served in the Charleston Light Dragoons. A series of marriages joined most of the lowcountry's wealthiest families together in complex networks that became the foundation for elite society. Charleston was the center of lowcountry finance, culture, and pleasure, and it brought lowcountry families into contact during social seasons. Out of these social gatherings grew the bonds that would cement the region's elite together, and it was the offspring of these prominent families who joined the dragoons.[43]

Fraternal and social organizations also brought together the city's economic and social elite. One notable Masonic lodge, Union Kilwinning Lodge No. 4, was considered to be the city's most exclusive lodge. Among its prewar members were Captain Benjamin H. Rutledge, Dragoon Benjamin F. Huger, and Dragoon Thomas A. Middleton.[44] Another popular lodge for dragoons was Landmark Lodge No. 76, which counted among its members Dragoons John Harleston and Edward Harleston Jr., Miles Brewton Pringle, John Robertson, W. R. Davis, and Lionel C. Nowell.[45] The Charleston Club was yet another organization that hosted the city's favored sons. Chartered in 1852, the club's founding membership comprised the city's and state's most prominent men, and future dragoons such as Ralph S. Izard, John W. Lewis, and Alex Rose. Other Charleston Club members included dragoons who were elected to membership after the war, such as Benjamin H. Rutledge and Benjamin F. Huger. William Howard Russell, correspondent for the *London Times,* visited the Charleston Club on April 15, 1861.[46] He accompanied Confederate congressman William Porcher Miles, former South Carolina governor John L.

Manning (father of future dragoon Wade Hampton Manning), and Confederate senator James Chesnut, husband of Civil War diarist Mary Boykin Chesnut
and cousin by marriage to future dragoon William L. Kirkland.[47]

The most exclusive Charleston organization with close ties to the dragoons
was the St. Cecilia Society. Founded in the mid-eighteenth century as a musi-
cal society, it had evolved by the mid-nineteenth century into a social organization that held balls in January and February for the city's elite. So secretive
were the dates of these affairs that white-gloved slaves were sent to members'
homes to deliver invitations.[48] The society's membership was kept secret, but
the names of society officers appeared on invitations to various balls. Among
these officers were relatives of dragoons, including Henry A. Middleton, father
of future dragoon Francis K. Middleton and cousin of future dragoon Oliver
H. Middleton Jr., whose father served as vice president of the St. Cecilia Society in 1843 and 1845. William Bull Pringle, father of future dragoon Miles
Brewton Pringle and uncle of future dragoons John Julius Pringle, Joel Roberts
Poinsett Pringle, and Dominick Lynch Pringle, was on the society's board of
managers in 1845.[49]

Belonging to an elite militia company required money as well as social
standing. Of those members whose dates of enrollment and resignation are
listed on the dragoon roster, the average time of service was five years.[50] During that period they expended a substantial amount of their own money,
including fifty dollars ($1,030 in year 2000 money) for a uniform, plus the cost
of an acceptable horse and necessary equipment.[51]

Membership itself conferred status, but the independent and proud young
members did not necessarily fulfill their obligations to the dragoons, for, like
other militia units, interest in and commitment to the dragoons waxed and
waned. In 1839, four years after its incorporation, the troop was struggling to
assemble a quorum (fifteen members) for its regular meetings. The company
failed to have a quorum at meetings on August 5, 1839, November 1, 1839,
December 20, 1839, and February 13, 1840.[52] The following month the unit did
have a quorum present and took steps to ensure better attendance in the
future. On March 17 members proposed a resolution, passed on April 14, that
lowered the number of members necessary for a quorum.[53]

Low attendance at regular meetings speaks volumes about service in a volunteer militia troop and life in the lowcountry. In the line militia, an unautho-
rized absence from muster could result in a court-martial or nonjudicial
review and punishment. Volunteer units, however, handled attendance problems internally. A dragoon had only to pay a fine for each meeting that he
missed. For the extra expense of belonging to a volunteer troop like the dragoons, members gained special consideration, something to which they were
accustomed, and a reprieve from militia duty for as long as they could pay or
until the unit agreed on stronger disciplinary action. Absent dragoons were

usually fined and received no other penalties. If a dragoon failed to pay his dues, however, he could face expulsion or feel pressure to resign. In fact, most dragoons who left the unit prior to the Civil War either resigned or were expelled because they failed to pay dues.[54]

In keeping with the troop's role as a social organization, much of the unit's activities involved the collection of dues. From September 1858 to July 1861, the highest amount due from a member was $48.25 ($993.47 in 2000), owed by J. P. Laborde, who eventually paid his late dues. Of 171 dragoons who were delinquent during this nearly three-year period, 116 (or roughly 68 percent) settled their accounts after notification. Delinquent members averaged $8.61 ($177.28) in dues owed, signaling either a habitual tendency by dragoons to pay bills late or an inability to manage personal finances.[55]

Although failure to pay dues was commonplace, the unit was willing to grant special consideration to some members but not to others.[56] In certain circumstances, the troop made individuals honorary members and nullified any outstanding dues. This occurred most often with older, long-standing members, such as James L. Rose, president of the South Western Railroad Bank.[57] Other longtime members, however, were not as fortunate. The unit expelled C. J. Cogdell for failure to pay his dues nine years and seven months after he first joined the unit. Similar circumstances surrounded the expulsion of William Thompson and C. Manly Smith, both of whom served for over ten years before being expelled. In these two cases the unit decided not to move the individuals to the honorary list, perhaps because the expelled members had contributed little but longevity.[58]

Inconsistencies in the application and enforcement of dragoon regulations indicate that it was more akin to a social club than a military organization. The unit's constitution detailed a series of fines that members were to pay when they violated company rules. Some of these offenses, such as missing a unit muster or attending muster with improper equipment or uniform, were outlined in federal and state militia statutes. Other transgressions, such as being thrown from a horse or violating a series of military or social protocols while on duty, did not appear in the statutes but were unwritten unit customs or regulations. The company's secretary often recorded and detailed the misdeeds in a "List of Difficulties."[59]

In keeping with the unit's likeness to a social organization, dragoons could pay their fines in food or drink for their comrades. Members regularly paid their fines with items such as champagne or "Charleston Light Dragoon Punch," a concoction that contained at least two varieties of liquor as well as sugar and lemon juice.[60] In other instances, the guilty parties "drank" their fine, rather like modern college fraternities.[61]

Aside from violations involving attendance, other infractions stemmed from alcohol consumption, poor military training, or a combination of both.

A common offense was that of being thrown from a horse, a problem that suggested possible intoxication. On April 1, 1859, at the company's anniversary parade, Dr. C. L. Meyer threw away his sword while on parade and received a fine. The same day the unit fined E. H. Yates for "milking his female horse." On March 31, 1859, the day prior to the anniversary parade, Richard H. Colcock was fined for "a hoist," having someone assist him in mounting his horse. A. Schrien was fined for "expecting his pistol to go off without cocking it . . . and remarking it was the hardest pistol trigger he had ever seen." Joseph Cohen made the list for "a daring feat of leaping a ditch 2 ft. wide and one inch deep losing his stirrups & bridle & saving his life by the aid of the Captain & his horse's main, supporting himself by his feet having [been] caught in his horse's main by his spurs."[62] After the 1854 mission to escort condemned prisoners to Walterboro, Warren Wells received a fine for "shooting himself." The wound was not fatal, and company members found the incident quite amusing.[63] These and other incidents, some likely lubricated by dragoon punch, demonstrate that volunteer militia service, even in a supposedly elite unit, did not meet the standards for professional military behavior.

At the beginning of the Civil War, the Charleston Light Dragoons had been incorporated for some twenty-five years, and the dragoons who served with the unit during wartime were in many ways similar to the organization's founding members.[64] They belonged to the region's wealthiest circles, and many were the sons of older members. Members generally lived in Charleston for extended periods to ensure that they could attend musters when called. During the war, however, a large number of men from other districts joined the dragoons, with most coming from Beaufort and Colleton Districts, where the unit was stationed. Ralph E. and Thomas Elliott and Bohna C. and Theodore DuPont were all from Beaufort District, while Josiah Bedon and W. H. Bellinger were both from Colleton District. In a few instances, recruits came from districts in the midlands (table 1). Four of these were Joel R. and Robert Adams and James and English Hopkins, all of whom came from lower Richland District.

The unit's wartime membership was made up overwhelmingly of those who planted rice and cotton and those who marketed it (see table 2). Recruits from outside of Charleston District included a large number of planters, while most dragoons from Charleston were clerks for commission merchants, although a substantial minority included clerks for retail merchants, railroads, and banks.

The primary responsibility of factors was to arrange for the sale of their clients' crops; however, their business and personal relationships with these planters were much more complex.[65] Factors often handled the purchase and hiring out of slaves. They sometimes acted as bankers for planters seeking small loans. They even served as financial advisors, purchasing stock for clients and voting their proxies.[66]

Table 1—Unit members and district of origin

District	Number	Percentage
Charleston	87	54.375
Colleton	25	15.625
Beaufort	21	13.125
Georgetown	8	5
Richland	4	2.5
Sumter	3	1.875
Darlington	3	1.875
Clarendon	3	1.875
Kershaw	2	1.25
Marlborough	2	1.25
Lexington	1	0.625
Fairfield	1	0.625
Total	**160**	**100**

Source: United States Bureau of the Census, *Eighth Census of the United States (South Carolina), 1860* (Washington, D.C.: Government Printing Office, 1865); *Directory of the City of Charleston. . . . 1860. Vol. 1.* (Charleston, S.C.: W. Eugene Ferslew, 1860), microfilm 291, pp. 33–145, SCHS.

Note: Table based on the 160 dragoons whose district of origin could be located and who served with the unit while it was in Confederate service (after March 25, 1862). For those members with residences in multiple districts, the listing with the largest amount of property, if a planter, or place of business was used as district of origin.

The bonds between planters and factors had always been close, but before the lowcountry economic decline of the early nineteenth century, "trade" was considered to be an unfit profession for a "gentleman." By the 1830s, however, many members of the social elite had turned their efforts toward founding and operating commission merchant firms in Charleston.

These businesses were the logical place of employment for planters' sons who wished to learn the basics of marketing their family's agricultural products. For the first few years of training, however, this was a costly endeavor. One factor wrote that young men worked for factors without wages and received compensation in the form of experience. Planters had to provide their sons with money for room, board, and expenses while they served as clerks for a factor.[67]

The long-term benefits of an apprenticeship with a factor could be great. With the needed background in commerce a younger son could open his own commission merchant business or work as a partner in another firm. Consequently, when planters sent their sons to work for commission merchants, they

Table 2—Unit members by occupation

Occupation	Number	Percentage
Clerks/Factors	30	31.58
Planters	22	23.16
Clerks/Retail	16	16.84
Physicians	5	5.26
Students	5	5.26
Attorneys	4	4.21
Maritime	4	4.21
Miscellaneous	4	4.21
Clerks/Railroads	3	3.16
Clerks/Bank	2	2.11
Total	95	100

Source: United States Bureau of the Census, *Eighth Census of the United States (South Carolina), 1860* (Washington, D.C.: Government Printing Office, 1865); *Directory of the City of Charleston. . . . 1860. Vol. 1.* (Charleston, S.C.: W. Eugene Ferslew, 1860), microfilm 291, pp. 33–145, SCHS.

Note: Based on the 95 members who entered the dragoons after the unit was in Confederate service (after March 25, 1862) and whose professions could be identified. When a member was a planter and also a physician, the profession matching the place of residence was used.

were tightening the bonds between their agricultural pursuits and trade, while providing a future for their sons. One of Charleston's largest commission merchant firms, John Fraser and Company, employed three dragoons: H. D. Burnet, Benjamin F. Huger, and J. D. White. Other merchant firms employed dragoons as well: J. Waring Boone was a clerk for Missroon and Company; Thomas H. Colcock and E. W. Mikell were clerks for Colcock, McCally and Malloy; Edward Harleston Jr. worked for W. H. Conner and Company; John Harleston worked for J. and F. Dawson; Charles Henry and Thomas A. Middleton were clerks for Middleton and Company; Alfred Manigault was an employee of H. Trapman and Company; Edward Martin worked for William & J. C. Martin; John J. McPherson worked for C. Atkinson and Company; H. M. Neyle was a clerk for J. A. Winthrop and Son; Edward W. Nowell was a clerk for Henckel, Tunno and Nowell; Lionel C. Nowell and S. W. Simons were clerks for Huckenwrath, Lesene, & Huger; James W. O'Hear was a bookkeeper for O'Hear, Roper and Stoney; Percival Porcher was a partner in P. J. Porcher and Boya; Joel Roberts Poinsett Pringle was a partner in Coffin and Pringle; James M. Prioleau was a clerk for Porcher and Lindsay; George E. Pritchett was the owner of George E. Pritchett; B. S. Rhett was a clerk at Rhett and Robson;

Alex Rose was a clerk for Green, Trapmann and Company; and J. G. Thurston was a clerk for Robertson, Blacklock and Company.[68] In all, Charleston's commission merchant houses employed at least thirty dragoons in some capacity (see table 2).

In many cases, the dragoons employed were the children, siblings, relatives, or owners of the firm in question. Thomas H. Colcock (of Colcock, McCally, and Malloy), Thomas A. Middleton (Middleton and Company) Edward Martin (William and J. C. Martin), Edward W. Nowell (Henckel, Tunno and Nowell), James W. O'Hear (O'Hear, Roper and Stoney), Percival Porcher (P. J. Porcher and Boya), Joel Roberts Poinsett Pringle (Coffin and Pringle), George E. Pritchett (George E. Pritchett), and B. S. Rhett (Rhett and Robson) were all involved in family commission merchant enterprises.[69]

Clerks for the city's rice and cotton merchants, especially those operated by established members of the social elite, were not simply bookkeepers hired for their professional abilities. Businesses in nineteenth-century Charleston were small, tight-knit organizations. Clerks were members of the same social class as the owner, young men who moved in the same circles, attended the same churches, belonged to the same clubs, and, during the social seasons, attended the same parties. They associated professionally and socially, and developed friendships based on these associations. These men were being groomed to operate their fathers' plantations or to become factors and partners in business, with the ultimate goal of owning a plantation.[70] For these young men at the outset of war, membership in the dragoons was a welcome respite from the monotony of the counting house.

As the war progressed, the dragoons' membership continued to change. Gradually, the unit received new recruits from its area of operations, notably Beaufort and Colleton Districts (see table 1). Some of these men were not strangers to Charleston; they had lived in the city periodically and had some previous ties to the dragoons. Others of substantial wealth and prestige seldom visited the city but chose to live on their plantations, having little interest in the workings of Charleston's elaborate social system.[71]

Of the men who joined the dragoons from Beaufort and Colleton Districts, most were planters, and over half of all dragoons who served during the Civil War carried the surname of the state's largest planters.[72] At least twenty-two of these were involved directly in planting.[73] Almost all were the sons of planters and lived either on their parents' plantations or owned their own plantation nearby. Joel R. Adams, age sixteen at the war's outset, was the son of lower Richland District planter James U. Adams, who had nearly $500,000 ($10.3 million in 2000) in assets.[74] Walter Blake Jr. was the son of Walter Blake, who was worth $300,000 ($6.18 million) and owned or managed for his father, Joseph Blake, more than six-hundred slaves.[75] Two other dragoons, Bohna C. and Theodore DuPont, were the sons of Beaufort District planter Charles C.

DuPont, whose worth in real estate and personal property exceeded $200,000 ($4.12 million).[76] Dragoon B. R. Burnet lived both in Charleston and at Woodburne Plantation in Colleton District, where his father, Andrew William Burnet, owned 176 slaves and had a net worth of $148,000 ($3.05 million).[77] One of the wealthiest dragoons in his own right was William Bell. At age twenty-three Bell owned both Pine Grove Plantation in Charleston District and a home in Charleston, and he had assets of $142,000 ($2.92 million), which he had inherited from his deceased father.[78]

A number of other members were the sons of planters but supported themselves as physicians or attorneys. Ralph E. Elliott was a trained physician and the son of the Honorable William Elliott, a prominent Edisto Island planter.[79] P. J. Maxwell was a physician and the son of Georgetown planter William Rivers.[80] Several others, including, H. W. DeSaussure Jr., John R. Waring, and M. N. Waring, were physicians.[81] Josiah Bedon was an attorney, although his father was a planter. Commissary Arthur P. Lining and Captain Benjamin H. Rutledge were attorneys as well.[82]

Although in the minority, men employed in various other businesses did join the unit. First Sergeant John C. Bickley was a wood dealer in Charleston. E. H. Darby was a clerk of the North Eastern Railroad, while Sergeant James A. Miles was a clerk of the South Carolina Railroad. E. T. Gaillard was a clerk for Bowen, Foster, and Company, dealers of embroideries and laces. W. S. Lance and J. J. Miles were clerks for Johnston, Crews, and Company, retailers of dry goods. A. McDowell Wragg was a clerk for Andrew McDowell, retailer of wholesale dry goods. Miles Brewton Pringle was an employee of Gravely and Pringle, retailers of hardware and cutlery.[83]

Most dragoons followed agricultural or business pursuits, and a few ventured into politics. The unit's commander, Captain Benjamin H. Rutledge, and Gabriel Manigault were signers of the Ordinance of Secession.[84] Others were the sons of politicians. General William Hopkins, the father of Dragoons James and English Hopkins, had been a state representative and a signer of the Ordinance of Secession.[85] Wade Hampton Manning was the son of former governor John L. Manning, who had called out the dragoons in 1854. Ralph E. Elliott's father, William Elliott, had served as a state representative and state senator. Thomas Alston Middleton was the son of John Izard Middleton of Crowfield Plantation in Georgetown District, who had been Speaker of the South Carolina House of Representatives and a member of the South Carolina State Senate.[86] Taken together, these experiences and backgrounds left the dragoons with a feeling of self-worth that was magnified by the general high regard of their fellow citizens.

By the outset of the Civil War, the Charleston Light Dragoons had taken their place as the premier cavalry unit in the state. Roughly sixty-nine years had elapsed since the unit's founding, and another thirty-five years had passed since its incorporation. Its members' uniforms were readily recognizable to the city's residents, as were the men who wore the uniform. The dragoons, like most volunteer militia companies on the eve of the Civil War, viewed their forthcoming service with confident anticipation. Past experience had convinced them that whatever circumstance lay before them, unit members, as always, would conduct themselves with the deportment expected from men of their elevated position.

Chapter 2

SERVICE AND CHANGE

This war and what is connected with it seems to absorb every thought
and feeling.

Susan M. Middleton

T he Charleston Light Dragoons had long protected and epitomized the
lowcountry's white minority and a way of life that had generated great
wealth. In 1860, however, the dragoons, like other volunteer militia companies
in South Carolina, were called to active duty to protect the state from a seem-
ingly dangerous enemy, one intent on the immediate destruction of their
world. Within months of South Carolina's secession, Union forces, through
blockade and invasion, threatened the security of the region's wealthiest slaveholders. The presence of the enemy on the state's shores so early in the conflict
created great alarm in the lowcountry. Many of the area's wealthiest residents
would join the dragoons in the hope of countering this apparent threat to their
most cherished values and dreams.

In 1860 Charleston was not only the center of the lowcountry world, it was
also at the epicenter of events that would shake the American nation's founda-
tions. In May 1860 Charleston hosted the Democratic National Convention at
Institute Hall on Meeting Street. There, lower South delegates staged a walk-
out over the convention's failure to adopt a plank calling for a federal slave
code for the territories. This caused a rupture in the national Democratic Party
and led to the election of Abraham Lincoln to the presidency.[1]

On November 7, 1860, the South Carolina General Assembly voted to hold
a convention to consider the merits of secession. This body met in Columbia
on December 17, 1860, but quickly adjourned to Charleston.[2] On December 20, 1860, the delegates gathered at Institute Hall to sign the Ordinance
of Secession. The building was filled with over three thousand spectators,
who wanted to witness the historic act. In attendance were members of the
General Assembly and Governor Francis Pickens. The clerk of the South Carolina House of Representatives called each convention delegate forward to sign
the ordinance. Onlookers especially cheered delegates from St. Philip's and St.
Michael's Parish, Charleston's oldest and wealthiest area. Among the parish's
delegation was Captain Benjamin H. Rutledge of the Charleston Light Dragoons, a man who would play a signal role in the unit's story during the coming war.[3]

News of secession generated enormous martial enthusiasm among Charlestonians and South Carolinians. To celebrate the event, local artillery units fired

salutes as cheering crowds thronged the streets. Bands played and militia companies, including the Charleston Light Dragoons, paraded through town. Young men fixed blue cockades and palmetto leaves to their lapels to indicate their readiness to serve their now independent state. On the following day, December 21, local militia units marched to the Mills House to hear recently elected Governor Francis Pickens make a stirring address in which he proclaimed that South Carolina, without reluctance, stood ready for war should it come. In the days that followed, other militia units joined the parades and festivities occurring throughout the city, while the dragoons remained in active service, escorting dignitaries and marching through the streets. These dramatic military displays stirred the city's young men, who rushed to enlist.[4]

The state, however, did not have to rely entirely on individual militia companies for its defense. The General Assembly already had laid the foundation for the creation of a larger volunteer force. On December 17, 1860, just three days prior to secession, the General Assembly had adopted legislation creating a more permanent military force out of the militia units that were then drilling statewide. This measure authorized the governor to receive into twelve months' service volunteer infantry, cavalry, and artillery units made up of militia companies, provided that they could field the requisite number of officers and men.[5]

The dragoons quickly volunteered for service. Like that of many other militia units, membership in the Charleston Light Dragoons swelled as a wave of patriotism swept the state. Seven new members joined after Lincoln's election, thirteen more on January 1, 1861, and another seven before the end of the month. This was the largest accretion in any three-month period since 1835. The suddenly expanded unit served as part of the 4th Militia Brigade's cavalry force, headquartered in Charleston.[6]

The glamorous nature of cavalry service accounted for some of the unit's popularity with potential recruits. The literature of Sir Walter Scott had instilled in young men romantic notions of knights mounted on steeds engaging in personal combat with evil foes. Cavalry units, especially units such as the Charleston Light Dragoons, saw themselves as the heirs to this knightly tradition. Practical reasons also made cavalry service preferable to service in the infantry. Riding was always less strenuous than marching, so Charleston's cavalry companies found plenty of recruits.[7]

In the days immediately following secession, local militia units moved to seize federal installations. On the night of December 25 and early morning of December 26, 1860, Major Robert Anderson, commander of the eighty-man federal garrison on Sullivan's Island, shifted his command from Fort Moultrie, which was vulnerable to attack by land, to the unfinished Fort Sumter at the mouth of Charleston's harbor.[8] In early January President James Buchanan ordered an unarmed merchant vessel, *Star of the West,* to resupply Anderson's garrison at Fort Sumter. On January 9, 1861, Confederate guns drove the ship away.[9]

Nearly six weeks after taking office, President Abraham Lincoln sent a similar relief expedition to resupply Anderson and his men. During the afternoon and evening of April 11, throngs of people from the surrounding countryside began crowding into Charleston to watch the anticipated Confederate bombardment of Fort Sumter. They were not disappointed. A little after 4:00 A.M. on April 12, 1861, Confederate batteries opened fire on the post. Charlestonians and visitors to the city watched the shelling from the waterfront, the Battery, and the porticoes and roofs of nearby homes. Several miles away on Sullivan's Island, the Charleston Light Dragoons, relegated to serving as a mobile force to guard against a Union landing, awaited the battle's results.[10]

For those dragoons who envisioned military service as an adventurous interlude in their otherwise dull lives, the next few months were a disappointment. Following the Confederate capture of Fort Sumter, the Charleston Light Dragoons remained briefly on Sullivan's Island, until General P. G. T. Beauregard relieved the company from duty for a few weeks. During that time, Captain Rutledge wrote to Colonel Lucius B. Northrop, a friend and the Confederate commissary general, to inquire whether the Confederate War Department planned to accept mounted men from South Carolina, and if so, under what conditions.[11]

By July the company was once again on duty in Charleston and was fulfilling one of its traditional functions as a ceremonial escort. On July 26, 1861, it served as an honor guard for the bodies of Charlestonians who had been killed at the battle of Bull Run. Emma Holmes wrote that "the Dragoons in their summer uniform of pure white" and other militia companies met the bodies at the depot and escorted them to the city hall. During the procession the dragoons were in the place of honor as the lead unit.[12]

On September 12, 1861, the dragoons served as an escort for a number of involuntary visitors to Charleston. Following the battle of Bull Run, Confederate authorities dispersed Union prisoners to cities throughout the South. Colonel Michael Corcoran, twenty-five Union officers, and men from the 150th New York Zouaves were transported to Charleston to be held in Castle Pinckney. Of this event Emma Holmes wrote, "The whole Rifle Regiment & Dragoons were ordered out to receive them, as it was feared the Irish & rabble might attempt to mob them."[13]

On November 7, 1861, Brigadier General Roswell Ripley ordered the dragoons to move to Pocotaligo in Beaufort District, which placed the unit much closer to military action.[14] Several days earlier, on November 2, Governor Pickens had warned all residents living near the coast that a large Union fleet was heading for South Carolina. By November 4, after passing through a severe storm off of Cape Hatteras, the fleet had assembled off the coast near Port Royal, in a position to strike at the Sea Islands or Beaufort. From their position in Beaufort District, the Charleston Light Dragoons served as pickets to warn of a Union strike into the interior and defend the Charleston and Savannah Railroad. Not only was the railroad of crucial importance as a transportation link, it also was an integral part of Confederate defensive arrangements for the region. In conjunction with the telegraph, the railroad allowed local commanders to rush reinforcements to any threatened area between the two cities.[15]

Although Governor Pickens had given area residents two days' warning of the Union fleet's arrival, their concern grew more acute when the fleet anchored off Hilton Head Island. Commanded by Flag Officer Samuel Francis DuPont, the flotilla included seventeen warships with transports carrying twelve thousand soldiers and six hundred Marines. Confederate general Ripley suggested that all residents of Beaufort evacuate the town on November 4, so families quickly packed their belongings and prepared for departure.[16]

Planters on neighboring islands were much less worried about the Union threat and made plans to observe the November 7, 1861, Union assault on Forts Beauregard and Walker. They gathered at Land's End Plantation on St. Helena Island and on Hilton Head Island to watch the action. Much to their horror, DuPont's warships pounded the Confederate fortifications for four hours. Among the Confederate soldiers defending Fort Walker were future dragoons Josiah Bedon and William A. Boyle. Bedon was captain of the Summerville Guard, Company C, 11th South Carolina Infantry. Boyle was a 2nd lieutenant in the same unit, and he commanded the fort's 42-pounder guns.[17]

At 12:30 P.M. Confederate generals Thomas F. Drayton and Ripley ordered their troops to withdraw from Fort Walker and Hilton Head Island. Panicky planters gathered their belongings and fled. For the most part, their slaves refused to leave, excitedly anticipating the changes that would accompany the arrival of Union forces. The Confederate garrison retreated to the ferry prior to abandoning the island.[18]

Across Port Royal Sound, Confederates manning Fort Beauregard withdrew to St. Helena Island, only to abandon it the following day. Beaufort's white residents heard of the calamity and boarded steamships headed for Charleston or Savannah. Again, most slaves decided to stay. Having lost their land and slaves, the planters of the Sea Islands near Port Royal Sound were ruined financially and became the state's first white refugees. Some sought shelter with friends and relatives nearby. Nannie DeSaussure, wife of Dragoon H. W. DeSaussure Jr., who resided in nearby Robertville in St. Peter's Parish, later wrote of the "long procession of carriages and wagons" that entered the town filled with "occupants not knowing what to do or where to go." These

CHARLESTON LIGHT DRAGOONS AREA OF OPERATIONS, 1861 - 64

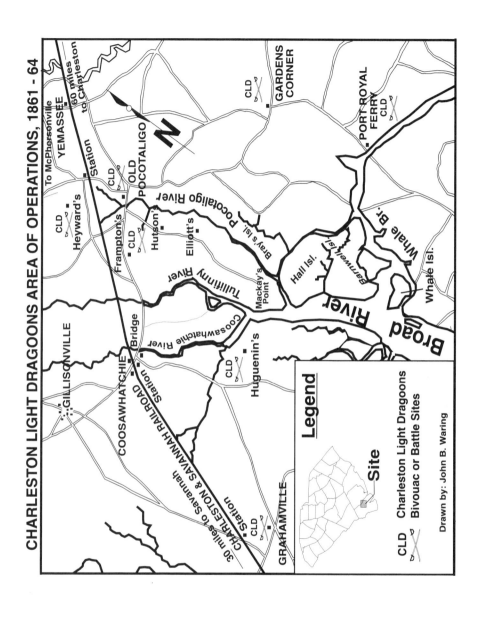

Legend

Site

CLD Charleston Light Dragoons
Bivouac or Battle Sites

Drawn by: John B. Waring

refugees found comfort in the parish, while others traveled to Columbia or towns spread across the midlands and upstate.[19]

After the battle of Port Royal, large areas of Beaufort District were in Union hands or were subject to Union raids. This meant that Confederate forces, including the Charleston Light Dragoons, would serve for extended periods of time at picket posts in the district's lower portion. There they acted as a crude early warning system for Confederate commanders, who hoped to prevent Union destruction of the railroad and to block any further Union movement into the interior.

The fall of the Sea Islands and Beaufort had one other repercussion for the dragoons. Many of the men who had lost or feared the loss of their estates in Beaufort District joined the dragoons. Of the 175 men who served in the unit during the war, at least twenty-four lived on or owned property there. Some of these recruits lost substantial fortunes when their families abandoned planta-tions and homes in November 1861. Among these was Ralph E. Elliott, whose father lost Newberry Plantation and his home in Beaufort. The family of Thomas Elliott also lost a house in Beaufort. By enlisting in the dragoons, these men hoped to protect their homes and nearby assets and to recover what they had lost. Their service, in turn, provided the unit with a valuable resource: men who intimately knew the area of operations.[20]

Several days after Union forces captured Beaufort, Confederate general Robert E. Lee, commanding the Department of South Carolina, Georgia, and East Florida, ordered Captain Joseph C. Ives, an engineer on his staff, and an escort of ten dragoons to conduct a reconnaissance of the town. The dragoons found it abandoned, except for a few slaves, and returned to Confederate lines without incident. A few days later Captain Ives and another detachment of dragoons conducted a reconnaissance of Daufuskie Island with similar results. During these and other missions to occupied areas, the dragoons noted, with surprise, that former slaves had returned to work even though the planters had fled. Unit members never seemed to realize that these freedmen had returned to work for themselves on what they now considered their own land. Instead, the dragoons were convinced that the former slaves were eagerly awaiting the return of their masters.[21]

When not conducting reconnaissance or serving as pickets, the dragoons suffered from the routine and boredom of camp life. During their months of service near Charleston, they had grown accustomed to the excitement of the city, especially during the epochal events of April 1861. In Beaufort District, however, there were few white residents near camp, and so there was less con-tact with the outside world. After Union forces captured Port Royal, the dra-goons set up camp close to the enemy. In mid-November 1861 the unit moved its headquarters to Roseland, the plantation of Julius Huguenin, where it joined several other commands along with the commissary and quartermaster supplies for the district. There the dragoons were responsible for picket duty near the Pocotaligo River and Port Royal Ferry.[22]

In November 1861, while at Huguenin's plantation, the Charleston Light Dragoons and the Rutledge Mounted Rifles were mustered out of state service because their three-month enlistment period had ended. When these units reassembled to be mustered once more into state service, the composition of each had undergone substantial changes. Until that time the ranks of the Rutledge Mounted Rifles, like the dragoons, had included a substantial number of prominent Charlestonians. That unit's commander, Captain William L. Trenholm, was the son of blockade runner and Confederate financier George A. Trenholm, who had supplied his son's unit with new cloth for uniforms, English saddles, and breech-loading Sharps carbines. Despite these advantages, morale in the troop was low because of Captain Trenholm's strict discipline.[23]

In comparison to other companies, the dragoons were in "a state of complete want of discipline," and the pace of their camp life was much slower than that of other units. When the bugler sounded reveille, "it was often a half hour before the men formed ranks for roll call. Occasionally at midday there would be a mounted drill."[24]

For the dragoons, familiarity, blood kinship, social elitism, and lax discipline combined to create a favorable environment for building unit cohesion. Prominent Charlestonians, including Gabriel and Alfred Manigault, left the Rutledge Mounted Rifles and joined the dragoons because, as they said, "most of our friends were there." Membership in the dragoons seemed attractive to the Manigaults because the company "was made up of the sons of Lowcountry planters, with some few from the middle country, who did not require rigid military rules for duty to be enforced," while the Rutledge Mounted Rifles were composed of "an entirely different material—men whom none of us knew."[25]

Camp life for the dragoons was in many ways as unremarkable as that of other Civil War units, Union or Confederate. And despite the importance of honor to the planter elite from which the company originated, the behavior of unit members was sometimes less than honorable. While bivouacking at Huguenin's plantation, Dragoons John Robinson and Allen Miles killed one of the owner's sheep and served mutton to their fellow dragoons. Mr. Huguenin learned of the sheep's slaughter and complained immediately to the commander of a nearby Tennessee infantry regiment. He never suspected the dragoons, nor did their officers, who joined Huguenin in disparaging the Tennesseans and their "low moral tone."[26]

Several months later, the dragoons showed a similar disregard for the property of another prominent local planter, leading to a confrontation that shocked many of the planter elite. While camped at the edge of William Heyward's plantation, the dragoons tore down his outbuildings and fences to build horse stalls and a covered dining area. They also regularly poached deer from Heyward's deerpark to supplement their rations.[27] These actions, as well as the similar behavior of other units stationed nearby, incensed Heyward (known throughout the state as "Tiger Bill" for his fierce temper). By the spring of 1863 Heyward, who was then sixty-three, had challenged all of the officers and men of the Charleston Light Dragoons, insisting that he would fight each of them one at a time. He posted flyers throughout the area branding the dragoons "consummate scoundrels and cowards." Lieutenant Lionel C. Nowell tore down one of the flyers and issued a challenge to Heyward, which he did not accept. In early July 1863 Heyward went to the Pocotaligo train station to post more notices, and there he met Dragoon Captain Richard H. Colcock, who grabbed the flyers from Heyward. Enraged, Heyward struck at Colcock's face with a pair of pliers in an attempt to blind him. Colcock "fell upon" Heyward and the two struggled in front of nearly one hundred spectators, none of whom attempted to help the elderly Heyward. Instead, bystanders yelled for Colcock to "kill the old brute."[28]

Although the incident resulted in only minor injuries to the two men, members of the planter class were appalled at the ungentlemanly behavior of the participants. Susan Middleton wrote, "It would have been better I think to have borne posting and everything else without redress from so old a man."[29] Dragoon Gabriel Manigault, a distant relative of Heyward, called the affair "disgraceful," and speculated that its origins lay in an ongoing feud between Heyward and his neighbors. Manigault classified Heyward as a planter of the "old regime," well traveled (having been to Europe twice), and "of elegant manners in his own house," who considered himself superior to nearby planters, whom Manigault classified as "utterly untraveled and consequently narrow minded and provincial."[30]

Angered by the behavior of the dragoons, Heyward undoubtedly viewed Colcock and his unit as representatives of those planters who had accumulated wealth but lacked the intangibles (travel, education, and, most important, manners) that set their class apart. Through his altercation with Colcock, both he and the dragoons had disregarded certain rules of behavior that character-ized them as gentlemen. In this instance, the war had eroded antebellum ideals and practices.

Theft, destruction of personal property, and brawling were only some of the vices that the dragoons acquired while in camp. The letters of Francis K. "Frank" Middleton are replete with references to the boredom that he and the rest of the unit experienced. In a letter to his sister Harriott, he commented, "There is little here to vary the monotony of life, mounting guard, going on picket duty, drilling, running half a dozen races a day, cleaning our horses and our arms, and playing cards constitutes our everyday camp life." In the same letter, he asked for three decks of cards.[31] Such behavior reflected the contradiction between the popular vision of soldiers as chivalrous protectors of the South and the reality of their behavior. The women of the planter class, like most civilians of both North and South, expected their soldiers to be virtuous in their thoughts and actions.[32] Horse racing and card playing were not activities of which women on the home front approved. After receiving a series of letters like this, it is not surprising that Harriott wrote that she questioned the character of her younger brother.[33]

Although frowned upon by home folks, racing horses seemed a natural form of entertainment for a cavalry unit. Each man had at least one mount, and in a unit whose members were as wealthy as the dragoons, many of the horses were of outstanding breeding and quality, at least during the war's early months.[34] Participation in this sport, however, could be hazardous to man and beast alike. On one occasion Dragoons Edward Lowndes and D. G. Ferguson raced their horses down the avenue of oaks at Huguenin's plantation until they came upon a wagon drawn by four mules and obscured by dust. Unable to stop, Ferguson slammed into the team of mules, knocking all four down. The impact of the collision threw him from his horse, which ended up under the wagon's wheels. Observers quickly rushed to the scene only to find that while Ferguson suffered from minor scrapes and bruises, his horse was apparently dead. Several dragoons failed to revive the animal until one kicked it in the ribs, after which it quickly regained its feet and bolted off.[35]

Other cavalry companies regularly challenged the dragoons to horse races, often with large sums of money riding on their outcomes. One of the unit's animals was a champion quarter with a remarkable string of victories. Members of a nearby cavalry troop, which the dragoons described as "innocent guileless countrymen," visited their camp to seek a race against the famed animal; they brought $100 of their comrades' money as a wager. The other outfit's animal was a shaggy gelding with a long winter coat and was ridden by a young boy. Initially, the dragoons felt guilty about the match, thinking it unfair to pit their horse against such a pathetic rival. They were surprised, however, when the gelding easily beat their horse. They soon discovered that the other company had brought the horse (a champion in its own right) a great distance and had kept its coat long to conceal the animal's physique.[36]

Horse racing not only could prove costly but also weakened a cavalry company's combat readiness. Cavalry mounts suffered terribly during the war's early months because the men often had little experience in caring for horses. The Charleston Light Dragoons, like many former militia units, were experienced riders. Their horses suffered, however, from being mounted with sporting saddles that were inappropriate for military use. And unlike Union cavalry, Confederate horsemen had to provide and feed their own mounts, for which the government paid them forty cents per day.[37]

In a letter to his sister, Frank Middleton bemoaned the condition of his animal. The "poor horse looks miserably . . . its back is again sore from another accident it met with some time since." He complained of being "a dragoon without a mount."[38] It is unclear whether the "accident" he alluded to was the result of racing or of some other cause. Regardless, Middleton, like many of his comrades, spent much of his time during the war searching for a suitable mount.

Drinking undoubtedly compounded the problems caused by horse racing. The consumption of alcohol, mostly in the form of champagne, wine, or fortified punch, had played an important role in the outfit's antebellum activities. As outlined in the troop's "List of Difficulties," punishment for any violation of company rules usually resulted in the guilty party providing the troop with champagne or some other alcoholic beverage.[39]

The members of the troop, being from wealthy families, were accustomed to consuming the finest wines and champagnes, which they actively sought during the war. On one occasion Frank Middleton and his friend John J. McPherson took a wagon and a team of horses to Middleton's sister Isabella's St. Peter's Parish plantation to retrieve "a number of boxes" of French wine. Upon arrival, however, Middleton discovered his sister and her family were in Savannah. Their slaves informed Middleton that they did not have the keys to the house and that recently they had discovered soldiers attempting to break into the dwelling, though the intruders had fled before gaining entry. Upon close investigation, Middleton discovered that the soldiers had damaged the wine cellar but had not taken its contents. Given the obviously precarious storage of the wine, Middleton "concluded to force the staple and help myself, which I did, carefully replacing it afterwards, and nailing up the window again." To compensate his sister for the wine, he "searched everywhere for some champagne . . . but could find none to send to her."[40]

Even though the dragoons' service experiences in some ways resembled those of other commands, company members had lived comfortably before the war and attempted to maintain a familiar lifestyle in camp. To facilitate this, they brought a fair number of servants with them into military service. Although it is not clear exactly how many male slaves served with the unit, they were numerous. Three of these, Alfred Brown, William Brown, and William Roddin, appear in the Compiled Service Records on the unit roster while it was in state service, though little else is known about these men or their duties.[41] Early in the war the dragoons formed messes of four or five members who would combine their resources and share food, wine, and accommodations when available. Slaves played an important role in this process by purchasing or gathering food and cooking for the mess, and also by acting as valets for their masters.[42]

That the dragoons considered their servants to be valuable assets in camp is beyond doubt. Early in the conflict Frank Middleton wrote to his mother to request a body servant, asking for "Richardson or some strong reliable person."[43] During the next two weeks he twice repeated the request, explaining that, "the expense will be trifling." He even offered to leave the selection of the servant to the family, as long as his mother did not "send a stupid one."[44] His entreaties were successful within the month, and he reported that his new servant, Wally, appeared to enjoy camp life.[45]

The Charleston Light Dragoons, as men of wealth, were accustomed to having house servants, and they attempted to re-create a domestic environment in camp. Dragoon Edward L. Wells wrote, "We are not obliged to do our cooking, washing, or to attend, except when on picket, to our horses, there being a sufficient number of negroes in camp to attend to these things."[46] Twenty years later he added that early in the war the unit's servants "were good, and some of the cooks excellent."[47] Reflecting the dragoons' dependence on their slaves, Frank Middleton suggested that a prospective recruit "should by all means bring a servant with him, he could not do without one."[48]

The structure of each mess even allowed for a specialized division of labor. In one mess, Gabriel Manigault's slave Stephney, a family coachman, served as a horse groomer, carpenter, and mechanic. Meanwhile, Frank Middleton's servant served as a cook for the mess, while Lewis Vanderhorst's servant Quash Stevens served as a waiter.[49] For slaves, working as a cook for the unit could be quite lucrative; a good cook "could get $20 a month as some of the most inferior get $15."[50] Regardless of their specialized skills, servants had to be capable of performing most tasks. Oliver H. Middleton Jr. commented about his slave, "Tom is very useful and answers all purposes so far, he washes for me, etc."[51]

Other slaves received high praise for their service as well. Frank Middleton wrote that he was going to send his servant William home for "a week or two," and he noted that "he has been very steady" in camp and "gives great satisfaction to the mess." Middleton continued in this paternalistic tone by explaining that William "is so good humored and tells the truth so often that I think he deserves a little holiday."[52]

The dragoons especially noted the virtues of slaves who died in service. Frank Middleton wrote, "Our mess has met with a great loss in Mr. [William L.] Kirkland's boy Tomson." Tomson died as the result of tonsillitis, or a similar ailment, with his throat swelling until he suffocated "in the greatest agony." Middleton referred to him as "one of the best and quickest servants I have ever known."[53] Gabriel Manigault's servant Robert contracted typhoid fever while in camp and, despite Manigault's attempts to get him to a physician, died shortly after being sent home. Manigault commented that the loss "grieved him much." Robert, who was only eighteen at the time of his death, had served Manigault for four years and "was slowly becoming a capable servant."[54]

It is not surprising that dragoons expressed such sentiments concerning slaves who had died in service. Like most of the planter class, these men clung to the belief that, if given the choice, most slaves would choose bondage over freedom. This attitude was evident in Frank Middleton's early letters. After the fall of Port Royal Sound on November 7, 1861, the area's planters had fled quickly with their families, leaving behind most of their slaves. Following reconnaissance missions to Union-occupied areas, Middleton claimed that these slaves were "perfectly orderly" and had continued to work without the presence of their masters.[55]

Middleton's faith in his slaves weakened somewhat over the length of his service. As mentioned, after he requested that his family send a slave named Richardson to him in late 1861, his father instead sent him a slave named Wally. Middleton at first seemed pleased with Wally's performance but soon wrote home that he was "sending Wally back in a few days. He will not answer." He asked his mother if there was "no person on the plantation pa could let me have, any intelligent person who can clean a horse, will answer . . . I can not get along very well without a servant."[56] This quick change in Wally's attitude is probably attributable to the nature of military service itself. Just as young men joined units and quickly grew homesick and tired of camp life, Wally could have realized that life at the elder Middleton's plantation was more to his liking. He therefore may have sulked or worked inefficiently so that he would be returned to his family.[57]

This incident and the specter of slaves deserting nearby plantations and escaping to Union forces affected Middleton's view of those he once simply had assumed were faithful and loyal slaves. In the letter praising his new servant William, Middleton informed family members that he was sending him home to Weehaw Plantation for a short "leave." He then inquired of his sister if she believed that William would run away during the trip home.[58]

The apparent fidelity of some servants raises important questions concerning their motivations. How did they view their roles? With no direct evidence from the slaves themselves, it is difficult to document their attitudes toward service. Undoubtedly, many slaves viewed military service as an act of self-preservation and were willing to ingratiate themselves with their masters for future benefits. Others served the dragoons for wages.[59] Still others had more personal reasons. One dragoon, Lewis Vanderhorst, served as caterer for his mess and often sent his servant, Quash Stevens, to the plantation of Vanderhorst's father on the Ashepoo River to retrieve "pork, eggs, chickens, and other good things."[60] Stevens ventured even farther afield in search of provisions later in the war. At one point Vanderhorst gave him "$60 and sent him up into Barnwell district about thirty miles with orders to buy what he could."[61] The slave returned with a large quantity of provisions for the mess.[62] This trip, and others like it, would have provided plenty of opportunities for escape, but Stevens always returned to Vanderhorst. The accounts of various dragoons indicate that Quash Stevens was a mulatto. Born either in 1840 or 1843, he was possibly the son of Elias Vanderhorst, who had fathered other mulatto children from the same mother, and the half brother of Dragoon Lewis Vanderhorst.[63] Such a circumstance would help explain Stevens's faithful service to Vanderhorst. Interestingly, no dragoons seemed to have remarked on any resemblance between the two men: even if true, discreet silence on such matters was expected.[64]

Considering the large number of slaves in camp, some probably ran away. It is just as likely that other cooks and servants stayed with the unit as long as it remained in the lowcountry, close to their homes and families, and as long as they were paid for their services.[65]

As the Charleston Light Dragoons continued to serve in the South Carolina lowcountry, a number of members sought assignments elsewhere, presumably to gain relief from picket duty, which was extremely unpleasant in that area. During much of the spring, summer, and fall, the area's high temperatures could make even routine activities arduous. During those months mosquitoes and sand gnats were unbearable, attacking any exposed skin.[66] Winter months were rainy, and though it very rarely snowed, the wind that constantly blew over the marshes and rivers was penetrating. All of these factors, coupled with the lack of accustomed camp amenities, made picket duty undesirable and other assignments an attractive proposition.[67]

Many dragoons were successful in their bids for temporary reassignment. Of the eighty men who served in the unit from November 7, 1861, to February 10, 1862, when it mustered out of state service, sixteen were detailed at some point during the three-month period. Because unit members became quite familiar with the rivers and marshes of Beaufort District, some dragoons served as guides. Others were detached by order of General Ripley with no reason given.[68]

Of greater concern to maintaining the troop's strength was the departure of twenty-five other members who left the unit for a variety of reasons at some time during their three months of state service. The enlistment of nine dragoons expired on February 7, 1862, and these men failed to reenlist. Three dragoons left after acquiring physicians' certificates claiming that they were unfit for duty. The remainder departed on a furlough or received new appointments and transferred to other commands.[69]

Problems with maintaining state units at effective strength in the lowcountry were widespread during the war's first year. On December 24, 1861, General Robert E. Lee complained to the state adjutant general about the depleted nature of South Carolina units, especially the cavalry companies in his department. Lee noted that the Charleston Light Dragoons had roughly forty-five men available for service. He suggested that all depleted units be reorganized because it was very expensive to "retain in service companies of such strength."[70] Hoping to alleviate its manpower problems, the company placed an advertisement in the *Charleston Daily Courier* that ordered all members not detached on special duty to report to camp within ten days. Failing to do so, "their names will be published in the daily papers of Charleston as no longer being members of this Corps, and their arms will be demanded forthwith," which no doubt would have caused great embarrassment for the absent members.[71]

At the same time, there was talk among unit members of the company's possible reorganization. Confusion existed about the amount of time left in the current term of service because the General Assembly had passed legislation on December 21, 1861, that had superseded the January 1861 act establishing a military force for the state's defense. The new legislation extended the term of enlistment for units in state service from one year to three years. Whether the dragoons automatically would have their service extended or whether they would have to reorganize and enlist for one or three years of Confederate service or for the war's duration remained unclear. If the unit underwent reorganization, it would do so in February 1862, the three-month anniversary of their enlistment in state service.[72]

The unit's officers were clearly uncertain about the company's future. In late December 1861, Captain Rutledge visited General Lee to inquire about his plans for the dragoons. Lee noted that the recent legislation "relieved" every militia company, but he had chosen to keep the dragoons in service. He offered the company the choice, however, of staying in service or being relieved to return to Charleston for reorganization and reenlistment. The company voted for the latter option, but Lee reconsidered and informed Rutledge that he would have to keep the company in service because he "wanted cavalry."[73]

Lee's decision reflected his confidence in the dragoons and their commander, despite the unit's apparent lack of discipline and affinity for avoiding the customary sacrifices of military life. The dragoons had successfully escorted his staff officers on numerous reconnaissance missions and had proved their knowledge of the area. Captain Joseph C. Ives of Lee's staff had even requested that the company be detailed to serve as scouts on the Sea Islands.[74]

Soon after meeting with Rutledge, Lee, perhaps realizing the urgency of quickly having the unit back in service, decided to allow the dragoons to return to Charleston, reorganize, and then reenlist for Confederate service. On February 10, 1862, the dragoons left state service.[75] On February 16, 1862, the company met at the Charleston Hotel and voted to volunteer for twelve months of Confederate service. As in peacetime, the company appointed a committee to take applications for new members. Those interested in joining the company were asked to visit Cornet James W. O'Hear at the firm of O'Hear, Roper, and Stoney. The dragoons also unanimously reelected their officers.[76] Any hopes of quickly reorganizing, however, soon faded. By March 2 the unit still had not found enough members (seventy-two were needed) to muster into service.[77] The new department commander, General John C. Pemberton, was in such desperate need of the dragoons that he informed Rutledge that he would take the company back into service with fifty members if the state adjutant general would agree.[78] Members of the unit, veterans and recruits alike, gathered at the Charleston Hotel to elect the company's officers. Again, each officer was reelected (yet another sign that old-fashioned deference was alive and well in Charleston), and befitting the unit's usual emphasis on sociability, the next evening the officers treated the unit to the company's potent punch at an engine house near Wentworth Street. A few days later, the Charleston Light Dragoons departed for McPhersonville, Beaufort District, where they were mustered into Confederate service for one year.[79]

The unit could not quickly find recruits because the initial enthusiasm for the war had waned during the previous year. Even for the renowned Charleston Light Dragoons, attracting new volunteers had grown difficult. Many of the region's wealthiest men, the sort who had joined the dragoons in the past, had received commissions with other commands or were serving as aides or adjutants to generals.[80] In addition, some veteran dragoons did not reenlist, having decided that three months of military service was more than enough.[81]

Yet at same time, several planters, some who already had lost large amounts of property during the war's first year, joined for the first time during the spring of 1862. Others who had stayed on their plantations to continue rice production either enlisted in an outfit such as the dragoons or faced being drafted according to the terms of the Confederate Conscription Act of 1862.[82]

Following this reorganization, many of the new recruits were older than those who had joined a year earlier. Of the ninety-four volunteers whose enlistment ages are recorded in the Compiled Service Records, the average age was twenty-seven and a half. One-third of the unit's new members were thirty or older, and four were forty or older. In contrast, only eleven members were in their teens (table 3).

Men in their thirties and forties clearly preferred membership in the Charleston Light Dragoons to more rigorous service in an infantry regiment. Undoubtedly, they saw service with the cavalry as less taxing, and service in the dragoons as even less demanding, than infantry service. The unit's privileged position in the local Confederate command was widely known. Recruits from the social elite could serve with longtime friends and relatives, men whom they considered to be their social equals. Furthermore, they could serve close to their plantations, overseeing agricultural production while benefiting from access to produce or livestock to supplement their rations.

For the families of the Charleston Light Dragoons, the euphoria that had swept through the city following the fall of Fort Sumter was short lived. In July 1861 the results of the war's first major engagement brought the realities of war home to many of the lowcountry's residents. Henry A. Middleton Jr., son

Table 3—Unit members by age

Age	Number	Percentage
17–19	11	11.70
20–29	48	51.06
30–39	31	32.98
40–49	4	4.25
Total	94	100

Source: National Archives, War Department Collection of Confederate Records, RG 109. Compiled Service Records of Confederate Soldiers Who Served in Organizations from the State of South Carolina. Microcopy 267, 4th South Carolina Cavalry, rolls 24–30.

Note: This table is based on the 94 members whose age at the time of enlistment is identified in the Compiled Service Records, and who enlisted in the Dragoons while it was in Confederate service (after March 25, 1862).

of Henry A. and Harriott K. Middleton and brother of Dragoon Frank Middleton, was mortally wounded in the first battle of Bull Run. He was the family's second oldest son and its hope for the future. He had assumed management of the family's plantations in Georgetown District in 1855 and enlisted in the Washington Light Infantry when the war began. He was buried in the graveyard of St. Philip's Church, Charleston's oldest congregation.[83]

His death and the deaths of other prominent Charlestonians cast a shadow over the city. Susan M. Middleton, Henry's cousin, wrote to his sister, "Oh— are these not dreadful days? Each hour seems to bring its own sad tale—And many say there are darker ones still in store for us—in spite of this great victory—the brilliancy seems very faint—amidst all this sorrow and suspense."[84]

The correspondence of the Middleton women provides an insight into the high expectations women had for family and friends who joined units such as the dragoons. Six months after Henry's death, his sister Harriott wrote that "our life is so sad—so utterly ship wrecked . . . as Mama was saying just now, 'everything in our lives is at an end.'" Alice, another of the Middleton sisters, described Henry as a brother, father, and husband to the family's women, "the one stable thing" in their lives that could not be tempted.[85]

By way of contrast, Dragoon Frank Middleton seemed no such paragon. Harriott explained that she was "very fond of him" but had doubts about his character after his letters from camp demonstrated that he regularly partook in its vices.[86] Although Harriott never defined "character" in her letters, it is fair to assume that her definition involved Victorian ideals of morality. Her estimation that her brother Henry "could not be tempted" stands in contrast to the behavior of her other brother.[87]

Within two months of the personal losses sustained at Bull Run, the dragoons' families faced substantial material losses as well. In the wake of the Union capture of Cape Hatteras on the North Carolina Outer Banks on August 29, 1861, Confederate officials, fearing that Charleston was the next Union objective, began evacuating the more exposed islands near the city. In early September General Roswell Ripley advised all planters on Edisto Island to remove their valuables and to leave their homes by September 12. This order was of particular interest to Ella Middleton Rutledge, wife of Dragoon Captain Rutledge, since their plantation was located on the island and she had recently given birth. The Middletons soon thereafter abandoned their home in the hope that they would return to it in better times.[88]

The Middleton women, and the women of other wealthy Charleston families, faced the war's early tribulations by attempting to rely on long-established antebellum standards of decorum for people of their social caste. In Charleston these ideals remained in place for some time during the war, and aristocratic women were quick to oppose any break in convention. An exchange between Isabella Middleton Cheves, Frank Middleton's sister, and an unnamed dragoon illustrates the manner in which war and military service had disrupted social conventions. One of Middleton's comrades and friends called at his home in Charleston while on leave. George, one of the family's servants, answered the door and announced the arrival of the gentleman, who wished to speak with a member of the family. Isabella went to the door only to find the visitor (presumably drunk) lying prostrate on the street outside. Surprised, she asked the man his business, whereby he informed her that he was seeking "protection for the night." He referred to George, one of the family's house servants, as "this damned nigger boy," impolite and offensive language for genteel company, especially when directed at a trusted family servant. The man also touched his cap repeatedly in what seems a nervous attempt to show respect for Isabella. Obviously appalled at such behavior, Isabella curtly informed the dragoon that Mr. Middleton was not in town and he would have to look elsewhere. The visitor, who was not familiar with the city, then asked for directions prior to departing.[89]

More than likely, the dragoon was acting like other soldiers, men who had spent months in camp surrounded by other men, with very few opportunities to socialize with women. In Victorian America, women were considered paragons of virtue and therefore a positive moral influence on men. Without their presence, soldiers could rapidly grow depraved. In this instance, the social distance between the vices of camp life, located miles away from the city and civilization, and Charleston south of Broad Street would have left the visitor ill prepared to adjust his manners and behavior to suit the Middleton women.[90]

Because the women of the city's most prestigious families, like most women North and South, could not serve in combat, they contributed in other ways.[91]

In some instances they provided assistance to aid societies.[92] For the most part, however, they viewed their role as that of moral guardians, serving to protect Southern values and ideals on the home front. This also meant defending the cause of secession through their rhetoric, their letters, and their prayers, all tasks conducted in the private or domestic sphere. As protectors of all that was sacred at home, they deplored anyone of their class whose actions conflicted with established rules of bravery, honor, or patriotism.[93]

This need to pressure friends and family into maintaining their commitment to the cause is evident in an incident involving a friend of the Middletons who visited some of the family in Flat Rock, North Carolina. In a conversation, Dragoon Henry Seabrook, a twenty-four-year-old planter from Edisto Island, asked the women if they had read his Unionist speeches prior to the war. He also spoke of the war and a battle on Edisto Island where he had witnessed the death of a young Union soldier, whom he referred to as a "poor little fellow." The women were "shocked and disgusted," and "seemed ready almost to kill *him.*" To compound matters, Seabrook told Ella Middleton Rutledge, wife of his commander, that if he ever charged with the dragoons, he would do so with his eyes shut. Furthermore, he insisted that he found comfort in the proposition that a dragoon was seldom injured unless he fell from his horse. In angry response, Ella cried, "What would happen to us if all our soldiers were like that?"[94]

This incident signified far more than the shortcomings of a dragoon who seemed too lighthearted in discussing the Confederate cause. It illustrates a growing gap between the expectations of those on the home front and those in camp. In Seabrook's comments an increasing cynicism with the struggle is visible, while the ladies' comments and actions reveal their lack of patience for those unwilling to support their cause wholeheartedly.[95]

As the women of the planter class witnessed the changing attitudes of the men whom they had sent to war, they found their own attitudes changing as well. The loss of loved ones forced some women to wonder if the central tenets of their privileged world could survive the war.[96] Women who had been forced to evacuate their homes wondered, not surprisingly, whether their menfolk would any longer be able to serve as the families' patriarchal protectors.[97]

During the war's first year, the lowcountry's wealthiest male residents found that the conflict not only called their accustomed social roles into question, it endangered their ability to provide for their families. Many men who were too old to serve in the dragoons continued in their usual professions, but being a planter, factor, or merchant became a difficult struggle. Even a prosperous factor, such as William C. Bee, who headed the firm W. C. Bee and Company, realized that the blockade might well ruin his business, so he founded the Importing and Exporting Company of South Carolina, also known as the Bee Company.[98] Despite remaining successful, Bee lamented the war's impact on his family. He feared for the safety of Charleston and Savannah.[99] He worried about his son James, a dragoon who was expected to report to camp but had run a fever, "for a fortnight past." Nor did garrison life apparently suit his other son, John, a lieutenant in the 1st South Carolina Artillery, then stationed at Castle Pinckney. And already the high inflation that would plague the Confederate economy had reached South Carolina. "I do not know how you get along in Columbia for food," he wrote to his daughter. "We shall have to make due with a plate of soup and rice, and be thankful for that." Bee even began to worry about being able to provide for his family.[100]

Others who were in need of capital continued to grow rice. Henry A. Middleton, father of Dragoon Frank Middleton, remained at Weehaw, the family's main plantation in Georgetown District, to ensure its continued rice production while preventing the flight of his slaves to Union vessels stationed off the coast. He sent his wife and daughters to safety in Flat Rock, North Carolina. Middleton was concerned with his slave property because of its relative value when compared with his other property. Aside from over 270 slaves, Middleton owned real estate valued at $300,000 ($6.18 million in 2000) in Newport, Rhode Island, which he feared losing due to the Federal Confiscation Act of 1862. If this property were lost, his family's only remaining assets were its Georgetown District land and slaves.[101] Middleton, therefore, was reluctant to abandon these last vestiges of his prewar wealth. Instead, he chose to risk the loss of his slaves and property to generate needed capital during a time of increasing uncertainty.

During the war's first year, the material circumstances of most dragoons and their families changed dramatically. The Union blockade of South Carolina ports and the capture of Beaufort prevented the region's rice and cotton planters from selling their crops in European markets. Moreover, the blockade threatened slavery, as Union naval patrols encouraged slaves living on coastal plantations to flee their masters.

The region's wealthy had abandoned homes on the Sea Islands, and many never regained their property. The Union capture of Port Royal Sound created the area's first refugees, some of whom lost most of their assets and were forced to rely on the assistance of family or friends. Even those refugees who had other estates and slaves often faced greatly reduced material circumstances.

Although these events raised the stakes of service for the Charleston Light Dragoons, their day-to-day existence remained relatively comfortable and uneventful during the war's first year. Service for the dragoons was a refuge from many of the troubles that their families were experiencing. On the home front the women of the planter class experienced material and personal losses, and the dragoons' fathers witnessed the gradual collapse of the lowcountry economy that had generated and sustained their wealth. The soldiers themselves, however, were part of a Confederate military system that, for that first year at least, protected them and kept them away from any heavy fighting. They would eventually have to fight, but until that point any gallantry, suffering, and death remained confined to their imaginations.

Chapter 3

A TASTE OF WAR

Their bullets came as thick as hail.

Frank Middleton

On March 25, 1862, the Charleston Light Dragoons began their Confederate service. In the ranks were prewar members and wartime veterans, plus their friends, family, and prewar business colleagues. Over the next two years more recruits trickled into the company, men from areas where the dragoons were stationed or from areas through which the company passed. Most hailed from wealthy and respectable families, and although they were late to enlist, their service in the Charleston Light Dragoons provided the new members with some social continuity. To maintain exclusivity, the dragoons continued to elect new members, a dragoon tradition that survived the changes wrought by war.[1]

The newly elected members of the company served and associated with men of their same class, just as they would have in a peacetime militia unit. This was also the case for those who already had some wartime service. Men who sought to escape the responsibility of command and staff positions in other outfits were more than willing to serve as enlisted men in the Charleston Light Dragoons. The unit's reputation for exclusivity made service in its ranks nearly as prestigious as being an officer in other, less renowned companies. In addition, for new and old members alike, camp life, most notably the quality of food and drink, helped maintain some semblance of gentility and set them apart from ordinary Confederate soldiers. It would take combat to introduce the dragoons to experiences similar to those had by other companies with less refined tastes and less aristocratic members.

Among the late arrivals to the company were four members of the Pringle family, including Miles Brewton Pringle, son of William Bull Pringle and Mary Mott Alston Pringle. Pringle's family resided in the Miles Brewton House, a large brick home on King Street in Charleston, and owned plantations in Georgetown District. Three cousins, John Julius Pringle, Joel Roberts Poinsett Pringle, and Dominick Lynch Pringle, also enlisted.[2] They were the sons of John Julius Izard Pringle and Jane Lynch Pringle. J. J. I. Pringle owned a home in Newport, Rhode Island, two Black River plantations, Greenfield and White House, and a house in France, where the family resided before the war. At the war's outset the three sons had been studying at Heidelberg.[3] In her famed diary, Mary Boykin Chesnut wrote of their almost epic journey back to South

Carolina. To return, all three had "walked, waded, and rowed in boats, if boats they could find; swam rivers when boats there were none." Chesnut concluded by pronouncing, "brave lads are they. One can but admire their pluck and energy."[4] Their background and dash made them ideal candidates for membership in the dragoons, and between September 1862 and May 1864, each brother found his way into the unit.[5]

Such men joined the Charleston Light Dragoons because, as long as the unit was in the lowcountry, it offered a refuge from danger for those who qualified for membership. In many cases the company also became a refuge from responsibility. Some of the newest members had served uncomfortably and perhaps unsuccessfully as officers in other commands. The former was the case with William L. Kirkland, a physician and native of Camden, in Kershaw District. He also owned Rose Hill Plantation, which Mary Boykin Chesnut described as "a most beautiful country seat. Live oaks in all their glory, camellias as plentiful on the lawn as the hawthorn in an English hedge."[6] Kirkland's plantation and Long Brow, an adjacent plantation belonging to his mother, were situated on the Combahee River, the dividing line between Beaufort and Colleton Districts, an area that was vulnerable to enemy attacks.[7]

Kirkland had previously served as an aide to General Roswell Ripley. Ripley blamed Kirkland and Rawlins Lowndes, another aide and former dragoon, for a fiasco at the battle of South Mountain (September 14, 1862), where, at a critical juncture in the action, Ripley became lost and led four brigades of infantry off into the woods and completely out of the battle.[8] After losing favor with Ripley, Kirkland returned to Rose Hill, where he joined the dragoons and narrowly avoided serving in the state reserve regiments, which were composed of men between the ages of thirty-five and sixty-five. Even after he enlisted with the Charleston Light Dragoons, a local reserve captain sent a party of men to their camp to arrest him. The dragoons and other local units protected Kirkland's nearby property, and that he could draw provisions from his plantation—"butter, turkeys, etc."—made him "quite an acquisition" in the eyes of the other members of his mess.[9]

Other new recruits were former officers who had failed to be reelected. Such was the case with Josiah Bedon, an attorney before the war from Walterboro in Colleton District. He had been the first person elected captain of the Summerville Guards, Company C, 9th South Carolina Infantry, which later became the 11th South Carolina Infantry. Afterward, he had served as a lieutenant in the 2nd South Carolina Battalion before enlisting as a private in the Charleston Light Dragoons. Like Kirkland, and unlike most dragoons, Bedon was a combat veteran. He had received a debilitating wound in the foot at the battle of Seven Pines on May 31, 1862, and was still limping when he joined the unit on April 11, 1863. For Bedon, service with the dragoons offered many of the same benefits that other members received and also allowed him to serve in a mounted unit, which was much easier for a disabled soldier than service in the infantry.[10]

A number of dragoons moved in and out of the unit throughout the war, using the prestige of membership as a stepping-stone to other appointments. William Bell joined the Charleston Light Dragoons in 1858 and was a member until he organized a cavalry company and was elected its captain. When his unit was transferred to the light artillery, Bell resigned his commission and rejoined the unit. Soon thereafter he was detailed to organize and operate the labor bureau in Charleston and build heavy fortifications about the city. He returned to the dragoons again in 1864.[11]

Some dragoons had been militia officers before the war but had lost their positions once hostilities began. Such was the case with Ralph E. Elliott. The son of William Elliott, both a state representative and state senator, a large-scale planter and an opponent of secession, Elliot had been a beat captain in the South Carolina State Militia before the firing on Fort Sumter. After hostilities began, Elliott lost his position and joined the Beaufort Artillery. Soon thereafter he won a seat in the South Carolina legislature. His family abandoned their home in Beaufort during the Union invasion in early November 1861, and his father died in Charleston in February 1863. In October 1863 he joined the Charleston Light Dragoons.[12]

At least one of the men who joined the unit in late 1862 was a renowned adventurer. John Harleston, son of a prominent lowcountry planter, had gone to Texas to fight Indians with the Texas Rangers when he was twenty-five. He returned to Charleston when South Carolina seceded and joined a militia company serving on Morris Island. He grew bored with his service, however, and signed onto the privateer *Savannah* as first officer. When the USS *Perry* captured the *Savannah* in 1861, Harleston and his fellow prisoners were paraded through New York City. They were charged as pirates and confined in a New York City prison nicknamed "The Tombs." Confinement was so trying for Harleston that he asked his mother to pray for his death.[13] The crew of the *Savannah* was tried but not convicted. Eventually they were exchanged as prisoners of war. Upon arriving home in Charleston, Harleston joined the Charleston Light Dragoons and remained with the unit until 1864.[14]

Most of the men who joined the company during the war did not complete their service in the Charleston Light Dragoons. A majority of dragoons used service in the company as a stepping-stone to appointments as officers, transfers to noncombat positions, or permanent detachments. A large number were dropped from the company's rolls during 1864, when regulations regarding the size of Confederate cavalry units forced the company to reduce its numbers. Of the roughly 176 men who served in the company during its Confederate service (after March 25, 1862), at least 85 left the unit before the war's conclusion (table 4).

Table 4—Final disposition of unit members

Disposition	Number	Percentage
Detached	26	16.35
Discharged, Appointment	25	15.72
Discharged, Health	4	2.52
Dropped, Reduction	30	18.87
Completed Service	74	46.54

Source: National Archives, War Department Collection of Confederate Records, RG 109. Compiled Service Records of Confederate Soldiers Who Served in Organizations from the State of South Carolina. Microcopy 267, 4th South Carolina Cavalry, rolls 24–30.

Note: This table is based on the 159 members whose terms of service could be identified and who began service after the unit was mustered into Confederate service (March 25, 1862).

Of those who left, thirty (the largest group) were dropped from the company's rolls in 1864 to reduce the unit to regulation strength. Some twenty-six unit members ended their service on permanent detail. An almost equal number were discharged to become officers in other units or to accept political appointments. Despite the number of older recruits, only four dragoons were discharged for health reasons.[15]

This large exodus of men from the company's ranks raises questions about unit morale and the nature of duty itself. Yet there is no evidence that service was overly demanding or daily duties exceedingly taxing. In terms of personal comfort and command informality, few combat units in Confederate service had the advantages that the Charleston Light Dragoons had. A more plausible explanation for the departure of company members involves both their social positions and the prestige that accompanied membership in the unit. Dragoons belonged to the most prominent families in the Confederacy, and they used this circumstance to their advantage to gain Confederate military and political appointments.

To attain positions of increased responsibility and stature, dragoons usually sought and received the recommendations of local commanders and company officers prior to corresponding with their congressman, William Porcher Miles. Miles had served as mayor of Charleston and as a U.S. congressman for Charleston before the war. He had been a fire-eater in the years prior to secession, and later he became a Confederate congressman, a position that he held for the war's duration.[16]

As a Confederate congressman, he received a number of requests regarding appointments. In early 1861 Gabriel Manigault, who would later join the Charleston Light Dragoons, petitioned for Miles's assistance in securing the position of secretary of legation to France or to the Court of St. James. Although Miles could not grant either request, he generally was accommodating to dragoons seeking appointments. For example, Wade Hampton Manning, son of former South Carolina governor John L. Manning, mentioned Miles's friendship with his father in requesting a recommendation.[17] Thomas A. Middleton wrote to enquire if Miles could assist him in securing an appointment as a lieutenant in the Confederate army. Arthur P. Lining also requested Miles's assistance in securing a commission in the Confederate army, explaining that he "had been excluded [from a] position, whilst commissions have been lavished upon those . . . who in many instances, are not a whit more competent than I, and whose claims were certainly not entitled to as much consideration."[18] Upon receiving letters such as these from dragoons, Miles forwarded the requests to Confederate secretary of war James Seddon. Miles in effect served as the gatekeeper for most of the appointments that dragoons received. He wrote to Seddon and Confederate president Jefferson Davis of each applicant's merit, most often describing each dragoon as a "gentleman of character and position."[19]

In some cases, however, dragoons wrote directly to members of the Confederate cabinet or to the president. John W. Lewis, a forty-four-year-old planter from Colleton District, wrote to Seddon and requested either a discharge or a transfer to the Engineer Department so he could be closer to his plantations and his large family. In another instance, Dragoon Albert Rhett Elmore wrote to both Seddon and Davis seeking an appointment. In his letter to Davis, Elmore wrote of the president's friendship with Elmore's parents.[20] As men accustomed to benefiting from their family's position and power, the dragoons naturally expected that personal connections would continue to serve their interests during the war.

Those dragoons who remained with the unit following reorganization soon learned that duty in Beaufort District could be both strenuous and hazardous. On May 29, 1862, Union troops launched a raid on Pocotaligo in Beaufort District with the goal of seizing and burning the Charleston and Savannah Railroad bridge there. This force, under the operational command of Brigadier General Isaac I. Stevens, set out from Port Royal Ferry and advanced north until it was met by a Confederate force under Colonel William S. Walker, commander of the Third Military District. Walker's men halted the Union thrust short of its objective in a running battle near Pocotaligo. Stevens's troops then retreated to Gardens Corner as night fell. The Charleston Light Dragoons and other cavalry units rushed to the scene of the battle, most arriving late on the evening of May 29. That night the unit advanced close to the enemy pickets in Gardens Corner before bivouacking for the night. It was their first forced march, and the day had been hot. When they halted for the evening, they found that other Confederate soldiers had drained all of the local wells.[21]

Walker, fearing the confusion of a night action, decided to wait until morning to press his attack, but the Union troops used this respite to withdraw back across the ferry under the cover of darkness.[22]

The dragoons' actions on May 29 and 30 highlighted their poor physical conditioning. Still exhausted from the heat and forced march on the day of the battle, they faced an even hotter day on May 30. They were physically drained and rode to Pocotaligo Station to catch the train back to their camp at Grahamville, while a small detachment led the horses back. The dragoons arrived at the station "in a jaded and exhausted state," and as they lay on the platform, their fatigue was so apparent that the local telegraph operator criticized the unit "as very unpromising material for soldiers."[23]

The engagement also revealed a serious weakness in Walker's cavalry. Most of the mounted troops in the Third District, including the Charleston Light Dragoons, were armed only with sabers and sidearms, and a few had shotguns. Consequently, the Union raiders had badly outgunned their Confederate opponents during the battle.[24] To remedy this problem, the dragoons' officers proposed equipping the men with rifles, a suggestion that many of the troopers stridently opposed. As yet unfamiliar with the realities of Civil War combat, the more naive and romantic types considered rifles to be "unbecoming weapons for light cavalry."[25] Undoubtedly, they were unaware that many other Confederate cavalry units, especially in the western theater, had discarded their sabers early in the war.[26]

These men knew little of the history of dragoon units. Beginning in France around 1600, dragoons had long been armed with muskets and were trained to dismount and fight on foot. As dragoons became more enamored of the charge and more reluctant to fight dismounted, European armies developed light dragoons, who served as scouts, conducted reconnaissance, and skirmished with enemy formations while dismounted. In this latter role, muskets were quite valuable. Dragoons had served well on the American frontier, where they seldom had opportunities to use their sabers.[27] And despite the South Carolinians' supposed affinity for the sword, its members refused to seriously study its use. Gabriel Manigault, the company's commissary, had taken fencing lessons in Europe prior to the war and had also acquired knowledge of sword drill from an ex-sergeant of British light cavalry named Henry W. Moran in Charleston. Considering himself something of an expert, Manigault tried to instruct one squad of dragoons, but his pupils soon tired of this because he "wanted to teach them too much."[28]

Considering the romantic antebellum Southern image of the cavalier or knight, it is understandable that unit members disdained rifles. Both the Southern upper class, including the Charleston Light Dragoons, and the New England Brahmins were imbued with the idea of "knightliness." Characterized as "an exaggeration of honor," knightliness was a set of ideals derived from romantic imagery epitomized in the novels of Sir Walter Scott. To those who subscribed to the tenets of knightliness, warfare was seen as a contest, similar to a joust, in which knights bravely and nobly pursued victory. The ideas of gallantry and courage associated with knightliness were most prevalent in the cavalry, the branch of service that most closely resembled the knighthood.[29]

In addition to their knightly pretensions and commitment to the saber, the dragoons had successfully performed the duties of light cavalry thus far without shoulder arms. In private wartime correspondence, Captain Benjamin H. Rutledge identified his command as the Charleston Light *Hussars,* using the designation of an especially flamboyant type of light cavalry.[30] In official correspondence, the unit remained the Charleston Light Dragoons.[31]

Despite the protests of some troopers, Colonel Walker and Captain Rutledge agreed to send Lieutenant Lionel C. Nowell to Richmond to procure rifles. Before Nowell could leave Charleston, however, General John C. Pemberton gave him permission to draw rifles from a recently arrived blockade-runner. The weapons were .577 caliber short Enfield rifle muskets made in Great Britain. They were longer than cavalry carbines but shorter than the long Enfield or the .58 caliber Springfield rifle musket used by many infantry units.[32] The distribution of these weapons to the men apparently elicited additional grumbling in the ranks.[33]

The Charleston Light Dragoons experienced other, potentially more disruptive changes in 1862. Several months after its reorganization, the unit faced the loss of organizational and operational independence. In August 1862 rumors circulated throughout the lowcountry that all independent cavalry commands would be consolidated into regiments. Many independent units scrambled to join with similar outfits to create their own regiments. The 3rd South Carolina Cavalry attempted to incorporate the Charleston Light Dragoons into its ranks, over the objections of many dragoons. Not surprisingly, troopers feared losing their independence and their many privileges, including the unit's large number of servants and its oversized private tents. Opposition also hinged on familial ties and personalities. The commander of the 3rd Cavalry, Colonel Charles J. Colcock, was the brother of dragoon 1st lieutenant Richard H. Colcock, the unit's least popular officer. If the dragoons joined the 3rd Cavalry, Captain Rutledge would be promoted to major while Richard Colcock would become captain of the dragoons, a situation "not desired except by a few of the men." Rutledge gave his unit the option to join the 3rd Cavalry, but the men, continuing their unit's own democratic traditions as well as reflecting the attitudes of many volunteers early in the war, voted against joining the 3rd South Carolina Cavalry.[34]

Unfortunately for the dragoons, the decision to remain independent was not a long-term option. In late August, General Pemberton recommended that Captain Rutledge be promoted to colonel of a cavalry regiment to be organized from lowcountry units. The dragoons were to become part of his regiment.[35] Around the same time, Pemberton informed Major William Stokes of the 2nd South Carolina Cavalry battalion that all of the cavalry units in the lowcountry were to be consolidated into regiments. Stokes's battalion would join another battalion, an independent company, and the Charleston Light Dragoons to form Rutledge's regiment. News of Rutledge's promotion to colonel was disconcerting to Stokes, who was slated to become lieutenant colonel of the regiment, despite the fact that he outranked Rutledge. Perhaps as early as late August, Rutledge visited Stokes to discuss the matter. What transpired at that meeting convinced Rutledge that he would need to utilize his personal connections to ensure his promotion.[36]

On September 3, 1862, Rutledge wrote to Colonel Lucius B. Northrop, a close friend and Confederate commissary general, to ask for assistance in securing the promotion. He complained to Northrop, "Parties have gone on to Richmond for the purpose of defeating the appointment if possible." Rutledge claimed he had known nothing of Pemberton's recommendation until the general had submitted it, arguing that "'the war of *Influence*' is a war from which I have always recoiled." He did not, however, recoil from using influence for himself. He asked Northrop to present the question to his friend President Jefferson Davis. Northrop only had "to let the President . . . understand *who* I am and *what* I have done so that I may not be quietly put aside to gratify the aspirations of mere self seekers." Rutledge's letter was not altogether self-serving. He also asked Northrop to make sure that Third Military District commander Colonel William S. Walker received a promotion to brigadier general.[37]

Whether Stokes actually sent an emissary to Richmond on his behalf is unclear. While on medical furlough, he received letters claiming that his battalion opposed being thrown into a regiment. In one, J. R. Massey, adjutant of Stokes's battalion, argued that Rutledge was in quest of "a commission hunted down by political influence." Under considerable pressure from his officers and men, Stokes wrote to Rutledge formally protesting consolidation. In a reply of October 16, 1862, Rutledge admitted that he was "not surprised at the wish of the Battalion to retain their separate organization," because his command, the Charleston Light Dragoons, also opposed consolidation. But, he continued, "unless the General [P. G. T. Beauregard] has changed his opinion entirely within 48 hours, your battalion will be obliged to enter into some regiment or other." That being said, Rutledge expressed his hopes that Stokes's battalion would become part of his regiment. He concluded by offering to send Stokes's letter of protest to Beauregard for a final decision.[38]

Two days later, Beauregard, who had recently replaced Pemberton as departmental commander, decided the fate of Stokes's battalion and the Charleston Light Dragoons. On October 18, 1862, he advised General Samuel Cooper, Confederate adjutant and inspector general, of the "unorganized condition" of the cavalry in his department. He requested authority to reorganize the department's cavalry into two regiments, one of which would comprise Stokes's battalion, William P. Emanuel's battalion, the Charleston Light Dragoons, and another company. Based on Pemberton's suggestion, Beauregard recommended Captain Rutledge of the Charleston Light Dragoons for colonel, Major Stokes for lieutenant colonel, and Major Emanuel for major. He added that "this proposed organization has the consent of Majors Stokes and Emanuel."[39]

It was by no means clear how influential Northrop had been in securing the promotion, but apparently based on the last line of Beauregard's letter, Stokes changed his mind about protesting consolidation. Perhaps he realized that opposition would be futile. Born of a prominent family, Rutledge was a well-known attorney before the war, a delegate to the Secession Convention, and a highly regarded officer. He commanded a socially and politically powerful company that had found favor with Generals Lee and Pemberton since the war's outset. Beauregard, who had been in Charleston in 1861, knew of the dragoons and their commander, and respected his predecessor's recommendation. In contrast, Stokes, a St. Bartholomew's Parish planter who lived near Branchville, had fewer political or social connections than the men of the Charleston Light Dragoons.[40]

For his part, Stokes resented the dragoons even before consolidation. Following the skirmish at Pocotaligo on May 29, 1862, he complained of inaccurate newspaper reports that had reported the dragoons' participation in the skirmish, even though they had been assigned to his command and had not been involved. His conclusion was that "City papers like to puff City companies."[41] Yet if he had continued to oppose consolidation, Stokes might have lost his promotion to lieutenant colonel and still ended up being absorbed into a less than desirable regiment.

Unlike Stokes, the commander of the new regiment's other battalion, Major Emanuel, lost his command and was not promoted. This was undoubtedly the result of his failure to appease the planters of Georgetown District. Emanuel, a Jewish farmer from Marlboro District who had graduated from the Citadel, had commanded most of Georgetown District's defense forces during the war's first year. Local planters such as Henry A. Middleton, father of Dragoon Frank Middleton, had complained about Emanuel's indecision and ineffectiveness as a commander.[42] He had failed to prevent a series of Union raids up the Black, Waccamaw, and Pee Dee rivers that had carried off a number of slaves.[43] His performance in Georgetown dissipated whatever political influence Emanuel might have exerted, and he did not protest the consolidation of his command into a regiment commanded by Rutledge, a junior officer.

Before the consolidation became official, military events in Beaufort District threw the dragoons into combat for the first time. On October 22, 1862,

Union major general Ormsby M. Mitchel, the newly appointed commander of the Department of the South, launched another raid to destroy the Charleston and Savannah Railroad bridge over the Pocotaligo River. In addition, Mitchel later claimed that his goals were to make a "complete" reconnaissance of the Broad, Coosawhatchie, Tulifinny, and Pocotaligo rivers, while testing his department's ability to move a Union force rapidly into enemy-held territory. By doing so, he sought to gauge the strength of Confederate forces guarding the Charleston and Savannah Railroad and have his men destroy as much of it as possible in a single day. Mitchel's force consisted of 4,500 men.[44]

The operation was no hastily planned exercise. Mitchel sent scouts and spies to all critical points on the railroad and dispatched a party to cut the telegraph wires between local Confederates and Savannah and Charleston. His scouts had examined all tributaries of the Broad River, gauging their depths and searching for viable landing points. Furthermore, he had his engineers convert two large flat boats into artillery transports with hinged aprons.[45]

Facing this amphibious assault were the Confederate troops of South Carolina's Third Military District, including the Charleston Light Dragoons. The district commander, Colonel William S. Walker, had only 475 men, of which seventy would have had to serve as horse holders in any fight, to face any immediate threat. In addition to his numerical advantage, Mitchel also believed that he held the advantage of surprise, since he could strike at any point in the Third District, which included hundreds of miles of coastline and rivers. Walker, however, hoped to counter these Union advantages. Out of necessity, he violated the military maxim of concentrating forces in the face of a superior enemy, instead spreading his command at picket posts throughout the district to serve as an early warning system. Like other units, the Charleston Light Dragoons performed this duty on a rotating basis. Through this intelligence network, Walker hoped to receive timely news of Union movements and then telegraph Charleston and Savannah for reinforcements that would arrive via the Charleston and Savannah Railroad.[46]

For this strike into enemy territory, Mitchel decided on a landing at Mackay's Point, a peninsula formed by the Broad and Pocotaligo rivers. From there his forces would push northward until reaching and destroying the railroad bridge near Pocotaligo. A wide country road running the length of the peninsula was to provide the Union troops an ideal avenue of approach, while the rivers would protect the column from flank attack. The distance to be covered was seven or eight miles, and Mitchel estimated that his force could easily accomplish all of its objectives and return to their embarkation point within twenty-four hours.[47]

Before the operation's commencement, Mitchel became ill, so he placed operational control of the mission in the hands of Brigadier General John M. Brannan, commander of the department's first brigade. Brannan's force arrived off Mackay's Point at 4:30 A.M. on October 22, but a transport ran aground and delayed the offloading of troops by four hours. Meanwhile, Brannan dispatched a small force up the Coosawhatchie River to destroy the railroad bridge at the town of Coosawhatchie.[48]

At 9:00 A.M. Confederate pickets informed Walker of the Union landing at Mackay's Point. Walker quickly telegraphed Brigadier General Hugh W. Mercer in Savannah to rush reinforcements to Coosawhatchie, and General P. G. T. Beauregard in Charleston and Brigadier General Johnson Hagood in the Second Military District to send troops to Pocotaligo Station. He then ordered part of his forces to concentrate at Coosawhatchie to protect the railroad there, while ordering the remainder of his troops, the Charleston Light Dragoons included, to gather just north of the advancing Union force near Caston's (known as Hutson's) Plantation.[49]

The dragoons, numbering nearly sixty men on the day of the battle, had recently rotated off picket duty near Port Royal Ferry. Several men were preparing to leave for Combahee when the orders arrived from Colonel Walker. Captain Rutledge quickly mounted the troop and began moving his men toward the advancing Union column, some seven miles distant.[50]

Brannan realized early on the morning of October 22 that he had lost the element of surprise. His men had failed to capture Walker's pickets at Mackay's Point, and Confederate pickets captured on nearby Bray's Island informed their captors that they had known of the forthcoming Union raid for days. Nonetheless, Brannan landed his troops and marched them five-and-one-half miles northward to a Confederate redoubt near the plantation of George Elliott. There they ran into Confederate cavalry, infantry, and artillery. The Confederate force briefly stalled the Union advance before withdrawing along Mackay's Point Road, burning all bridges in the vicinity.[51]

This delaying action bought time for Walker to gather his forces near Frampton's Plantation, which was a mile and a half to the north. The Confederate delaying force also briefly defended a causeway and bridge on Caston's Plantation, before retreating slightly north to Frampton's Plantation. There Walker deployed his men on either side of the road, behind a marsh that stretched the length of the Confederate front. A narrow causeway with a bridge crossing Frampton Creek bisected the position, and retreating Confederates pulled up boards from the bridge as they crossed. Woods skirted the edge of the marsh on both sides of the causeway, forcing Walker to place his artillery in an exposed position near the causeway, where his guns could do greater damage to the advancing Union troops.[52]

The Charleston Light Dragoons arrived at Frampton's Plantation just as Walker's troops finished disabling the bridge. As they deployed, a Union gunboat on the Pocotaligo River opened fire on the unit, but its shells passed harmlessly through their formation. Yet the fire may well have unnerved some of the men. Many Civil War soldiers remarked on how waiting to go into a fight, especially when under artillery fire, aroused more anxiety than actually marching into battle.[53]

Colonel Walker placed the dragoons in the Confederate center, just to the right of the road. They dismounted, and horse holders led the animals to the rear. The company quickly sought concealment in the tall marsh grass, along with the rest of Walker's troops. As Brannan's men moved up the road, Confederate artillery again opened fire, this time with devastating effect.[54] Union artillery attempted to respond but quickly ran short of ammunition. Brannan tried to sweep the Confederates from their position, by ordering his first brigade forward, with disastrous results. The brigade advanced against the Confederates but "were twice driven out of the woods with great slaughter by the overwhelming fire of the enemy, whose missiles tore through like hail."[55]

Unfamiliar with the surrounding terrain, Brannan continued to press the assault through the marsh. Walker knew that his position was weakest on his right flank, which was vulnerable to attack by Union forces if they were able to cross the marsh and wade across Frampton Creek. The Confederates defended their position for forty-five minutes before Union troops began to cross Frampton Creek. With casualties mounting among his exposed gunners, Walker ordered a withdrawal to the next defensive position.[56]

Until that point, Confederate losses, with the exception of the gun crews, had been light. The withdrawal of Walker's troops under fire, however, resulted in numerous casualties. Among the dragoons, James M. Prioleau was severely wounded. Comrades placed him on a spare horse and sent him to the rear. Also wounded were Privates J. J. A. O'Neille, Edwin C. Holland, and J. Dubose Porcher.[57]

The dragoons and the rest of the Confederate forces retreated to Old Pocotaligo, the original site of settlement on the Pocotaligo River, which was south of Pocotaligo Station. The road leading to the town crossed a long causeway through a marsh before reaching a thirty-foot bridge that spanned the Pocotaligo River. As the last of Walker's troops crossed the river, they pulled up the boards from the bridge. Walker deployed his men to the north and south of the road along the riverbanks. Once again, he positioned his artillery in the center, where it could sweep the approaches to the causeway. Walker held the Charleston Light Dragoons as a strategic reserve a half mile to the rear.[58]

Brannan's pursuit of the retreating Confederates was delayed while his engineers repaired the bridge over Frampton Creek. Once across, his command quickly marched to Old Pocotaligo, where, Brannan later reported, "the rebels opened a murderous fire on us."[59]

As the battle progressed, the Charleston Light Dragoons waited at the rear of the Confederate line. Soon wounded soldiers began to stream past, spreading rumors of disaster, claiming that the Union forces had crossed the bridge, that most Confederates were killed or wounded, and that the artillery was out of ammunition. These reports had a demoralizing effect on the dragoons. During such times Civil War units were often motivated to stay in ranks by the threats or cajoling of officers.[60] Such was not the case with the dragoons on this occasion. Though they may have considered withdrawing, they stayed in place, and Walker ordered the dragoons forward at the double quick. He instructed the men to shout as they advanced to deceive the Union troops into believing that Confederate reinforcements had arrived at nearby Pocotaligo Station on the railroad. One dragoon later recalled that Lieutenant Richard H. Colcock drew his sword, brandished it above his head, and rushed forward with the dragoons cheering and advancing behind him. The Confederates already engaged soon echoed these cries. In his official report of the action, Walker described how at the "crisis of the fight I ordered up the Charleston Light Dragoons. That corps came forward with an inspiriting shout and took up position on my left, which wanted strengthening."[61] Undoubtedly, the effect on the dragoons was as heartening as it was for other Confederate troops. Yelling, whether it was a Rebel yell or a Union huzzah, tended to relieve tension for soldiers entering combat.[62]

The dragoons' advance temporarily inspired Walker's command, but it also revealed weaknesses in the company's officers. After arriving at its position in the Confederate line, the unit's leadership collapsed. Frank Middleton later commented, "As our officers did not appear to know how to act, the men very prudently scattered and took to the trees and creeping up as near to the enemy as the ground allowed, commenced firing." He pointedly remarked, "From first to last there was no discipline on our side it was a free bush fight from beginning to end."[63]

The dragoons' advance temporarily improved the Confederate rate of fire, but in response, Brannan committed more reinforcements to the Union line, and their fire "began to increase in intensity until their bullets came as thick as hail . . . a rat could hardly run from tree to tree without being hit." In response, the dragoons crowded behind the large live oaks to protect themselves from the Union onslaught. Simultaneously, the Confederate fire slackened and nearly ceased until around 4:00 P.M., when Lieutenant Colonel Patrick Henry Nelson's 7th South Carolina Infantry battalion, a unit of over two hundred men, arrived from Pocotaligo Station. Walker quickly committed this unit to relieve some of the pressure on his line.[64]

Across the river, Brannan was reaching his breaking point. At each of Walker's defensive positions, Brannan had ordered frontal assaults on the Confederate lines. In each instance his men had attacked with vigor and suffered significant casualties but had been unable to drive their opponents from the field. Instead, they had exchanged small-arms fire with the smaller Confederate force. The Union artillery had faced ammunition shortages all day and, as a result, had been unable to silence the Confederate batteries. As night approached, Brannan realized that he would be unable to reach the railroad bridge, so he ordered a withdrawal to the landing craft.[65]

As the Union force retreated, Walker sent elements of his cavalry in pursuit, while keeping the rest of his command, including the Charleston Light Dragoons, at Old Pocotaligo to counter the Union raid at Coosawhatchie if needed. He did not know until later that his troops there had driven the Union raiders away from the railroad, which sustained only minimal damage.[66]

Despite the apparent breakdown in company command, the official reports of the dragoons' role in their first battle were favorable. Walker noted that Captain Rutledge had been "cool and collected in both fights," and related how his "gallant corps" had reinforced the Confederate line and convinced their opponents that a large body of reinforcements had arrived. Perhaps to their surprise, the dragoons found their new Enfield rifles indispensable in battle. A dragoon later wrote that at the height of the action one trooper remarked to Rutledge, "Thank God! for the Enfields, Captain. I was dead against them, but now I say, bless *God,* and bless *you* for the Enfields."[67]

The dragoons' performance was both character revealing and noteworthy. In the last two phases of the action, the unit members sought cover when under fire. Thus their actions did not meet the ideals of knightliness to which so many Southerners of their class aspired. Nor did their officers live up to expectations. At key moments during the battle, these men could have set an example by actively directing the unit's fire or issuing words of encouragement to calm the enlisted men. Lieutenant Colcock was conspicuous during the final advance, but no evidence suggested that any other officer met this first stern test of combat leadership very well.[68]

However true that might be, Walker and his men had clearly won the day. Confederate casualties totaled 163 (21 killed, 124 wounded, and 18 missing). In comparison, Union casualties totaled 340 (43 killed, 294 wounded, and 3 missing). Relying on accurate and timely intelligence, rapid concentration of forces, and effective use of terrain, Walker overcame the Union numerical advantage and prevented the destruction of the Charleston and Savannah Railroad bridges.[69]

For the Charleston Light Dragoons, the battle was their first real fight and first victory, though a costly one. Of the roughly sixty men present, some forty-five were engaged, and the rest acted as horse holders. The unit suffered nine casualties (all wounded), or 20 percent of its combatants. Among the wounded were Edwin C. Holland, James Hopkins, Sergeant Benjamin F. Huger, Gabriel Manigault, J. J. A. O'Neille, J. Dubose Porcher, Miles Brewton Pringle, James M. Prioleau, and Lewis Vanderhorst.[70]

Having survived the terror of battle, the wounded dragoons faced a new kind of terror. Ideals of courage dictated that soldiers suffer bravely, although once admitted to a hospital, the wounded could receive little support from their comrades, who in many cases were far away. Such isolation could make life in the hospital especially miserable.[71] To compound matters, Civil War medicine was rudimentary at best. Because minié balls, the war's most common small-arms projectile, caused significant soft tissue and bone damage, the primary surgical procedure was amputation. It has been estimated that fifty thousand amputations were performed during the war.[72]

It is not clear from the available records whether any dragoons wounded at Pocotaligo underwent amputations. None died of their wounds, but the physical and mental damage they suffered was apparent. J. J. A. O'Neille suffered a fractured left leg and remained on sick furlough through October 1864, when he became an employee at the Ordnance Works in Charlotte, North Carolina. James M. Prioleau, wounded seriously in the right thigh, reported back for duty in January 1863 but was detached several times during the next two years. He eventually served as a brigade mail courier and clerk for the medical purveyor in Macon, Georgia.[73] Miles Brewton Pringle, shot in the lower leg, had the ball removed and received a medical furlough that lasted until December 1862. The wound's lingering effects, however, and what may have been post-traumatic stress disorder, began to take a toll on Pringle. In April 1863 family members unsuccessfully petitioned for an appointment that would shield him from further combat. He continued to serve with the dragoons until September 1864, when he gained a position as a quartermaster officer. A medical board classified him "fit only for light duty" shortly thereafter.[74]

Another wounded dragoon, J. Dubose Porcher, also sought a position far from the front, but with more success than Pringle. Wounded slightly in the hip, Porcher remained on sick furlough through December 1862 before returning to service. Seven months later he sought and obtained an appointment as a war-tax collector, and he received his discharge from the dragoons on July 1, 1863.

Those dragoons who were transported to the hospital in nearby McPhersonville experienced firsthand the shortage of supplies that plagued so many makeshift wartime hospitals. During the fight at Old Pocotaligo, Gabriel Manigault had been struck in the left eyebrow by a pistol ball or buckshot, which exited from the right side of his nose. He rode six miles to McPhersonville, where a Confederate hospital was located in the village church. There were few "suitable beds," and Manigualt was told to lie on one without a mattress. The following day Dragoon Dr. Isaac Gregorie offered Manigault a mattress from his father's nearby plantation. Dragoon James Hopkins, from lower Richland District, lay across from Manigault. During the battle Hopkins seemed to have been seriously wounded in the side, so the dragoons placed him on a horse and sent him to the rear of the battle. Manigault claimed that he saw a minister praying over Hopkins as though he would die. General William Hopkins, James's father, and the rest of his family learned of his wound and took a train from Richland District to Charleston and then to Pocotaligo, then traveled to the hospital to see Hopkins. His family noted that he was in good spirits and anxious for the surgeon to remove the ball, which he declined to do. Some time later, however, Hopkins, who had recovered from the wound, stood, retrieved his jacket and hat from his bed, and walked quickly out of the hospital. Manigault later claimed that Hopkins had found in his pocket the ball that he thought had penetrated his side and implied that Hopkins departed the hospital due to embarrassment. Regardless of the circumstances surrounding Hopkins's wounding and recovery, he remained on sick furlough for six months before returning to the unit to experience combat again.[75]

Following the battles of October 22, 1862, the dragoons returned to picket duty near Port Royal Ferry and Mackay's Point, much as they had done in previous months. One commented on the equipment and refuse that the retreating Union forces had left behind. The road, he said, "was strewn with ammunition, canteens, soda crackers and quantities of bundles of lightwood . . . dipped in pitch, for the evident purpose of firing any buildings or railway bridges."[76]

Several days later, on October 29, Captain Rutledge and his command were on parade for General Beauregard when Colonel Walker received word that a Union gunboat was shelling the woods near Pocotaligo. He quickly ordered Rutledge to take the Charleston Light Dragoons and two other companies and inflict as much damage as possible on the vessel. In the words of one dragoon, Rutledge's face "lengthened out immensely." The gunboat, however, withdrew before the Confederates could reach Pocotaligo.[77]

By late November 1862, the dragoons had learned of Rutledge's forthcoming promotion and the unit's consolidation with other units to form a cavalry regiment. Rutledge requested that General Beauregard return men who had been detached from the dragoons. Colonel Walker approved the request, and as a reminder of the unit's favored position in the Third Military District, he wrote, "This gallant and efficient corps is capable of turning the fortunes of a day, I therefore approve of any measure calculated to increase its efficiency."[78]

On December 16, 1862, the Charleston Light Dragoons, the St. James Mounted Riflemen (commanded by Captain Thomas Pinckney), and Majors Stokes's and Emanuel's battalions were officially consolidated into Rutledge's Regiment of Cavalry (later the 4th South Carolina Cavalry). As expected, Rutledge became colonel of the new regiment, Stokes was made lieutenant colonel, and Emanuel, major. The Charleston Light Dragoons became Company K of the regiment, and the new company commander was Richard H. Colcock, making him the junior captain in the regiment.[79] With the exception of Emanuel's battalion and Captain Pinckney's company, the units that made up the new regiment had served together in the Third Military District. This offered little consolation to the dragoons, who regretted losing Rutledge and feared the changes that might accompany consolidation. One commented that Colcock, the new commander, "will not suit us at all." Some dragoons believed that Rutledge would be the only efficient regimental officer, since "Stokes, the lieutenant colonel, although a very amiable well meaning man is a perfect cypher, and Emanuel the major is a German jew and quite inefficient."[80]

By February 1863, two months after the formation of Rutledge's Regiment of Cavalry, little had changed for the dragoons. The unit was still encamped near Pocotaligo, though they had moved to a cornfield on "Tiger Bill" Heyward's plantation. Colonel Rutledge had not yet brought the components of his new regiment together, and although he had recently assumed command of all cavalry in the area, he made the dragoons' camp his headquarters. He also began to fill vacant regimental positions with dragoons. As commissary for the dragoons, Gabriel Manigault had befriended Rutledge during the previous year in the hopes of becoming regimental quartermaster. Manigault, age thirty, was the son of Charles and Elizabeth Heyward Manigault. Charles Manigault had attained most of his wealth from his wife, who was a daughter of Nathaniel Heyward. Charles Manigault's worth in 1861 was close to $500,000 ($10.3 million in 2000), including Gowrie, his Savannah River plantation, and the slaves that worked it.[81] Gabriel Manigault had studied extensively in Europe before becoming a physician. His brother Alfred, age twenty-three, was also a dragoon. The two had joined the unit on January 1, 1862, and although Gabriel had been wounded at Pocotaligo, he had quickly returned to service and earned the respect of his fellow dragoons.[82]

Like the elder Manigault brother, Oliver H. Middleton Jr. attained a position on Rutledge's staff through patronage. Middleton joined the dragoons on January 4, 1863. At age seventeen, he was one of the youngest members of the outfit. He was Rutledge's brother-in-law and the son of Oliver H. Middleton, an Edisto Island planter who owned over 250 slaves.[83] The younger Middleton entered the unit as a private and became a member of his cousin Frank Middleton's mess, which was composed of dragoons nearly twice his age. Frank Middleton wrote of Oliver Middleton Jr. that "he is entirely too genteel for camp, but this will probably wear off."[84] Soon thereafter Rutledge offered Oliver Middleton Jr. the position of private secretary, undoubtedly as a favor to Ella Middleton Rutledge (Middleton's sister and Rutledge's wife) and her parents.[85]

As dragoons, Manigault and Oliver Middleton Jr. were members of the best equipped and supplied mess in the company. When they moved to regimental headquarters, they joined Rutledge's mess, which was the worst supplied in the unit. The dragoons, who had always valued their physical comfort, had, according to the desires of each mess, constructed log cabins in which to eat and sleep. They also provided their own rations. Rutledge, perhaps intending to set a good example, continued to sleep in the open.[86] If he hoped to inspire a more military behavior in the Charleston Light Dragoons, he was disappointed. Frank Middleton considered Rutledge to be "too lazy or too penurious to have a shanty built to eat under."[87] To rectify this, Gabriel Manigault and his servant Stephney constructed a log cabin in which Rutledge and his staff could eat and entertain other officers. Manigault also assumed duty as caterer to the mess.[88]

For their part the dragoons, with the apparent permission of their officers, maintained their distinctive habits. In early May 1863, as word spread of the regiment's gathering at Pocotaligo, the dragoons feared that the company would be thrown together with the rest of the regiment, subject to the same discipline, and undoubtedly forced to associate with men of lower social standing and more humble economic status. Accordingly, they took steps to ensure that their privileged position in the Third Military District would not change. Colcock and the other company officers visited Walker, now brigadier general and Third Military District commander, and received permission to camp away from the regiment and "be as independent as before."[89] Walker granted this permission because he "recognized the difference between the Dragoon company and the rest of the men," so he "did what he could whenever it could be done without exciting jealousy . . . for them to be an independent company."[90]

During the spring of 1863, the 4th South Carolina Cavalry moved from Pocotaligo to McPhersonville. This was no easy task for the dragoons due to the large amount of baggage that they had accumulated.[91] Once this task was completed, the individual companies drilled as a regiment on a weekly basis, a process that benefited all of the companies and gradually led to the regiment's proficiency in necessary cavalry maneuvers. The dragoons and the rest of the regiment also assumed responsibility for nearby picket posts.[92] The forces under Major Emanuel (two companies) were headquartered at Green Pond and were assigned to picket stations along the Combahee River on the border between Beaufort and Colleton Districts.

During this period Union troops periodically made reconnaissance forays into Confederate territory. On one such occasion a railroad superintendent noticed that the telegraph line had been cut, and local troops from the 4th Cavalry and tracking dogs captured the guilty party as it attempted to return to its landing craft. Captain Thomas Pinckney of the 4th Cavalry unsuccessfully attempted to interrogate the Union telegraph operator, who refused to give information regarding Union troop dispositions. Pinckney then asked his men to acquire some whiskey and sent to the Charleston Light Dragoons for John Robinson (nicknamed Porgy), who was instructed to ply the telegraph operator with liquor and record his observations. Pinckney reported to Gra-hamville on inspection duty and returned to discover that the operator had given little information and "drank our man under the table."[93]

On June 2, 1863, three Union riverboats and several hundred men moved up the Combahee River, burned four plantations and six rice mills, and seized over seven hundred slaves. Major Emanuel's two companies, which had recently been transferred to the area from Georgetown District, failed to prevent the destruction, and later the owner of Newport Plantation accused Captain Pinckney's company of looting the burned plantations after the Union troops departed. For his conduct during the raid, Emanuel faced a court-martial. In his report of the action, Brigadier General Walker claimed that he had provided instructions and maps to Emanuel and had also issued a circular to planters advising them to move their slaves into the interior or risk their loss.[94] Pinckney requested that a court of inquiry be convened, so that he could be cleared of any wrongdoing. He and his men were subsequently found to be innocent of the charges, and he later learned that the plantation overseer had stolen the items in question from the plantation.[95]

The plantation owners on the Combahee River had gambled that Union forces would not attack. Some undoubtedly hoped that their slaves would continue to cultivate rice, while others may have been unable or unwilling to move their people inland. Regardless, their decisions to keep their slaves near the coast cost them dearly. Among those who lost plantations and slaves was Dragoon William L. Kirkland. Union troops burned his Rose Hill Plantation, as well as his mother's plantation, Long Brow, and carried off all but a few slaves.[96] Kirkland was ruined, and news of his misfortune quickly spread.[97]

As a direct result of this raid, the Charleston Light Dragoons, who had been stationed at McPhersonville in Beaufort District since May 9, 1863, received orders to proceed to Green Pond on June 18, 1863.[98] Along with Company G, they served under Lieutenant Colonel Stokes, who replaced Emanuel as the local commander.[99] Again the dragoons camped apart from the other company, a situation that irritated Stokes. Walker, however, had granted the unit permission to establish its own bivouac, and it continued to enjoy this privilege.[100]

After the Union raid on the Combahee plantations, the dragoons and other troops at Green Pond spent more time trying to prevent slaves from fleeing to Union forces, a task that proved nearly impossible. When large numbers of slaves did escape, however, local commanders expressed no sympathy for their owners. Stokes remarked that it was impossible to prevent escapes with the small number of troops at his disposal, and that "the planters are to blame for keeping their negroes here."[101]

While the dragoons were performing picket duty in Beaufort District during the spring and summer of 1863, lowcountry residents and soldiers turned their attention to Charleston. In April a Union ironclad fleet attacked Fort

Sumter. Confederate artillery guarding the harbor's entrance soundly repulsed the Federals, doing damage to several vessels and sinking the USS *Keokuk.* In an attempt to capture the city, Union brigadier general Quincy A. Gilmore, commander of the Department of the South, decided to attack the Confederate fortifications on the islands guarding the mouth of the Charleston harbor. Instead of thrusting toward James Island as an earlier Federal force had done, Gilmore decided to attempt to reduce the Confederate fortifications on Morris Island. His plan called for the island's capture, the reduction of Fort Sumter through an artillery barrage, and the establishment of access to the harbor for the Union ironclad fleet, the arrival of which would force a Confederate withdrawal from the city.[102]

After successfully capturing the Confederate positions on the southern end of Morris Island, Gilmore turned next to Battery Wagner. As the Union assault on the Confederate defenses intensified, General Beauregard detached the Charleston Light Dragoons from the 4th South Carolina Cavalry on August 18, 1863, and ordered the unit to report to General Roswell Ripley in Charleston. The troop arrived there the following day and for two nights camped at Hempstead, the home of Lieutenant Lionel C. Nowell. Two days later the company moved to the Washington Racecourse on the Charleston Neck.[103] While at the racecourse, Ripley sent a detachment of nine dragoons, commanded by Sergeant Benjamin F. Huger, to Battery Gregg, which was located on the northern tip of Morris Island. Various detachments had drawn lots to determine who would participate in this dangerous mission, and Huger's men had lost.[104]

Upon arriving at Battery Gregg, where they occupied a small dugout within the fortifications, Huger and his men served as couriers, carrying messages between that post and Battery Wagner, three-quarters of a mile to the south. Located nearby were the detachment's mounts, five horses that previous couriers had left behind. When Battery Gregg received a communication intended for Battery Wagner, a dragoon would mount one of the horses and carry the message there. These couriers were under naval artillery fire from the moment they left Gregg's fortifications to the moment they arrived at Wagner. For the last quarter mile they were also under small-arms fire from Union sharpshooters located farther down the beach. After delivering the message, the rider would stay at Battery Wagner until the time came for him to make the return trip to Battery Gregg with another message. Troopers performed this duty on a rotating basis, so that each dragoon shared equally in the hazards of the job. All of this was great sport for observers and combatants, both Confederate and Union. Union gunners targeted the couriers, while Wagner's defenders cheered each successful delivery and rushed to any dragoon who was dismounted before reaching his destination.[105] On August 30, another detachment of dragoons relieved Huger and his men. They would be the last dragoons sent to the island.[106]

As Union siege lines moved inexorably closer to Battery Wagner, Confederate commanders, defenders, and civilians in Charleston realized the position's vulnerability. On September 5, Confederate engineers informed General Beauregard that the battery was untenable, and he ordered the Confederate garrison on Morris Island to withdraw from its location on the evening and early morning of September 6–7, 1863. John Harleston, one of the four dragoons at Battery Gregg, later commented that Confederate commanders forgot to include the couriers in their withdrawal plans. As the Confederate garrisons were loading transports, Harleston and his comrades freed their horses, located a skiff, and left the island. Despite the dangers associated with courier service on Morris Island, no dragoons were killed, though most involved were injured slightly by falling or being knocked from their horses.[107] Shortly after Confederate troops abandoned the island, a witness to the battle there wrote of "the courage and faithfulness of the cavalry employed as couriers on Morris Island." He noted that, while there, "members of the Charleston Light Dragoons performed that duty, and I never saw a moment's hesitation though the peril was often terrific, and had to be encountered alone."[108]

While the two detachments had been serving on Morris Island, the remainder of the company acted as guards at the Ashley River Bridge at the foot of Charleston's Spring Street. There they protected the bridge from fire, examined the passes and passports of those who crossed it, and arrested anyone who looked suspicious.[109] Following the withdrawal from Morris Island, the detached dragoons returned to duty with the company. Life for those dragoons who stayed behind contrasted sharply with the dangerous duty on Morris Island. Servants would escort dragoons to the bridge for duty, take their horses back to camp, and then return with them the following day just prior to their masters' relief from duty. When not on guard detail, unit members would visit their homes and nearby plantations. Gabriel Manigault returned to his home on Gibbes Street on many nights when he was off duty.[110]

For many dragoons, a trip to a home south of Calhoun Street became increasingly dangerous. A Union battery located in a marsh near Morris Island began shelling Charleston on August 21, 1863. Union gunners initially targeted the area near St. Michael's Church, at the corner of Broad and Meeting streets. By the end of 1864, Union artillery had damaged many buildings south of Broad Street, home to the city's most prestigious families. Many residents left the city after the bombardment began. Those who remained slowly grew accustomed to the dangers that now haunted this once-desirable location.[111]

Dragoon Ralph E. Elliott was in Charleston when the shelling was at its height. He had volunteered to carry dispatches to town in hopes of seeing his brother, who was supposedly staying at the Mills House. Upon arriving in the city, Elliott noted that sixteen shells had fallen on Charleston between morning and 3 p.m., killing one woman, wounding one man, and otherwise doing little damage. Elliott, however, had a close call that day. He hitched his horse on King Street, and a shell shattered the post to which the animal was tied, tearing off its reins. Fortunately for Elliott and his horse, the projectile failed to explode.[112]

Despite the dangers of the bombardment, Charleston remained a healthier environment for the dragoons than Beaufort District. The unit's two years of service in and around the marshes had weakened the older soldiers' health. After arriving in Charleston, Alfred and Gabriel Manigault began to suffer from fevers, and at different times between late 1863 and early 1864, they appeared before medical boards seeking sick furloughs. Gabriel Manigault recovered after a short leave to Augusta during the latter part of the year. His brother Alfred, however, continued to suffer from chills and fever, which would keep him off of active duty for several months.[113]

Throughout the summer and fall of 1863, little new occurred to disrupt the Charleston Light Dragoons' routine of guard duty. Yet the unit's privileged status remained unmistakable. In September the company was chosen to escort Confederate president Jefferson Davis during his trip to Charleston. Two members even served as couriers for Davis. One month later the unit was transferred to a line of earthworks, near Magnolia Cemetery, that extended from the Ashley to the Cooper River. There they served as guards, as they had on the Ashley River Bridge, helping to control who entered or left the city limits. They also established a new camp at Accabee, an old plantation on the Ashley River near Six Mile Road.[114]

Indeed, the dragoons remained closely tied to their traditional plantation world, still free to enjoy the benefits of serving their country near their homes and other great estates. Gabriel and Alfred Manigault, despite their fevers, held a dinner for several friends and the French consul at Marshland Farm, seven miles north of Charleston, enjoying "choice Madeira" and French brandy, which the guests later shared with Confederate sentries as they passed back into the city.[115]

Despite such social diversions and regardless of other breaks in camp routine, the unit became increasingly weary of picket duty near Accabee. This was especially true of the men from Beaufort, who felt farther from friends and family than ever before. One of those who longed to return home was Ralph E. Elliott. He lamented the drudgery of guard duty and its exposure to the elements, and he thought of seeking less demanding service closer to home. In early December 1863, he complained in a letter to his mother about the cold weather, cold food, and lack of sleep that accompanied the life of a sentry on the Charleston Neck. His mother suggested that he seek a position nearer to home on the staff of Brigadier General Beverly H. Robertson, commander of South Carolina's Second Military District. Elliott agreed but informed his mother that he would need the assistance of an "outsider" such as his brother-in-law or mother. He wrote of how these relatives might approach Robertson to ask General Beauregard to detail Elliott to staff duty. Otherwise, Elliott wrote, Dragoon Captain Richard H. Colcock would never allow him to be detailed, unless of course, he were one of Colcock's "bootlicks," which he was not.[116]

As one dragoon was seeking an assignment as a staff officer closer to home, another was anxious to leave his staff position and return to the company. While the Charleston Light Dragoons remained in Charleston, the rest of the 4th South Carolina Cavalry continued to serve in Colleton and Beaufort Districts. For Oliver H. Middleton Jr., separation from the company caused such anxiety that he chose to give up a position on the regimental staff to rejoin the troop. He had served with the dragoons for close to a month before becoming Colonel Rutledge's personal secretary, and Middleton and the rest of the regimental staff had bivouacked with the unit prior to its departure for Green Pond on June 18, 1863.[117] During that time Middleton had grown accustomed to the unit's camaraderie. Several days after the company departed, he was complaining that "I find it very slow here—the dragoons being no longer within a minute's walk but at Green Pond."[118] By August, as the dragoons were being transferred to Charleston, Middleton decided to resign his position and rejoin the company. He complained to his mother about the boredom of camp life, while writing admiringly about Morris Island's Confederate defenders. Perhaps equally important, he was embarrassed over accidentally discharging his pistol and nearly shooting himself. He therefore, like many others, preferred service with the dragoons to service in a staff position.[119]

Soon after returning to the dragoons, Middleton wrote home to brag about the unit's newest, and most unlikely, recruit. Edward L. Wells was the son of Thomas L. Wells and Julia Lawrence Wells of New York. Wells's grandfather's second wife was Sabina Elliott Huger Wells, a South Carolinian and the sister of Judge D. E. Huger. Wells had visited South Carolina in 1860 and was treated quite well as a result of his pro-South sympathies. He quickly became enamored of plantation life while visiting with his Huger relatives.[120]

When the war began, Wells returned to New York, but he feared being conscripted into the Union army. Instead, he booked passage on a steamer bound for Nassau in the Bahamas, where he boarded the blockade runner *Fannie* and ran the blockade into Wilmington, North Carolina, on November 17, 1863. By December 1, 1863, he had returned to Charleston. Given his personal attributes and especially his South Carolina family connections, he moved easily among the state's most important political and military leaders.[121] He consulted with prominent Charlestonians on which military unit to join. Alfred Huger provided Wells with an introduction to Governor Milledge L. Bonham, who in turn provided him with letters of introduction to Confederate president Jefferson Davis and General Wade Hampton. Wells traveled to Virginia and consulted with Hampton and former dragoon Rawlins Lowndes, a member of Hampton's staff. Both men were sufficiently impressed with Wells that they persuaded him not to join a unit in Virginia but, instead, to return to South Carolina and join the Charleston Light Dragoons, "a company . . . composed of gentlemen entirely." Hampton promised Wells that he could always be transferred back to Virginia if the dragoons were not transferred there eventually.[122]

On December 30, 1863, Wells joined the Charleston Light Dragoons in Charleston, much to the pleasure of unit members, who were quite impressed that he had traveled so far to become a dragoon.[123] Wells wrote home to his mother on January 12, 1864, to explain why he had joined this company of Southern gentlemen. He enjoyed his new comrades and even believed that picket duty "agrees with my health extremely well. I never felt better in my life." His affinity for the unit was no doubt due to the goodwill of company members: "I have been received most kindly by all, whom I have met."[124]

While Wells and his new comrades coped with the boredom of picket duty on the Charleston Neck, the rest of the 4th South Carolina Cavalry experienced a similarly uneventful existence in Beaufort District. The regiment remained on duty there largely to counter Union raids, which seemed to free more and more slaves in the district and caused Rutledge great embarrassment.[125]

On November 24, 1863, near Cunningham's Bluff, a company of Union soldiers from a black regiment infiltrated Rutledge's lines and freed twenty slaves belonging to Daniel Heyward. The Union troops then broke into smaller groups and successfully eluded capture. On November 26, 1863, the *Charleston Mercury* erroneously reported that the Union force had marched to Pocotaligo Station unmolested before returning to their lines. Stung by the newspaper's criticisms and denying that his men had failed in any way, Rutledge wrote a letter to the editor, Robert Barnwell Rhett Jr. In this way, he hoped to set the record straight about the recent affair. Defending the vast coastline of the Third Military District, Rutledge observed, was futile unless he received reinforcement. Union forces could strike his portion of the lines at will because the sentries were so thinly spread. Rutledge asked Rhett to persuade his father, Robert Barnwell Rhett, a former U.S. congressman and senator and a proponent of secession, to pressure Confederate headquarters into sending more troops to assist with picket duty in and near the Third Military District.[126] The continued service of the dragoons in Charleston only exacerbated Rutledge's manpower shortage.

As 1863 ended, the Charleston Light Dragoons remained on duty near Charleston. Since they had entered Confederate service at Grahamville over a year and a half earlier, the unit had experienced both the boredom of camp life and the terror of battle. Among its ranks were men from the state's most prominent families, men who hailed from both far and near. The war had significantly diminished the material circumstances of all but a handful of its members and had destroyed the fortunes of many. The dragoons were no longer an independent company. They were now Company K of the 4th South Carolina Cavalry, and they had lost their popular commander to promotion. Yet despite the changes of the previous two years, the company had maintained its reputation as a socially elite command and a company of "gentlemen." It also had performed admirably in the field. As 1864 approached, its members faced an uncertain future with the knowledge, however, that they continued to hold a position of prominence among Confederate units in South Carolina. The Charleston Light Dragoons' reputation would be their undoing. In the coming year, unit members would learn that outside of the South Carolina lowcountry there were limits to the benefits of social and political position, and that this war would respect no man, no matter how prominent or privileged.

Chapter 4

CATACLYSM

They stood still, to be shot down in their tracks.

Mary Boykin Chesnut

The year 1864 began with little change in the Charleston Light Dragoons' routine. Of the 4th South Carolina Cavalry's ten companies, only the dragoons were detailed to Charleston, service that in many ways reprised their days as a militia company. Even though the blockade increasingly reduced the number of luxury items available to unit members (such as Madeira and other wines), duty at Accabee Plantation allowed the unit's men to make home visits. Charleston and nearby plantations offered numerous parties, some hosted by dragoons. Their lives still seemed far removed from those of most other soldiers, both Confederate and Union.

In contrast to the dragoons' relatively quiet and undemanding service, other militia companies from the city had been in combat since the war's outset. One unit, the Washington Light Infantry, had raised three companies and sent one to Virginia in May 1861, where, as part of Hampton's Legion, it participated in the first battle of Bull Run and afterward served in the Army of Northern Virginia. The remaining two formed part of the Eutaw Battalion, which, like the dragoons, had remained in the lowcountry. Unlike the dragoons, however, the Washington Light Infantry had defended Charleston during the battle of Secessionville on June 16, 1862, where it had halted a Union thrust toward the city. In addition, these two companies were part of the garrison of Battery Wagner during the Union assaults of July 18, 1863, and had been some of the last men to abandon Morris Island on September 6–7, 1863. In each of these actions, the Washington Light Infantry suffered substantial casualties, and the unit's members could claim with some pride to have defended Charleston in two major engagements, a claim that most dragoons could not make.[1]

In early spring of 1864 rumors swirled throughout the lowcountry that various local units would be sent north to join Lee's Army of Northern Virginia. Such rumors were not new. On May 31, 1863, Frank Middleton had written, "Our company has been very much exercised for the last month by rumours of our being sent out to the West or Virginia." Middleton continued, writing that "Gen. Wade Hampton has been moving heaven and earth to get Rutledge's regiment in his command." Nearly ten months later Hampton secured the unit's transfer. On March 18, 1864, the 4th South Carolina Cavalry was ordered to Virginia as part of a new brigade to be made up of the 4th, 5th, and 6th South Carolina Cavalry regiments. Brigadier General Matthew C. Butler, former regimental commander of the 2nd South Carolina Cavalry and a veteran who had served under Major General J. E. B. Stuart, was placed in command of the brigade. Confederate adjutant and inspector general Samuel Cooper ordered Butler's three regiments to proceed to Virginia in light marching order, including instructions to go with as little baggage as possible and with their wagons carrying only cooking utensils.[2]

For the 4th, 5th, and 6th South Carolina Cavalry regiments, the order was problematic. Besides limiting each unit's baggage, it also dictated that each company reduce its numbers to ninety-four members. During the war, the ranks of each of these regiments had grown rapidly until they overflowed with men.[3] South Carolinians had joined cavalry units stationed in the lowcountry to be close to home and, not coincidentally, to avoid excessive physical exertion and reduce the risk of becoming a casualty.

The directive to reduce the number of men in each unit was particularly odious to the officers of the Charleston Light Dragoons, who were forced to drop thirty men from the rolls. Colonel Rutledge later commented that the regiment's companies "were considerably cut down," and he lamented the loss of good soldiers and their horses.[4] He requested permission to drop from the rolls men on long-term details, so that he would be left with a regiment manned primarily by the most experienced, and therefore the best, troops in the regiment.[5]

Dragoon Captain Richard H. Colcock, with a few exceptions, used a fairly simple formula for choosing the men who would be dropped from the rolls. Following Rutledge's lead, Colcock released men who had served on long-term details away from the company. He also excused those who had joined the unit recently or who had been on sick leave for an extended period. The soldiers left in the unit's ranks were those with the longest service experience and the strongest company ties.[6]

Not all dragoons wanted to make the trip to Virginia. Ralph E. Elliott had written often of his displeasure with picket duty and the discomfort of being cold and wet, yet he asked to stay behind in Charleston and be assigned to another local unit.[7] Elias Ball used his connections to separate himself from the unit prior to its departure. He remained on the Charleston Light Dragoons' roster but petitioned Brigadier General Thomas Jordan, General Beauregard's chief of staff, to be detached from the dragoons for service as a mounted courier to Colonel Alfred Rhett, who commanded forces in Charleston. Jordan approved Ball's request but did so after the dragoons officially were under the command of General Wade Hampton. This incident irritated Hampton, and on his next trip to Charleston he "remonstrated" with Jordan about his decision.[8]

News of the brigade's departure caused great consternation among lowcountry families. Beaufort District residents and relatives and friends of those men serving in the 4th South Carolina Cavalry, especially the Charleston Light Dragoons, petitioned Confederate commanders and officials for the unit to remain in the lowcountry. These protesters were so vociferous and their social and political connections so great that the 4th Cavalry was late in departing for Virginia.[9]

Once it was clear that the unit would indeed make the trip, some families sought to shield their sons from combat. The parents of young Oliver H. Middleton Jr. pressured him to return to his previous position as personal secretary to Colonel Rutledge. Rutledge also tried to persuade Middleton to rejoin his staff, even holding out the prospect of Middleton receiving a furlough prior to the company's departure for Virginia.[10] Besieged by a doting mother and a colonel, Middleton explained that he nonetheless chose to remain in the ranks of the dragoons and to share their fate.[11] His refusal to rely on connections to avoid more dangerous duties was in sharp contrast to the actions of other dragoons such as Elliott and Ball.

Confusing orders, civilian lobbying, and finally logistical problems all delayed the unit's departure. There were no facilities at Pocotaligo to shoe the 4th Cavalry's horses because the lowcountry's sandy soil made horseshoes largely unnecessary.[12] In addition to the question of changing terrain, equipment issues hampered the regiment's movement as well. Rutledge sent Captain John C. Calhoun to Richmond to secure McClellan (or Jenifer) saddles for the regiment and have them forwarded to Columbia. These saddles were the most satisfactory for mounted service and were the least damaging to horses, better than those the unit had been using. For instance, Regimental Adjutant Gabriel Manigault, like members of the dragoons, used an English riding saddle, which, though of the highest quality, was completely unsuited for the unit's trip to Virginia and extended service. Worse still were the saddles of the "country companies," as the dragoons referred to the rest of the 4th Cavalry. One lieutenant even carried a small trunk attached to the rear of his saddle.[13]

Their impending departure from the lowcountry also raised other difficult questions for the dragoons. The unit had grown used to having servants and cooks in camp, but many questioned whether to take slaves with them to Virginia.[14] Oliver Middleton's mother offered her son two family servants and a lesson in how to treat slaves in times of crisis. She wrote that the two men, Tom and Lewis, were at his service and that he should not "consider them or their pleasure." Although Tom was sick, Lewis "would be trusty and useful and as for his wife and family, he has been with them ever since the war began so he cannot think it hard to leave them now."[15] Middleton declined his mother's offer and left the men at home.

Other dragoons were more reluctant to live without their slaves. Although Gabriel Manigault left Stephney Wilson, his servant for the previous two years, at home to recover from an illness, he replaced him with a slave named Zackey [Zachariah], who had previously worked as a field hand.[16]

The reduction of baggage and the uncertainty regarding the disposition of the unit's slaves signaled unwelcome changes in the unit's status. The Charleston Light Dragoons realized that their recent duty at Accabee had been less demanding or dangerous than duty in Virginia was bound to be. As before, they feared the loss of organizational independence and dreaded future service with companies that they considered to be socially and militarily inferior. So with much trepidation, the unit began its march northward.[17]

For the dragoons, the trip to Virginia proceeded in two phases. One-third of the 4th South Carolina Cavalry was furloughed, while the remainder left for Columbia on April 14, 1864, taking with them the horses of their furloughed comrades. Once the unit reached Columbia, it was to rest for a few days, and then those men who had been furloughed would arrive in Columbia and take the unit's horses to Virginia, while the remaining two-thirds of dragoons would be furloughed and then take a train to Virginia.[18]

Together for the first time in months, the entire 4th Cavalry began its trip toward Columbia and was entertained at various stops along the way. At Orangeburg, the ladies of a nearby women's college sang to the passing troops, an occasion that exemplified the deferential and subordinate roles expected of South Carolina women in sending their noble protectors off to war. Part of the company stopped and gallantly removed their hats until the ladies completed their serenade. Women from plantations brought food to the roadside to feed the cavalrymen. The brigade's other regiments received similar treatment, and Gabriel Manigault surmised that South Carolinians realized that this was the state's last brigade of cavalry and hoped earnestly that Confederate commanders in Virginia would not squander it.[19]

When the command reached Columbia, the troops entered a city overflowing with refugees, many from Union-occupied lowcountry districts. High rents in the city forced other refugees to scatter throughout the state, finding lodging in small towns and on plantations. Those who had moved their slaves to inland plantations early in the war were able to use their labor to grow food crops and ease the expense of living away from their homes.[20]

With such a large number of lowcountry expatriates in the city, many dragoons soon became caught up in a social whirl. Dances and dinner parties allowed members to meet, or get reacquainted with, their new division commander, Major General Wade Hampton, who had left Virginia to help expedite the movement of his newest brigade. The Hampton family had been famous in South Carolina for two generations, and the military exploits of the major general were such that most white South Carolinians were impressed with his character and his bravery.[21] These occasions allowed the dragoons to hold onto their more sumptuous ways of living for a few days longer.

To honor Hampton, the 4th and the 5th Cavalries each held a review at the Columbia racetrack. Many members of both regiments had received passes when the brigade was ordered to Virginia but had rejoined their comrades in Columbia, so the ranks of both units were full. During the Civil War sustained combat and attrition could quickly diminish a cavalry regiment to between three and four hundred men, so the full ranks of both the 4th and 5th Cavalries were as large as some cavalry brigades in Virginia. Gabriel Manigault later claimed that, due to the presence of the Charleston Light Dragoons in its ranks, more people gathered to witness the 4th South Carolina Cavalry's review than that of the 5th South Carolina Cavalry. He suggested that the increased attendance was due to the high proportion of members who had independent fortunes, had been officers in other commands, or hailed from the state's most prominent families. At a barbecue after the parade, Manigault found "it amusing to see the desire of the ladies to have a Drag [Dragoon] pointed out to them, so favorably were they known."[22]

As the regiment left Columbia to move northward, the outpouring of hospitality, often in the form of gifts of buttermilk or other food, continued. These roadside gifts proved timely, because the troopers were already feeling the pinch of reduced rations. Oliver H. Middleton Jr. wrote home that "something is wrong in the Commissary Department for our rations have been very scanty so far."[23] The dragoons moved to Camden and then marched through Lancaster, South Carolina, on the way to Charlotte, North Carolina. The company then moved through Concord, Salisbury, Lexington, Thomasville, and Greensboro, North Carolina. The march was made in warm weather, and the passage of so many men on a single road created great clouds of dust that begrimed the men farther back in the column. In Greensboro, it finally rained heavily, but this only increased the men's discomfort and fatigue.[24] The unit passed through Clarksville, Virginia, to Amelia Courthouse, where townspeople treated many of the dragoons to dinner.[25]

The company arrived in Richmond only one day late; a minor dereliction that nevertheless prompted a brusque rebuke from General Braxton Bragg, who was military advisor to Confederate president Jefferson Davis. The shortage of military saddles and the distance traveled from South Carolina to Virginia had taken a toll on the dragoons and their horses. The animals lost weight during the trip. When the unit was near Richmond, the regimental quartermaster had paid to have the unit's horses fed from a farmer's clover fields, but the animals clearly preferred grass.[26]

Upon arriving in Richmond on May 24, 1864, the dragoons marched through the city and bivouacked near a small church across town from their arrival point. Many of the men were fed that night by a Richmond woman whose daughter was engaged to a colonel from Charleston. In addition, women from nearby farms flocked to meet these dashing South Carolinians.

Upon returning to the regiment from Richmond, Surgeon Gregorie and Gabriel Manigault met "two buxom country girls," who "smiled with us and asked if any more South Carolina men would be traveling that way."[27]

Despite this warm reception, the company soon realized that food would be scarce. The Army of Northern Virginia was surviving on half rations, with each man receiving one-half pound of meat, usually bacon, and one pound of cornmeal or flour per day.[28] This was particularly distressing to the dragoons, who had grown used to the additional food they had acquired from the low-country's plantations.[29]

The sudden scarcity of rations made keeping a servant an onerous burden. Oliver Middleton quickly realized the wisdom of leaving his servant at home. He wrote to his mother that the seven men of his mess were having a difficult time feeding their two servants. He remarked that the soldiers had to get by on a daily ration of "six or eight small fritters and two or three scraps of bacon."[30]

The food shortages caused great resentment among the dragoons, who had long been able to avoid such hardships. After the war Edward L. Wells, the New Yorker who had joined the Charleston Light Dragoons, had little good to say about the cooks and servants after the unit arrived in Virginia. In an ironic reversal of roles, he christened them "tyrants of the most unmerciful kind," who took "good care not to starve themselves" while saving little food for their masters. He concluded that this behavior caused "much needless suffering" among unit members.[31]

Wells's comments denoted lingering postwar and post-Reconstruction resentment, but they also provide clues to the morale of slaves who accompanied the dragoons to Virginia. Wells wrote that Surgeon Gregorie's servant, Othello, was sullen after his arrival and guessed that "he had already had enough of 'following Hampton,' and was thinking of the pleasures and comforts of home."[32] If servant morale plummeted with the dragoons' transfer, it comes as no surprise. They, like their masters, were away from the lowcountry for the first time during the war. Like the rest of the Army of Northern Virginia, they had to subsist on reduced rations. Not surprisingly, Wells's attitude hardened toward the unit's servants as they became less of an asset and more of a burden to their masters.

The dragoons and their servants, however, had little time to grumble or adapt to their new surroundings in Virginia. Many company members scrounged for necessary equipment, such as military saddles or saddlebags; others struggled with excess baggage that had to be stored at the homes of South Carolinians living in Richmond.[33] Three days after arriving in the city, the unit rode toward Lee's headquarters, camping for the evening near the site of the battle of Yellow Tavern, where Major General J. E. B. Stuart had been mortally wounded on May 11, 1864, only thirteen days before the dragoons arrived in Richmond.[34]

Following its arduous trip from South Carolina, the 4th South Carolina Cavalry had 987 men available for service. Unfortunately, only four hundred horses had completed the journey fit for duty. Elements of Major General Jubal Early's corps, a battle-hardened unit, teased the green cavalrymen mercilessly, mocking their Enfield rifles and their homespun uniforms. Lieutenant Colonel Stokes of the 4th Cavalry, a tall, lanky man, was especially singled out for ridicule.[35]

Brigadier General Butler's brigade, including the 4th South Carolina Cavalry under Colonel Benjamin H. Rutledge, had arrived in Virginia at the height of Union lieutenant general Ulysses S. Grant's Overland Campaign, which began on May 4, 1864, with the objective of destroying General Robert E. Lee's Army of Northern Virginia through sustained battle. Grant had hoped to turn the right flank of General Lee, drawing his Army of Northern Virginia out of its trenches and into a "showdown battle" south of the Wilderness, a densely wooded area west of Fredericksburg.[36] Lee had countered Grant's initial thrust at the Wilderness on May 5 and 6, but Grant continued to move southward and the two armies sidestepped toward Richmond. On May 24, the date of the Charleston Light Dragoons' arrival in Richmond, Lee faced Grant from behind the North Anna River. Grant once again moved the Army of the Potomac southward and crossed the Pamunkey River between May 26 and 28. Unsure of Lee's whereabouts, Major General George G. Meade, commander of the Army of the Potomac, ordered the army's cavalry chief, Major General Philip H. Sheridan, to determine Lee's whereabouts by moving south toward Mechanicsville and the Chickahominy River.[37]

Opposing Sheridan was Major General Wade Hampton, the Army of Northern Virginia's senior cavalry officer, who had taken the late J. E. B. Stuart's place as nominal commander of all cavalry in the theater. General Lee had directed Hampton to provide him with intelligence about Grant's movements after crossing the Pamunkey River. Hampton moved the 4th and 5th South Carolina Cavalries from Atlee's Station to reconnoiter Union positions, aiming this probe toward the small crossroads village of Haw's Shop. Unbeknownst to Hampton, Sheridan had moved a division of cavalry numbering 3,500 men there to check on the location of Lee's army.[38]

On May 28, Colonel Rutledge's 4th South Carolina Cavalry and Colonel John Dunovant's 5th South Carolina Cavalry regiments were joined by Lieutenant Colonel John M. Millen's 20th Georgia Cavalry battalion to form a provisional brigade commanded by the 4th Cavalry's Rutledge, former captain of the Charleston Light Dragoons. Lieutenant Colonel William Stokes assumed temporary command of the 4th Cavalry. This new brigade joined Hampton's cavalry division, which now numbered 4,500 men. Among the units were Brigadier General Thomas L. Rosser's Laurel Brigade; Major General Fitzhugh Lee with Brigadier General William C. Wickham's Virginia brigade; Major

General Rooney Lee with Brigadier General John R. Chambliss's brigade; and parts of Colonel John A. Baker's North Carolina brigade.[39]

The complex organizational structure of Hampton's force played a crucial role in the events of May 28. Neither Rutledge, who was in temporary command of Butler's brigade, nor his superiors adequately understood the chain of command. Hampton believed that Rutledge would report to Rosser, the senior brigadier in Hampton's division. Rosser also assumed that Rutledge was under his command, but Fitzhugh Lee believed that Rutledge was assigned to him. Rutledge was unsure who his immediate superior was and whether Millen's battalion, which was attached to Butler's brigade, was under his command.[40]

Equally ominous, the ranks of the 4th Cavalry and the Charleston Light Dragoons had been thinned significantly. A number of the company's horses had sustained back injuries caused by civilian saddles. The 4th Cavalry had four hundred men and horses available for combat, only 40 percent of its total strength. Of those, there were only forty-seven dragoons, or 41 percent of the company. Perhaps more important, the dragoons entered battle with only one officer present. Captain Richard H. Colcock was suffering from a debilitating illness contracted while he had been on duty near the lowcountry marshes. First Lieutenant Lionel C. Nowell was in charge of the company in his absence, while 2nd Lieutenant James W. O'Hear was detailed to serve as acting adjutant for Lieutenant Colonel Stokes, the acting regimental commander. O'Hear replaced Lieutenant Gabriel Manigault, who served as Rutledge's acting brigade adjutant. The unit's only other officer, 3rd Lieutenant Edward R. Harleston Jr., had been detailed the previous day to return to Richmond and draw ordnance for the company.[41]

At daybreak on May 28, the dragoons awoke tired and hungry. Manigault, adjutant for the 4th Cavalry, noted that the boys received nothing to eat that day. He shared a small piece of cornbread with Frank Middleton and found members of the company "to be utterly out of spirits at the severe marching and the scarcity of food."[42]

After Hampton's officers received their orders, the Charleston Light Dragoons and the rest of the 4th Cavalry mounted their horses and rode northeast along the Atlee Station Road toward Haw's Shop in the vanguard of Hampton's cavalry. As his command approached Enon Methodist Church, one mile west of Haw's Shop, Hampton sent Wickham's brigade forward. Union cavalry located near the Haw House quickly engaged the Confederates. After a series of charges and countercharges, the battle degenerated into a dismounted action, with the soldiers of Union brigadier general David McM. Gregg's division battling Hampton's troopers in thick woods near Enon Church. Hampton deployed Wickham's and Rosser's brigades in a line that ran north to south and perpendicular to Atlee Station Road. Rosser's brigade was north of the road and Wickham's was south. Once in position, the Confederate cavalrymen dug shallow rifle pits and constructed barricades using fence rails. Hampton anchored his left flank on Crump's Creek to the north and his right flank on Mill Creek to the south. From this location, he invited the Union cavalry to attack what he considered to be a nearly impregnable position.[43]

Gregg's division rose to the challenge, with Colonel Henry E. Davies Jr. committing eight regiments to the fight in the woods. What had begun as a fluid contest of traditional cavalry tactics devolved into a fierce fight at close range, with neither side able to drive its opponent from the woods. Federals and Confederates alike grabbed whatever cover was available, firing relentlessly at fleeting targets glimpsed through the smoke-filled brush. At 11:00 A.M. Hampton decided to put more pressure on the Union line. He had held Rutledge's brigade in reserve on Atlee Station Road behind Wickham's brigade. Fitzhugh Lee requested that Hampton send the 4th Cavalry to prevent Union troops from breaking Wickham's line. Hampton relented and ordered Stokes to take the regiment to the Confederate right.[44]

After moving forward and just prior to dismounting, the Charleston Light Dragoons and the remainder of the 4th Cavalry witnessed two events that boded ill. The first was a mortally wounded lieutenant being taken to the rear; the second a courier being knocked from his horse end-over-end by a shell that killed the animal but left the rider only shaken. Yet unit members laughed heartily as the rider scurried back in the direction from which he came.[45] The 4th Cavalry dismounted, leaving every fourth man behind to hold the horses. As the men gave a Rebel yell, the regiment moved forward at the double quick, much as the dragoons had done at Pocotaligo. As they advanced, the company suffered its first combat death of the war. In a place where the trees spread and there was little underbrush, Alexander Robertson, a twenty-four-year-old planter from St. Thomas and St. Denis Parish, was mortally wounded.[46] Shortly thereafter, the 4th Cavalry arrived at its assigned position, where unit members crouched to avoid the fire of Union sharpshooters. Hampton, however, had second thoughts regarding the unit's placement and recalled it to its original position, forcing it to return through the same sort of fire that killed Robertson.[47]

On the Union side, Gregg had committed all of his available regiments to the assault on Hampton's line. He requested reinforcements from Sheridan, who disregarded nearby Union infantry, hoping instead to carry the day with cavalry alone. In a renewed effort at piercing the Confederate line, Gregg pushed his men forward north of Atlee Station Road. This advance quickly petered out. Believing this push had weakened the Union line south of the road, Fitzhugh Lee went directly to Stokes and ordered him to have the 4th Cavalry relieve Wickham's brigade of Virginians. The regiment shouted and advanced, extending the right flank of Wickham's line. And once again the

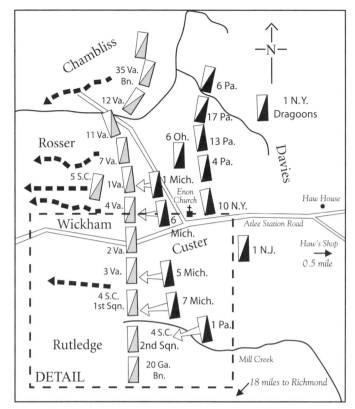

Battle of Haw's Shop, May 28, 1864, around 4:00 p.m.

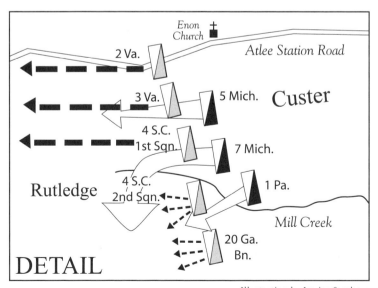

Charleston Light Dragoons suffered casualties during the advance. The company moved across an open field and toward its intended position in single file, and as they advanced, Percival Porcher was wounded severely in the leg, forcing the trailing dragoons to jump over his body as he writhed in pain. Timothy O'Brien was also shot in the right thigh, the first of two wounds he would receive as a dragoon.[48] The 4th Cavalry moved into position on both sides of a large ravine. Stokes and the first squadron manned the ravine's north side, while Captain Thomas Pinckney and the second squadron, including the Charleston Light Dragoons, took their places to the south of the ravine.[49]

As the action unfolded, Colonel Rutledge did little. Hampton and other superior officers moved Rutledge's regiment and brigade into action without consulting the former dragoon. When he needed to commit the 4th Cavalry to the fight, Hampton sent word to Stokes instead of Rutledge. He also was responsible for sending the regiment back to its original position. The second time the unit was thrown into the line, Fitzhugh Lee ordered Stokes to move to the support of Wickham. Neither general communicated with Rutledge and instead dealt directly with regimental commanders. Consequently, Rutledge and Lieutenant Manigault, his adjutant, remained near the 4th Cavalry's horse holders, mere spectators in one of the fiercest cavalry engagements of the war.[50]

As they entered the woods, the dragoons faced combat's chaotic horrors. Captain Pinckney moved them and the rest of the second squadron down a hill and into a ditch at its base, with "the enemy's fire thus passing over their heads."[51] On the left of the line was the ravine, into which "a considerable number of the men pressed." From this position the dragoons opened a heavy fire on their opponents, members of Colonel John P. Taylor's 1st Pennsylvania Cavalry, "many of whom were as close to them as thirty yards." The cover was thick, and it and the smoke made it difficult for the dragoons to spot targets. Edward L. Wells later wrote that most shots were "snaps, fired at faces only for a second thrust from behind a tree, or peering around a bush, or at the rifle flashes."[52]

On the right of the company's line there was far less undergrowth than on the left. Unlike their opponents, who were armed with breech-loading carbines, the dragoons were sometimes forced to expose themselves to load their weapons. Casualties quickly mounted. Sharing cover along this part of the line were Arthur Robinson and James Adger Jr. Robinson was shot through the head and died instantly, and the spent ball struck Adger in the head; the wounded Adger tried to drag Robinson's body away. Another dragoon, Josiah Bedon, a thirty-year-old attorney and planter from Colleton District, had apparently experienced a premonition about the fight, and before the dragoons' advance, he had left with one of his horse holders an image of his wife. He was mortally wounded.[53]

By 4:00 P.M. the battle had reached a fevered pitch. Major Generals Sheridan and Hampton both attempted to break their opponent's line, with little success. At this juncture, however, Rooney Lee asked Hampton to withdraw Chambliss's brigade, recently battered in a failed flanking movement and now anchoring the Confederate left flank. Hampton agreed, and Lee ordered the withdrawal. Chambliss's retreat, however, exposed the left flank of Rosser's brigade to Union attack, so Rosser ordered his men to withdraw. This in turn uncovered the left flank of Wickham's brigade, so Wickham ordered his unit's withdrawal. Finally, Stokes ordered the first squadron of the 4th Cavalry to pull back with the Virginians. The 4th Cavalry's second squadron and the Charleston Light Dragoons, however, received no orders to withdraw, and separated from the rest of the Confederate command by the large ravine, they failed to notice that the remainder of Hampton's command had relinquished the field.[54]

To the rear, Colonel Rutledge and Lieutenant Manigault remained with the horse holders. Undoubtedly chafing over being ignored as the fighting raged, Rutledge and his adjutant sought out Hampton to ask if they could rejoin their regiment, since the colonel's position as brigade commander "had become a sinecure." Hampton informed Rutledge, "the combat was over, its purposes accomplished, its troops ordered to retire." Hampton ordered the brigade's horses forward so that the troops could mount quickly and thus "prevent any confusion in that quarter." Neither he nor Rutledge knew that Stokes had left behind the second squadron and the Charleston Light Dragoons.[55]

The rapid withdrawal of Hampton's line prompted a Union pursuit. Captain Pinckney, commanding the isolated second squadron, later wrote that he witnessed men across the ravine moving toward the rear. Pinckney twice traveled up the hill to his squadron's rear in search of an officer who could tell him if he should retreat. On both occasions officers persuaded him to keep his men in place.[56] Shortly thereafter Lieutenant Nowell and the rest of the dragoons began to receive fire from their left. Nowell feared that the rest of the 4th South Carolina Cavalry had become disoriented and was firing into the dragoons, until Adjutant Theodore A. Jeffords from the 5th Cavalry arrived to tell him that the company was being flanked on both sides. When he discovered that part of the command was left behind, Fitzhugh Lee sent his aide, John Gill, to lead the remaining Confederates to safety.[57]

Around the same time, other commanders recognized the problem. Pinckney ordered the second squadron to fall back and went to the ditch to ensure that everyone was retreating. He stayed behind to get his men out and quickly realized that Union cavalry had cut off his escape. He moved to the left into the woods in hopes of evading the enemy, but a group of men from Brigadier General George A. Custer's Michigan brigade quickly captured him.[58]

Meanwhile, Stokes had discovered that he had left half of his regiment on the southern side of the ravine. His acting adjutant, Dragoon 2nd Lieutenant James W. O'Hear, had two dragoons acting as couriers, but neither lasted very long. Frank Middleton was shot in the back and taken prisoner as he moved through the encircling Union troops to inform the dragoons to withdraw.[59] The other courier, William L. Kirkland, the physician whose Combahee River plantation was burned in a Union raid the year before, was struck by a minié ball that entered his thigh and crushed his femur. Kirkland, however, managed to escape the advancing Union cavalrymen.[60] After losing both couriers, O'Hear attempted to extricate the dragoons himself, but he was quickly surrounded by Union troops. The previous day he had experienced a premonition of death, which perhaps increased his desperation. Troopers from Custer's Michigan brigade moved in on O'Hear and ordered him to surrender. Instead, he rapidly fired his pistols at the surrounding Union cavalry until he was shot in the face and killed.[61]

Since first entering the battle, the dragoons and other Confederates south of the ravine had withstood several Union assaults. They fought "coolly and intelligently," holding their portion of the line throughout the afternoon.[62] Upon realizing, however, that they had been flanked and were slowly being surrounded, their confidence evaporated. In combat, the psychological shock derived from a sudden turn of events could quickly alter a soldier's inclination to stand and fight. Indefatigable troops might quickly break and flee for their lives. Such was the case with the Charleston Light Dragoons, who broke for the Confederate rear.[63] As they fell back, they rushed past Hampton, who had learned of their dilemma and was bravely fighting to extricate them.[64]

Rushing through a gauntlet of fire at close quarters, the dragoons' rapid retreat through the encircling Union troops resulted in even more casualties. Sergeant Allen Miles and Benjamin Bostick had shared a rifle pit during the fight. As they quickly retreated toward the rear, Miles, who had been shot in the posterior at Pocotaligo, "begged Bostick to take his pistol." Having no place to put the weapon, Bostick declined the offer. The two "ran on as fast as they could" with the enemy "being not more than 30 paces from them on their flank as they ran." Seconds later, Miles, who was several steps ahead of his comrade, was shot in the back. Bostick later recounted, "I heard the ball hit him . . . distinctly. He swung around, his rifle flew from his hand, and he fell on his back." Bostick slowed his pace as he passed his fallen sergeant, who raised his hands slightly as if to ask for help. Bostick did not stop.[65]

Other dragoons fell during the withdrawal. Lewis Vanderhorst, one of the older and more popular dragoons, and T. G. Holmes, who was detailed as a clerk and an engineer for most of the war, also were killed. Most of the Union flanking fire came from the right of the retreating Confederates, and so several men were wounded in their right thigh or leg, and one in the right hand.[66]

The survivors halted at a rail fence, which they dismantled to form a barricade. Soon thereafter Stokes arrived and ordered the men back to their horses. One dragoon recalled seeing Benjamin F. Huger, a popular sergeant, limping toward the fence, but no one could remember seeing him reach the barricade. One of the dragoons rode back to the fence with Huger's horse. There he found the sergeant and helped him onto his animal. Huger refused to relinquish his pistol, claiming that he would use it on any surgeon who tried to amputate his wounded limb.[67]

Even after the withdrawal, confusion reigned. Rutledge and Manigault attempted to move the brigade's horse holders forward to meet the retreating Carolinians and Georgians. The 4th Cavalry's horse holders passed through a gate too narrow for the three horses in each man's possession, and the animals broke loose. Surviving cavalrymen, emerging from the engagement in twos and threes, had trouble finding their mounts. Yet there were few signs of panic, largely because Union cavalry had halted their pursuit of the fleeing Confederates.[68]

In terms of Rebel losses for this battle, the 4th South Carolina Cavalry, Rutledge's regiment, suffered the most casualties. The regiment took 400 men into battle and 127 (32 percent) were killed, wounded, or captured. And of the regiment's ten companies, the Charleston Light Dragoons suffered the heaviest losses. Nineteen of the forty-seven dragoons who participated in the battle of Haw's Shop (40 percent) became casualties.[69]

Three dragoons were captured by the Union forces. J. W. Evans, "a mere boy" in his first and only action during the war, surrendered without being injured.[70] The other two soldiers, William W. White and Frank Middleton, were wounded and captured. White had been a dragoon for seven years prior to the war and had served intermittently as a bookkeeper in the South Carolina Treasury Department during the conflict. At Haw's Shop he was shot in the right leg below the knee and was sent to the U.S. Army General Hospital in Alexandria, Virginia. There he recovered from the injury before being transferred to Old Capitol Prison in Washington, D.C., and eventually to Elmira, New York.[71] Frank Middleton, however, was wounded severely when a minié ball entered his back and pierced his lung. Union soldiers carried him to a field hospital at Summer Hill, near Hanover Courthouse. There several women, occupants of the home, cared for him until his death two days later, on May 30. He was buried in the family's yard.[72]

Nine dragoons were wounded during the engagement and treated by Confederate medical personnel. Percival Porcher, wounded in the left thigh, was taken to a field hospital near Richmond, where he died of gangrene on June 3, 1864. William L. Kirkland, who had his right femur shattered by a minié ball, was transported to General Hospital No. 9 in Richmond. Surgeons amputated his leg on May 30, and friends transported him to a private residence in hopes of speeding his recovery. Kirkland's leg turned gangrenous, however, and he died on June 19, 1864.[73] That the other wounded dragoons avoided a similar fate seemed miraculous. Gabriel Manigault wrote that "hospital gangrene and erysipelas were in the atmosphere of the city."[74]

For the survivors of the battle at Haw's Shop, their reduced numbers undoubtedly served as a sober reminder of their experience but also as a source of pride. Before the battle the men sensed that other outfits were jealous of their wealth and social position. For the survivors, however, combat changed the way they felt about their standing. Thereafter they believed that their courage under fire entitled them to the respect of other units within the regiment and brigade.[75]

Although the dragoons admired their own performance at Haw's Shop, their commanders feared criticism for the unit's high casualty rate. Shortly after the battle, Major General Hampton, the man most responsible for the Charleston Light Dragoons' transfer from the relative safety and comfort of the South Carolina coast, seemed quite concerned about the losses. He asked Lieutenant Manigault to provide him with a copy of his report as soon as possible, which Manigault did the following day.[76]

The battle's tragic outcome for the dragoons—and the whole of the 4th Cavalry's second squadron—resulted from command and communications failures. As the newly anointed cavalry chief for the Army of Northern Virginia, Hampton was leading his troops into their first major action since Major General Stuart's death. At Haw's Shop he failed to communicate with Rutledge and allowed subordinates such as Fitzhugh Lee to bypass the former dragoon and deliver instructions directly to his regimental commanders.

Colonel Rutledge also shared a portion of the blame. He had never commanded a regiment under fire, and at Haw's Shop he led a brigade in combat for the first time. Instead of placing himself near Hampton or with his troops once his unit was committed, Rutledge remained with the brigade's horse holders and thereby removed himself from the events that transpired. One eyewitness later accused him of cowardice for not advancing with his brigade. During the battle Brigadier General Pierce Manning B. Young, who commanded a brigade recently arrived from Georgia, came upon Rutledge and Manigault as they waited with the brigade's horse holders at a small house in the rear of the line. Afterward, Young reported to General Lee's headquarters that he found Rutledge and his adjutant "seeking protection behind a house." Manigault later wrote that he thought it "spiteful" of Young to make such a report because it did "much injury" to the two men, especially Rutledge, who was "anxious for promotion."[77] Due to his location during the battle, Rutledge could not have known that one squadron of his regiment (including his beloved Charleston Light Dragoons) had been left behind during the general withdrawal.

The greatest responsibility for the regiment and the disaster that befell it sat upon the shoulders of Lieutenant Colonel William Stokes, the 4th Cavalry's acting commander. Stokes was an able squadron commander, but at Haw's Shop he was in charge of the entire regiment for the first time. By placing the regiment astride a ravine, he invited disaster. During the retreat he did not give proper attention to ensuring that the second squadron received the order to withdraw. Consequently, half of the regiment was left in place and surrounded. Stokes's adjutant, Dragoon Lieutenant O'Hear, and his two couriers became casualties, and the 4th South Carolina Cavalry suffered the most casualties of any unit, Confederate or Union, engaged in the battle.[78]

At the company level, Lieutenant Nowell did an admirable job of steadying the dragoons and keeping them in the fight until they were flanked. As the only company officer present, he alone could not have halted their mad dash toward safety. The untested nature of the troops helped to explain the rout as well. After several engagements, veteran units could withdraw from combat without panic, stopping at a safe distance to re-form and fight again. Repetition of this maneuver in various drills decreased panic in the ranks during a battle. Veteran troops would also have realized that retreat was a military necessity, not an indictment of one's courage. The dragoons and the rest of the 4th South Carolina Cavalry had learned none of these lessons, although subsequent events would hasten their education.[79]

Following the battle, Nowell and the regiment's other remaining officers gathered survivors two miles from Haw's Shop in the rear of Major General John C. Breckinridge's division. The following day, May 29, 1864, they remained in camp, drawing rations for the first time in two days. Because the unit's servants were far to the rear, "food for once was plentiful."[80]

Probably for the first time since the war began, the company gathered around fires without forming into designated messes, and shaken survivors combined their resources to make do with their scant rations. This marked a notable unit transformation. Attrition had forced the men to disregard the established system of unit messes, each containing several members who shared servants and rations. Thereafter the company would constitute one large primary group, bound together by its members' survival, a kind of democracy of common valor and suffering.[81]

The day after the fighting at Haw's Shop, many soldiers' friends and acquaintances visited the dragoons' camp to hear about the battle and inquire about the casualties. News of the engagement quickly traveled to the dragoons' families. Some dragoons who had been furloughed in Richmond arrived to replenish the company's reduced ranks.[82]

On May 30, two days after the battle, the brigade comprising the 4th, 5th, and 6th South Carolina Cavalries was gathered at Mechanicsville, Virginia, south of Lee's army. There, for the first time, the brigade came under the command of Brigadier General Matthew C. Butler, who had arrived in the field on the evening of May 28. Butler was a combat-hardened cavalry commander, who had led the 2nd South Carolina Cavalry under Stuart. He had lost a foot to an artillery shell at Brandy Station, and after convalescing he was anxious to prove himself a capable brigade commander.[83]

Deciding to leave the 6th Cavalry at Mechanicsville, Butler gathered the 4th and 5th regiments to move toward Cold Harbor. Also accompanying Butler was Brigadier General Martin Gary and his small brigade of cavalry. With Gary was the 7th South Carolina Cavalry, a green unit that had only recently been consolidated. Once again Hampton called for a reconnaissance in force, with the intention of probing Grant's lines.[84]

With the arrival of the brigade's guide, Butler's command proceeded along Old Church Road, until lead elements spotted two Union cavalrymen fleeing from a house. Butler led his troops forward at a trot for nearly half a mile, then turned the formation into an open field on the right of the road. There he had Gary's battalion dismount and ordered them forward as skirmishers, leaving the rest of the brigade mounted and in place.[85]

Facing the Confederates was Union colonel Thomas C. Devin's brigade of cavalry near Old Church, a crossroads village that had once been the site of an early church. Devin had moved his men south on Bottoms Bridge Road until they crossed Matadequin Creek. He moved one squadron of the 17th Pennsylvania Cavalry farther south until they occupied the Barker family farm. There they were surprised to run into Butler's brigade as it moved north on Cold Harbor Road.[86]

As Gary's battalion moved forward, Colonel Rutledge, now in command of the 4th Cavalry, grew impatient. He was still smarting from recent failures and perhaps from accusations of cowardice at Haw's Shop. In addition, Major General Jubal Early had rebuked Rutledge that morning for not being able to read a map of the vicinity.[87] Rutledge undoubtedly was anxious to prove his worth in combat. As senior colonel, he had unsuccessfully commanded the brigade only two days prior, and he was anxious to lead the 4th South Carolina Cavalry forward as skirmishers. Military practicality, however, dictated that the regiment, which had suffered heavily at Haw's Shop, be held in reserve. Rutledge showed his displeasure at this by dismounting and lying down under a nearby tree.[88]

This episode was the first of several that set the tone for Rutledge's wartime relationship with Butler, the newly arrived brigade commander. In many ways Butler was the antithesis of Rutledge and the Charleston Light Dragoons. He was from the South Carolina upcountry, having grown to maturity in Greenville and Edgefield, and members of the lowcountry aristocracy had long disdained that region and its residents. Although Butler was from a politically prominent family, he had few lowcountry ties and was not a man of great wealth.[89] Regional rivalries and social differences therefore contributed to Rutledge's frustration with his new commander. To Butler, a veteran of Stuart's greatest victories and the survivor of a wound that nearly cost him his life and left him with a cork foot, Rutledge was little more than an inexperienced regimental commander.

As these events transpired, a battle unfolded that closely resembled the clash at Haw's Shop. Around 2:00 P.M. on May 30, Butler's skirmishers drove back the Pennsylvania cavalrymen to Matadequin Creek and were able to occupy portions of Barker's farm. Devin quickly committed more men to the battle, and the Pennsylvanians repelled Butler's skirmishers, once again occupying the farm.[90]

Butler realized that he had run into a large body of Union cavalry, and so he had the brigade dismount and sent it into action one squadron at a time. The Charleston Light Dragoons and the Rutledge Mounted Rifles were left in reserve.[91] This was probably because Hampton already had shown concern for the dragoons' losses, and it is possible that he impressed on Butler the need to protect the unit in future actions.

Butler committed the 4th South Carolina Cavalry to the west of Bottoms Bridge Road, where it drove back the Pennsylvanians and soon recaptured Barker's farm. To the east of the road, the 5th Cavalry occupied the farm of Spotswood Liggan. Devin in turn committed the 6th New York Cavalry to the right of the 17th Pennsylvania regiment and moved the 9th New York Cavalry to its left. Union brigadier general Alfred T. A. Torbert soon arrived and ordered the remainder of his cavalry division to move toward the fighting from Old Church. The first of these reinforcements to arrive on the scene was Brigadier General Wesley Merritt's Reserve Brigade. As part of Merritt's brigade, the 2nd U.S. Regulars replaced the 17th Pennsylvania Cavalry in the line and, along with the 6th New York Cavalry, began to drive back Rutledge's 4th South Carolina cavalrymen. This created a hole in the Confederate line, which Butler quickly rushed to fill.[92] He ordered the Charleston Light Dragoons (only twenty-eight of whom were present) to dismount and move forward into line. Lieutenant Nowell dismounted his men and led them into the fight. As at Haw's Shop, a handful of horse holders stayed behind.[93] The dragoons advanced on foot through a field until they reached the Liggan farm. There they filled the gap between the 4th and 5th South Carolina Cavalry regiments and quickly disassembled a rail fence in the Liggan yard to use for cover, while the Union cavalry retreated to the farm buildings.[94]

This tiny band opened fire on Union cavalrymen in the nearby outbuildings with the same intensity they had at Haw's Shop. As the fight progressed, George Armstrong Custer's brigade of Michigan cavalry arrived and launched an assault on the left flank of the 4th South Carolina Cavalry. Rutledge's regiment began to retire and was quickly flanked on the right by Merritt's brigade.

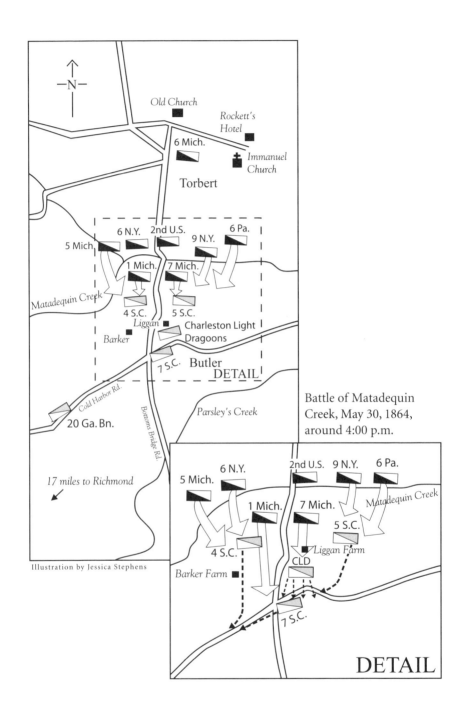

Old Church

Rockett's Hotel

6 Mich.

Immanuel Church

Torbert

6 N.Y. 2nd U.S. 6 Pa.

5 Mich. 9 N.Y.

1 Mich. 7 Mich.

Matadequin Creek

4 S.C. 5 S.C.

Liggan Charleston Light Dragoons

Barker

7 S.C. Butler

DETAIL

Cold Harbor Rd.

20 Ga. Bn.

Bottoms Bridge Rd.

Parsley's Creek

Battle of Matadequin Creek, May 30, 1864, around 4:00 p.m.

17 miles to Richmond

Illustration by Jessica Stephens

6 N.Y. 2nd U.S. 9 N.Y. 6 Pa.

5 Mich.

1 Mich. 7 Mich. Matadequin Creek

5 S.C.

4 S.C. Liggan Farm

CLD

Barker Farm

7 S.C.

DETAIL

Under this pressure, the 4th Cavalry rapidly abandoned the field and exposed the dragoons' left flank. In a replay of the events of May 28 at Haw's Shop, the dragoons at the Liggan farm soon came under fire from their left.[95] Realizing his men's vulnerability, Butler ordered a general withdrawal, and the unit stationed to the right of the dragoons pulled back quickly, leaving the dragoons to retreat through a gauntlet of fire, yet again repeating the scenario of two days before. Again, the dragoons fought well until realizing that their flanks were compromised. As the rest of the Confederate line fell back, the dragoons broke for the rear and the safety of their horses.[96]

The Union pursuit, as at Haw's Shop, inflicted still more casualties on the dragoons. James L. Bee, son of William C. Bee, factor and blockade-runner, was shot in the lower right leg. He was near a woodline on the Charleston Light Dragoons' left flank. Corporal Robert Adams, a planter from lower Richland district, stopped to assist Bee, only to be shot in the pelvis. Poinsett Pringle, one of three brothers who had joined the dragoons after an epic journey from Europe to Charleston, was mortally wounded and captured near the rail fence. Young Oliver H. Middleton Jr., Colonel Rutledge's brother-in-law and one-time personal secretary, also fell, the victim of a Union ball that entered his shoulder, angled downward, and pierced his lungs before exiting through his back. Union troops quickly captured the mortally wounded dragoon. Nearby William Bell was wounded twice, with one bullet entering his arm above his elbow and the other striking him in the hip. Disabled, he crumpled to the ground as Union cavalry advanced past his position. A Union straggler, however, continued to fire at Bell. Having missed the wounded dragoon with seven rounds, the frustrated soldier walked over to Bell, grabbed him by the collar, and escorted him from the field.[97]

Lieutenant Nowell, who had proved himself an able company commander at Haw's Shop, was again at his best during the dragoons' retreat. As panicked men fled from their positions, Nowell calmly held his ground and returned the Union fire to ensure that his men escaped. Eventually, he too was wounded and captured. In all, the dragoons lost fourteen of the twenty-eight members engaged in what became known as the battle of Matadequin Creek. Of those, thirteen (six of whom were not wounded) fell into Union hands. The Union pursuit of the fleeing Confederates was so intense that several dragoons chose to be captured rather than be killed or wounded.[98]

Other dragoons refused to surrender and rapidly outpaced their pursuers. Albert Rhett Elmore had joined the dragoons in August 1863 after serving as a private in Hampton's Legion and as sergeant major of the 7th South Carolina Infantry Battalion. At Matadequin Creek he and a group of comrades including Edward L. Wells, John Chisolm, Richard Martin, and Thomas Durant ran until they gained the cover of some pine trees and hid in a ravine formed by a branch. There they drank from the muddy water while trying to catch their breath. Elmore, believing that he could run no further, decided to surrender. Shortly thereafter, however, another Confederate cavalryman jumped into the ravine and informed the group (incorrectly) that black Union soldiers were in pursuit and giving no quarter to prisoners. Elmore and his comrades quickly found the strength to continue their flight to the rear.[99]

The dragoons and those near them were not the only fleeing Confederates —the entire Rebel line ran for their horses. Out-of-breath survivors, desperate to find their animals and make good their escape, moved up and down the line of horse holders. Dragoon Edward Trenholm, son of Charleston factor Edward L. Trenholm, was a horse holder at Matadequin Creek.[100] When he hurriedly tried to mount his animal, it threw him and rolled on him. The badly injured dragoon was carried to a Confederate hospital.[101] Corporal Robert Adams was not as fortunate. Having been shot in the pelvis while trying to assist James Bee, he retreated to the horse holders only to learn that another fleeing cavalryman had taken his animal. The rapidly advancing Union cavalry quickly captured him and Bee.[102]

Butler's troopers scattered in all directions as Confederate brigadier general Martin Gary attempted to form a rear guard to protect the fleeing Confederate forces. Among the fifty-odd men that he assembled were Colonel Rutledge and a detachment of the Charleston Light Dragoons.[103]

Once again the 4th South Carolina Cavalry and the dragoons had suffered heavy casualties due in part to communications and command failures. Butler, leading his brigade for the first time in combat, conceivably asked too much of his inexperienced regiments when he ordered a general withdrawal while his men were in close contact with Union cavalry. Consequently, the retreat quickly became a rout. He also failed to ensure that the Charleston Light Dragoons received the order to withdraw. As commander of the 4th Cavalry, Rutledge had been active in the fight, but he could not control his retreating companies, and he, like Stokes at Haw's Shop, also neglected to ensure that the dragoons withdrew in a timely manner. This oversight at Matadequin Creek probably resulted in a number of casualties among friends and family and, compounded by earlier failures, was an obvious indicator that he had much to learn about combat command and control.

For the dragoons, Matadequin Creek was eerily reminiscent of Haw's Shop. Once again they withstood Union assaults until they were flanked, and once again they received orders to retreat only after they were nearly surrounded. Another constant was the skillful and determined command of Lieutenant Nowell, who kept the company in the fight until the general withdrawal, when he attempted to cover his men's retreat until he was himself wounded and captured.

Dragoon Captain (later Colonel) Benjamin Huger Rutledge, circa 1861.
Photograph provided by Rare Books and Special Collections, Thomas
Cooper Library, University of South Carolina; used by permission of
descendants of B. H. Rutledge.

Dragoon Oliver Hering Middleton Jr., circa 1861. Courtesy of the South
Carolina Historical Society, Charleston, S.C.

Dragoon Josiah Bedon, circa 1861. Courtesy of the South Carolina Confederate Relic Room and Museum, Columbia, S.C.

Dragoon William L. Kirkland, circa 1860. Courtesy of the South Carolina Historical Society, Charleston, S.C.

Dragoon Edward L. Wells, circa 1860. From a copy, courtesy of South Caroliniana Library, University of South Carolina, Columbia.

Dragoon Alfred
Manigault, circa
1860. Courtesy of
the South Carolina
Historical Society,
Charleston, S.C.

Major General Matthew
Calbraith Butler, CSA,
circa 1863. Courtesy of
the South Carolina
Historical Society,
Charleston, S.C.

Dragoon (later 2nd Lt.) Gabriel E. Manigault, 1894. Courtesy of
The Charleston Museum, Charleston, South Carolina.

Dragoon William Bell, circa 1906. Courtesy of Paul G. Bell Jr.

Charleston Light Dragoons gathered at Magnolia Gardens by the monument to the Charleston Light Dragoons, May 10, 1910 (Confederate Memorial Day). Courtesy of the South Carolina Historical Society, Charleston, S.C.

The disaster of May 30 did not end for the dragoons as the day ended. Soon after dark, remnants of Butler's brigade slowly gathered near the site of the battle. Union cavalry had pursued the retreating Confederates, and Union pickets lay astride the road not far from where Butler's men attempted to rally. Butler, hoping to gain time to gather his command, ordered a detail of thirty or forty horsemen to move forward and push back the Union pickets under the cover of darkness. The remaining dragoons were a part of this detail, although all of the company's officers and noncommissioned officers were by this time casualties, ill, or dismounted.[104]

It was a moonless night, and the darkness of the woods through which the tiny band moved must have added to an atmosphere of impending catastrophe. Ahead of the column rode several members of the brigade, handpicked to scout Union pickets. The horsemen following in their wake were formed in a column of fours that was nearly as wide as the lane, with the Charleston Light Dragoons in the middle of the column. Sometime between 9:00 and 10:00 that evening, the group dipped into low ground near a brook. A Union picket fired on the guides, who turned their horses and galloped back toward the column. Hearing the pounding of approaching hooves, the men in the column's front ranks froze, and before the detail could react, the returning pickets, perhaps unaware of their comrades' precise location, slammed into them. Riders and horses panicked. Rifle fire erupted nearby. In the chaos that ensued, fleeing horses threw their riders, and several members of the detail were trampled. Survivors fled into adjoining woods to avoid capture; others lay on the road, badly hurt. Those still on their horses retreated quickly back down the road, dashing past Butler's headquarters and far beyond before finally stopping.[105]

All of the dragoons were unhorsed in the stampede. W. R. Withers and Otis B. Philips were both badly injured. J. M. Howell stumbled about in the dark until Union troops captured him. The rest made their way back to brigade headquarters, although some were unable to find their horses. Julius Pringle, known for his neat appearance, arrived in camp the next day without his horse or hat and with a handkerchief tied about his head to protect it from the sun.[106]

Around midnight, a livid Butler summoned Rutledge and Manigault to his brigade headquarters. Butler blamed Rutledge's men for the stampede, and his supposed slight of Rutledge the previous afternoon only added to the bad blood. Manigault later wrote, "There was a sharp parlay between the two for a few minutes, during which the colonel gave the general tit for tat." Butler announced that he longed for the days with his old regiment, the 2nd South Carolina Cavalry, rather than having to put up with the 4th Cavalry, for which he obviously had little respect. Rutledge and Manigault left the meeting shortly thereafter, once again to nurse wounded egos. Stokes later wrote that "nothing that Rutledge ever did was satisfactory at Brigade headquarters, and . . . it was the constant effort of every one there to belittle him."[107]

Rutledge's anger was not entirely misplaced. Over the course of two days the 4th South Carolina Cavalry had suffered far more casualties than Butler's old regiment, the 2nd Cavalry, had suffered during the entire war. Rutledge was particularly proud of his dragoons, now reduced to a pathetic handful.[108]

Neither the dragoons nor the rest of the regiment would recover from the events of May 28 through 30. At Haw's Shop they fought bravely in their first Virginia engagement. They gained confidence in their ability to stand in the face of battle until poor leadership and communication left many of them stranded on the battlefield and forced them to flee for their lives. Just two days later at Matadequin Creek, the company again fought well before abandoning the field of battle under similar circumstances.

The stampede on the evening of May 30 only proved what Butler should have known and what Rutledge already knew following the action at Matadequin Creek. The 4th South Carolina Cavalry in general, and the dragoons in particular, were demoralized or, as the soldiers might have put it, "played out." Their commanders' inexperience produced tragically high casualties, especially among the officers, and the men were physically spent. Manigault later wrote, "The truth was that our men were completely exhausted by the day's work. It had lasted from sunrise until well into the night."[109] The stampede on the evening of May 30 completed the demoralization of a fought-out regiment, already sadly reduced to a pathetic remnant of its former self by several days of hard riding and three engagements over a period of seventy-two hours.

Of notable significance was the large number of casualties that the unit had suffered. One study of the impact of casualties on combat effectiveness claims that a unit is ruined psychologically if it twice suffers casualties numbering one-third of its total strength.[110] In two battles between May 28 and May 30, over 40 percent of the dragoons engaged became casualties.[111]

No company could undergo three such heartbreaking disasters, lose so many critical leaders, and not have their morale plummet. Rutledge later wrote that "the accidents of Hawe's Shops, Cold Harbor and this Stampede, together with the loss by casualty of so many officers, who gave tone and character to this command, affected somewhat its temper and morale."[112]

Military failure and casualties, however, did more than diminish morale. The experience of combat molded the survivors into a unit that thereafter entered combat warily. Blind tenacity no longer seemed a virtue. Civil War soldiers, like fighting men throughout time, felt the need to prove themselves to their comrades and sister units during their first or second battle. In subsequent fights, however, they became less concerned with demonstrating their courage.[113] Their skills and efficiency as soldiers improved with combat experience up to a point. Beyond that, soldiers continued to gain experience but

lost enthusiasm for battle, and their effectiveness thus declined.[114] The dragoons experienced this deterioration in combat effectiveness following Matadequin Creek, only three days after the company's first battle in Virginia.
Thereafter the survivors adopted a more cautious and wary attitude toward
fighting, which would serve them well in future engagements.

After retreating from Matadequin Creek, the dragoons numbered roughly
a dozen men out of the once large, proud company that had arrived in Virginia
six days earlier. Only one company officer remained, 3rd Lieutenant Edward
Harleston Jr., and he was still on detached duty in Richmond. As a result, the
company was placed under the command of Lieutenant A. W. Cordes of Captain Pinckney's company.[115] For the first time during the war, the unit had not
been shielded from the worst aspects of military service. They had fought
alongside men they once would have treated with condescension, if not con-
tempt, and they had suffered heavy casualties. Their losses would shock the
South Carolina planter class and change forever assumptions regarding the
unit's elite and privileged character.

Chapter 5

TRANSFORMATION

*I was so fortunate, as to get from a knapsack a lot of nice crackers . . .
I relished them & blessed the provident spirit of the dead Yank, from
whose corpse I got the knapsack.*

Edward L. Wells

Following the battles at Haw's Shop and Matadequin Creek and the stampede of May 30, 1864, the survivors of the Charleston Light Dragoons could consider themselves veterans of some of the war's most intense cavalry combat. They were far from the South Carolina lowcountry both in distance and in circumstances. They had experienced privations and combat; only some had survived. The dragoons had shed their image as dandies unwilling or unable to fight but had also lost their pretensions of civility, and the coming year would intensify this transformation. By the war's conclusion they would be little different from any other Confederate cavalry company chewed up by the conflict.

On May 31, the morning after the stampede, Butler's brigade rode toward the Chickahominy River. Near Bottoms Bridge, the dragoons saw Robert E. Lee for the first time as he rode in a buggy along the Confederate line. The following day the dragoons and the rest of the brigade moved toward White Oak Swamp and bivouacked near Frazier's Farm, the site of a bloody 1862 battle still strewn with items from Union major general George B. McClellan's retreat during the Seven Days campaign.[1] The company remained there for two days before marching to Mechanicsville, another battlefield from the Seven Days campaign. The brigade at last received the McClellan saddles they had needed before leaving South Carolina, but new equipment could not heal the pain caused by the recent bloody engagements. The feud between Butler and Rutledge broke out anew. Butler accused Rutledge and the 4th South Carolina Cavalry of delaying the brigade's march, and Rutledge commented that his former commander, Brigadier General William S. Walker, was "much more considerate in what he said."[2] Spirits plummeted further when the dragoons realized that the campsite at Mechanicsville had recently been home to Confederate infantry who had left large numbers of lice in their wake.[3]

The Charleston Light Dragoons and the rest of the brigade drew rations and moved to Yellow Tavern, five miles north of Richmond, before turning northwest toward the Virginia Central Railroad. They halted within sight of the Blue Ridge Mountains on June 10, 1864, a cool, crisp night, and camped within three miles of Trevilian Station.[4] The dragoons did not realize that two divisions of Sheridan's cavalry were nearby, attempting to distract General Lee by destroying railroad stations before joining Major General David Hunter in the Shenandoah Valley. With Lee distracted, Grant would be able to move the Army of the Potomac across the James River and seize Petersburg, another important Confederate rail junction. Lee would then be forced to fight or flee.[5]

Sheridan began this raid on June 7, 1864, with close to 9,000 men, heading northwest for the railroad junctions at Gordonsville. Major General Hampton caught wind of this movement and raced 6,400 men from his division, Fitz-hugh Lee's division, and several artillery units to intercept the Federals. The Confederate column moved out on June 9, and by the following evening Hampton had placed himself in the path of Sheridan's troops near Trevilian's Station. On the morning of June 11, Hampton was riding with Butler toward his pickets when they met some of Butler's troopers retreating from advancing Union cavalry. Butler quickly ordered his brigade forward.[6]

The morning was cool. The dragoons, numbering twelve men plus Lieutenant Cordes, had had little to eat save cornbread, and some did not even have that.[7] The 4th Cavalry was the lead regiment as Butler's brigade advanced toward the Union cavalry. Seeing enemy pickets in the road, Butler ordered the first squadron of the 4th Cavalry to charge. This served little purpose, however, because the Union pickets simply moved off the road into the woods and continued to fire at the charging squadron, which soon backtracked to Butler.[8] Butler ordered the second squadron to dismount and form a line to the west of the nearby Fredericksburg Road. Rutledge took command of this squadron, which contained the few remaining dragoons, and deployed skirmishers, who quickly ran into Union troops and retreated to Rutledge's line situated along the brow of a wooded hill.[9]

Butler, realizing that he faced at least a brigade of Sheridan's cavalry, dismounted his entire brigade except for the first squadron of the 4th Cavalry, under the command of Captain John C. Calhoun, grandson of the famous South Carolinian.[10] Facing Butler once again was the brigade of Brigadier General Wesley Merritt, comprising three regiments of U.S. Cavalry Regulars as well as the 1st New York and the 6th Pennsylvania Cavalries. As at Haw's Shop and Matadequin Creek, the two sides fought dismounted in thick brush and tall grass. And again, the dragoons fought well in the dense woods that offered an excellent defensive position. Rutledge later claimed, "This position could have been held. The enemy advanced several lines, but were easily repulsed with loss."[11]

Despite the 4th Cavalry's success in this stage of the battle, Butler remained dissatisfied with Rutledge. Rutledge, having learned costly lessons from the two preceding battles, sent Manigault, his adjutant, to stay near the rest of the regiment so that Rutledge would have some command and control over the 4th Cavalry's second squadron. Seeing Manigault on horseback nearby, Butler ordered him to inform Rutledge that his men were making too much noise. Perhaps Butler thought Rutledge was revealing his position to the Union cavalry, or perhaps he felt it necessary once again to frustrate the colonel and his adjutant. Soon thereafter, Butler's horse was killed beneath him, and he was seen riding "a beautiful bay mare," the horse of Dragoon James Adger, who had been wounded at Haw's Shop.[12]

As the fighting intensified, so did the bad blood between Rutledge and Butler. Rutledge sent word to Butler that Union troops were flanking his command to the left and asked for reinforcements. Butler turned to the courier and responded, "Give my compliments to Colonel Rutledge and tell him to flank back." Rutledge was furious, commenting that his line was stretched to its limit and incapable of launching a flanking movement.[13] Having delivered this barb, however, Butler nevertheless asked Hampton for reinforcements, and Hampton sent Wright's brigade to Butler, who ordered them into action to secure Rutledge's left flank.[14]

The firing along the 4th South Carolina Cavalry's segment of the line was fierce, with the Charleston Light Dragoons again suffering casualties. Dragoon Thomas Lining, the company's color bearer, had stayed with the horse holders at Haw's Shop and Matadequin Creek. At Trevilian Station he traded places with a sick dragoon, who agreed to hold horses. Lining received a mortal wound in the femoral artery for his trouble. Nearby, Edward L. Wells also was wounded. He later wrote,

> I was hit by a flanking fire of the enemy, the bullet striking at an angle, about a quarter of an inch from my backbone in the small of the back. It did not penetrate far, owing to the angle at which it struck, & a leather belt, & two flannel shirts, through which it passed, & which broke the force of it considerably.[15]

Further to the left of the dragoons, Colonel Gilbert J. Wright's brigade tried to move into position in support of Rutledge but had a difficult time finding the 4th Cavalry in the thick woods. Their arrival on the firing line, however, caused yet more trouble for Rutledge. He later recalled that officers commanding units of Wright's brigade had ordered a charge, orders that Rutledge attempted to countermand. One witness reported that "Col. Rutledge remonstrated, insisting that he commanded the position. His remonstrances were unavailing." Most of the Confederate line moved forward, only to be hit by Union fire and be sent reeling back toward their original positions. Rutledge claimed that only a few members of the 4th Cavalry remained in position with him, and these checked the initial Union pursuit but were soon forced to retire.[16]

As at Haw's Shop and Matadequin Creek, the dragoons were nearly enveloped. Rutledge described their predicament: "Retreat to the rear was impossible, the ground being swept by the fire of both parties" so "to escape capture . . . [Rutledge] ran the gauntlet of their fire out to the right where the road lay."[17] Wounded and exhausted, Wells was at a Confederate field hospital when he was captured.[18] A former dragoon also was captured. To the rear of the 4th Cavalry at a bend in the road, Butler ordered Adjutant Manigault to dismount and find Colonel Hugh Aiken of the 6th South Carolina Cavalry in order to advise him to beware the heavy Union fire on his side of the line. Manigault carefully moved toward the far right of Butler's line in search of Aiken, who had been wounded earlier during the fight. Unaware of Aiken's injury, Manigault continued moving to the right of the Confederate line until two privates of Merritt's U.S. Cavalry captured him and escorted him to the rear of the Union position.[19]

Other dragoons became casualties during the withdrawal as well. J. Waring Boone was killed, as was William H. Fairly, who was serving as a courier, and Joseph M. Lawton was captured.[20]

As Butler's line stabilized nearly two miles to the rear, there was a lull in the battle. Early that morning George A. Custer's Michigan brigade had moved south on Nunn's Creek Road, which ran between the two wings of Hampton's command. Custer's men seized Hampton's wagons and wreaked havoc in the Confederate rear. At this time Dragoon A. Burgess Gordon was captured, along with many of the horse holders.[21]

Fearing that Custer would strike at Butler's rear, Hampton ordered Rutledge to mount two squadrons and drive south to stop the Union advance. Rutledge could gather only sixty men, and with these he drove back the Union pickets. But upon returning to where Butler's command had been, he found the position occupied by Union soldiers. Unaware of Butler's new position, Rutledge moved his command westward, following a group of Confederate officers until he joined Colonel Wright and his one hundred and fifty men. The two officers combined forces, but upon coming to a stream, Rutledge led his command downstream and Wright led his men upstream. Soon thereafter, Rutledge, who was suffering "severely" from dysentery and believed that he could not go farther, turned his command over to Captain Osborne Barber and ordered him to advance toward a Confederate artillery battery to the west. Although fearing imminent capture, Dragoon J. L. Brisbane refused to leave Rutledge. The two men rested for some time before moving toward the battery. As these events transpired, the remainder of the 4th South Carolina Cavalry, under the command of Lieutenant Colonel Stokes, helped Butler's brigade hold back the advancing Union forces to end the first day's battle.[22]

The following day the 4th South Carolina Cavalry again played a key role in the fight near Trevilian Station. Hampton ordered Butler's brigade to maintain a strong L-shaped position behind the Ogg House along the Gordonsville Road and a railroad cut. Butler placed the 4th Cavalry on the left, the 6th in the center, and the 5th on the right. Colonel Aiken of the 6th Cavalry had been wounded the previous day, so Rutledge again commanded the brigade.[23] Between 3:00 P.M. and nightfall, Union major general Sheridan ordered seven assaults against the Confederate position. Dragoon Wade Hampton Manning, son of former South Carolina governor John L. Manning, served as a courier during the battle. He delivered a message to Butler, who, although under heavy fire, stood perfectly still, while Manning attempted to dodge the flying Union shells.[24]

Rutledge, too, came under heavy fire in the fighting on June 12. A Union sniper shot three holes in his coat, grazed his cheek with a ball, and shot away part of his beard. The colonel bravely disregarded the near misses, and his men finally killed the Union sharpshooter.[25]

Following the failed final assault on their position, Butler's men counterattacked, driving Sheridan's cavalry from the field. During their retreat that night, Union forces abandoned Dragoon Edward L. Wells, whom they had captured a day earlier. The native New Yorker had been wounded the previous day and taken to a Confederate field hospital, where he and the other Confederate patients were left behind during the retreat of June 11. Union soldiers captured these men, and Union physicians treated them until Sheridan's forces retreated on June 12. Thereafter Wells and the other patients were once again in Confederate hands. Soon after this ordeal, Wells was admitted to a military hospital in Richmond but soon left to convalesce at Dragoon Benjamin F. Huger's "pineland place."[26]

As Sheridan retreated, the 4th South Carolina Cavalry, including the Charleston Light Dragoons, joined the rest of Hampton's troops in pursuing the Union cavalry. This movement culminated in the battle of Samaria Church, a running fight during which Hampton's and Fitzhugh Lee's forces literally chased Sheridan's troops for several miles. This engagement marked the end of Sheridan's raid; afterward Hampton's men were allowed to rest after nearly a month of continuous marching and fighting.[27]

Hampton's repulse of Sheridan also marked a new low point for the dragoons. The two-day battle of Trevilian Station nearly completed the company's destruction. Only twelve men had gone into combat on June 11. Three were killed, two captured, and one wounded, captured, and released, leaving a mere six dragoons. In addition, former dragoon and adjutant for the 4th Cavalry, Lieutenant Gabriel Manigault, was captured.[28]

It is not clear exactly how many dragoons took part in the fight on June 12. The previous day Rutledge had taken sixty men with him on the mission to drive back Union pickets. Undoubtedly, the dragoons were part of this detail. When Rutledge was too ill to continue on with the rest of his command, one dragoon stayed with him. The other five probably were with Captain Barber when he inadvertently stumbled into Union forces. Some of Barber's command was captured, while the rest escaped with Barber. These men therefore could have missed the battle on June 12.[29] The surviving dragoons participated in the pursuit of Sheridan's forces and the battle of Samaria Church. None of the dragoons were casualties during this last phase of the campaign.[30]

The fighting at Trevilian Station, following the costly battles at Haw's Shop and Matadequin Creek, was devastating for the 4th South Carolina Cavalry. Lieutenant Colonel Stokes estimated that the entire regiment mustered four hundred officers and men at the beginning of the campaign, but after Trevilian Station had less than one hundred men fit for duty. Of those, a half dozen or fewer were dragoons. This pitiful remnant could be proud of its record, as could the entire regiment and Butler's brigade. Sheridan claimed, "I have met Butler and his cavalry, and I hope to God I never meet them again."[31]

After the battle, few dragoons reported for duty. A number were in the regiment's reserve camp, unable to serve because their horses had galled backs. The unit had fielded only forty-seven men and horses for the battle of Haw's Shop, and its numbers declined precipitously afterward.[32] Periodically dragoons would join the regiment as horses became available, but these men were a company in name only.[33]

Although the Charleston Light Dragoons were far away from the South Carolina lowcountry during their month of combat in Virginia, news of their exploits and casualties quickly spread throughout their home state. Family members rushed to the aid of wounded loved ones, and all efforts were made to secure the bodies of those who had died. A grieving Oliver H. Middleton Sr. wrote to Congressman William Porcher Miles requesting aid in retrieving his son's body.[34] Family servants, some of whom had accompanied their masters to Virginia, were left with the task of returning their deceased masters' bodies, horses, and personal effects to the family. Percival Porcher, critically wounded at Haw's Shop, was sent to a field hospital near Richmond. Like other dragoons, he had left his servant Robert at home when the unit marched to Virginia. Fearing for her husband's life, Porcher's wife sent Robert to Richmond to care for him. Upon arriving, the servant learned of his master's death, but he could not secure transportation back to South Carolina for Porcher's body. Robert, according to family legend, walked the streets of Richmond begging for help until an officer took him to General Lee, who ordered artillery horses to convey the body home with a guard of honor.[35]

A number of dragoons were missing after the battles of May 28 through 30, and their families and friends desperately attempted to determine their fate. Enquiries often produced enough evidence for the family to determine what had happened to their relative. The family of Dragoon Allen Miles sought help from a number of sources to find him. From Northern sources, they learned that he had been shot in the back and abandoned on the field at Haw's Shop. No dragoons could account for him in prison, and the family received notice from a New York newspaper reporting Miles' death. Taken together, these sources left little doubt about the fate of the dragoon.[36]

Close family and social bonds always had connected the dragoons, and after combat operations in Virginia, these ties served as a network of information for the families of the missing. Word came of their fates not from the Confederate government, but from people close to the family. Such was the case with the family of Lewis Vanderhorst, who was missing following the battle of Haw's Shop. Ella Middleton Rutledge, wife of the 4th Cavalry's Colonel Rutledge, sister of Dragoon Oliver H. Middleton Jr., and cousin of Dragoon Frank Middleton, sent word to the Vanderhorst family verifying that Lewis had died in combat. Ella had received a letter from her aunt living in the North, Mrs. Elizabeth Middleton Fisher, which was delivered under a flag of truce. It contained information about the death of Ella's brother Oliver, as well as verifying the deaths of Joel Roberts Poinsett Pringle and Lewis Vanderhorst. Ella sent the note to her uncle, Alfred Huger, who forwarded it to the Vanderhorst family with his condolences.[37]

A wave of despair and frustration swept over the families and friends of those who had perished. Emma Holmes noted in early June 1864, "Each day brings sad tidings from Va. of the death, wounding, capture or missing of some acquaintance or friend" from skirmishes "from which nothing seems gained . . . while the most precious life blood is poured out like water."[38] In Camden, South Carolina, Mary Boykin Chesnut wrote of the battle of Haw's Shop as "that famous fight of the Charleston Light Dragoons" where "they stood still, to be shot down in their tracks. Having no orders to retire, they were forgotten, doubtless, and scorned to take care of themselves."[39] Her comments recalled the ideals of knightly courage that lowcountry families admired, but also suggested that civilians of her class resented what they considered to be the needless sacrifice of the dragoons, the fair flower of aristocratic manhood.

Dragoon casualties left a number of young, and not so young, widows among the state's wealthiest families. William L. Kirkland's wounding at the battle of Haw's Shop caused great despair, and then word of his death in Richmond from gangrene on June 19 drove his wife, Mary Miles Withers Kirkland, into an upper story room of their house. She emerged from this self-imposed exile on only one occasion during the rest of her life.[40]

The manifestation of Mrs. Kirkland's bereavement might have been more dramatic than that of other dragoons' wives, but it was by no means more heartfelt. Emma Holmes wrote that for Annie O'Hear, widow of James W. O'Hear, the anticipated birth of a friend's child "adds to the overwhelming grief for her husband, whom there can be little doubt was killed in that fatal battle [in Virginia] which has left desolation in so many other Charleston homes." Holmes described it as "the saddest of sights, a young girl of beauty, talents, refinement & wealth, whose mind is so clouded by melancholy as to be oblivious of the realities of the present."[41] Mary Boykin Chesnut also wrote of women left behind by fallen dragoons in the spring of 1864, describing Josiah Bedon's wife as the "loveliest of young widows." In contrast, she wrote that the face of Dragoon Converse Frierson's fiancée was hard, cold, and tearless.[42]

The expression of grief for fallen dragoons was not confined to lowcountry women. Throughout South Carolina members of the planter class sent and received letters of mourning that reported the loss of family and friends. This was an especially bitter pill because so many of the dead had been "gentlemen." Frederic Percival Leverett, a soldier in Virginia and son of a prominent low-country planter, related the Charleston Light Dragoons' story to his sister Mary. He corresponded with family members about acquaintances in the company who were killed, and commented that there "has been some gross mismanagement of the new Cavalry Regs." The blame, he thought, must rest with General Butler. Mary Maxcy Leverett noted that, only recently, the dra-goons had been in Columbia "at parties, balls & c. and now numbers of them are in the cold earth." She claimed that General Hampton had reprimanded General Butler "severely" for the loss of so many dragoons. She repeated rumors that the dragoons paid dearly for their reputation of easy living. They were "sneered at & laughed at," and "Gen. Butler (*upcountry man*) . . . treated them shamefully cursing & swearing at them, calling them 'silk stockings.'" To give them a taste of what war was really like, Butler reportedly had placed the dragoons in impossible positions against overwhelming odds. In turn, the dra-goons refused to retreat because their comrades and their commander mocked them and questioned their fighting abilities. As a result, "they held their ground, until surrounded, and the consequence is they were frightfully slaugh-tered."[43] If the rumors were true, and she failed to note this fact, the dragoons paid a very high price for upholding their notions of honor.

Although Mrs. Leverett's account is only partially accurate, it is indicative of the recrimination and resentment among those who lost family and friends from this most famous Charleston cavalry company of "gentlemen." To some, like Mrs. Leverett, Butler's envy and resentment were seen as the direct cause of the dragoons' heavy losses, and his upcountry origins helped to explain his behavior. To others, the dragoons' losses were viewed as the result of poor command decisions. Regardless of which explanation one accepted, the unit's casualties appeared needlessly high. In a brief announcement of William L. Kirkland's death in Richmond from gangrene, the *Charleston Mercury*'s editor summed up the feelings of the city and state's first families: "The rapid and apparently useless destruction of that favorite command, composed of young men of educated minds and high character has greatly shocked and distressed our people."[44]

Yet despite showing disdain for the unit's social origins, Butler had not caused its destruction. He had not been present at Haw's Shop; Rutledge had commanded the brigade there. Two days later at Matadequin Creek, Butler had held the dragoons in reserve, committing nearly every other unit in the brigade before finally calling the dragoons into battle. Butler *was* guilty, how-ever, of not subscribing to the presumptions of privilege to which Rutledge and the company had grown accustomed. A fighting general, Butler looked for opportunities to embarrass Rutledge and publicly display his disdain for the aristocratic colonel. And although Rutledge commanded the 4th South Caro-lina Cavalry, he was the quintessential Charleston Light Dragoon. Much that he gained in military service, he received through patronage. He expected But-ler to extend the same considerations to him and his unit that Generals Lee, Pemberton, Beauregard, and Walker had in South Carolina. When the requi-site deference was not forthcoming, Rutledge expressed his displeasure to fam-ily, friends, and anyone who would listen. Before arriving in Virginia, he wrote letters to the *Charleston Mercury* concerning his actions as commander of the 4th South Carolina Cavalry.[45] Stories of the company's costly valor at Haw's Shop and Matadequin Creek were known throughout the state. In none of the surviving correspondence, however, did Rutledge assume responsibility for the dragoons' combat performance or high casualties.

While their families sought to discover their whereabouts, a number of dra-goons, especially those who had been wounded, faced for the first time the uncertainty and tribulations of captivity. James Hopkins, who previously had been wounded at Pocotaligo in 1862, was captured at Matadequin Creek. Following the battle, Union guards led Hopkins and the other captured Con-federates on a forced march to prison. Still suffering from the ill effects of his earlier wound, Hopkins fell behind the column and eventually stopped in a ditch alongside the road. There a Union officer ordered him to march or be shot. Exhausted, Hopkins urged the officer to shoot him, but a "Hessian sol-dier" intervened and assisted Hopkins to the rear.[46]

For wounded Dragoon William Bell, the trip to prison was one of fear, pain, and fellowship. At Matadequin Creek he was shot in the arm and hip and cap-tured by advancing Union troops. Bleeding profusely, Bell offered his spurs to a guard in exchange for two canteens of water to clean his wounds. No doctors were available for the wounded Confederates, so Bell bandaged a severely wounded comrade who had been placed on the ground beside him. Later that day a Union surgeon informed Bell that his wounds were probably fatal, a diagnosis that Bell disputed. In order to receive medical attention, he crawled onto the front seat of an ambulance loaded with wounded Union cavalrymen.

Upon reaching a field hospital, Union doctors decided not to amputate his arm, but they could not extract the bullet lodged in his hip. Union soldiers placed him upon a mattress with Dragoon Joel Roberts Poinsett Pringle, who was mortally wounded. The next day, a Union clerk asked Bell to identify the bodies of two Confederate cavalrymen. One was Pringle, but Bell could not identify the second body, so the clerk placed Bell's name and information on the marker after Bell was transported to a new hospital. Bell and the other wounded Confederates were carried by wagon along railroad tracks, which elicited "the shrieks of the poor wounded fellows." They were then loaded onto a steamer that conveyed them to Lincoln Hospital in Washington, D.C.[47]

While undergoing medical treatment, William Bell benefited greatly from having family members who resided in the North. William W. White, a fellow dragoon who had been wounded and captured at Haw's Shop, wrote from Lincoln Hospital to Bell's uncle, Dr. S. H. Dickson, a professor at Jefferson Medical College in Philadelphia, to inform him of Bell's location and condition. Dickson corresponded with the Union surgeon general, Joseph K. Barnes, who wrote to Dr. J. C. McKee, the surgeon in charge of Lincoln Hospital. Barnes asked McKee to give Bell "his personal attention" and to provide him with anything that he requested that was not prohibited by law. The bill for all that he required was to be sent to the surgeon general. McKee followed Barnes's instructions and personally operated on Bell, who later commented that McKee "treated me with as much consideration as if I was a younger brother."[48]

For other captured dragoons, prewar financial and social connections were beneficial as well. Union troops had captured seventeen dragoons in three battles. As word arrived of loved ones alive and in Union prisons, the dragoons' families did everything in their still considerable power to ensure that imprisonment would be as short and as painless as possible. In one notable incident, John A. Converse, a resident of Montreal, Canada, and the uncle of Dragoon Augustus Converse Frierson (wounded and captured at Matadequin Creek), applied to President Lincoln for Frierson's release and included with his letter an endorsement from Senator Ira Harris of New York. Converse even offered to purchase two substitutes for the Union army and ensure that Frierson never again assisted the rebellion. His request, however, was denied, and Frierson died of his wounds while still in captivity on July 30, 1864.[49]

Other family members wielded similar influence on behalf of the imprisoned dragoons. Dragoon Edward L. Wells, who was briefly a prisoner during the battle of Trevilian Station, enlisted the aid of his family in New York to find and assist captured comrades. Women in the family gladly complied with Edward's wishes, though he had left New York to fight for the Confederacy. Wells's aunt, Sabina E. Wells, in addition to forwarding money to him, located imprisoned dragoons and assembled packages containing food and clothing for them.[50]

In contrast to other Confederate prisoners, dragoons and former dragoons such as Gabriel Manigault had a network of friends and family in the South and North. Upon arriving at the Union prison at Fort Delaware, Manigault contacted Harry Morris, a cousin in New York, and had him send money and clothes. He then purchased cooking utensils and rations for dragoons and other acquaintances from the regiment. One of his cousin's packages contained several French novels, including Victor Hugo's *Les Miserables*. Another cousin sent Manigault a pair of pants and boots of such high quality that he refused to wear them until he was released from prison.[51] Prior to the war, his father and mother had been close friends of Union admiral Samuel Francis DuPont, so the elder Manigault wrote to the admiral seeking his son's release. Although DuPont could not grant this request, he did visit Fort Delaware to ensure that the young Manigault had everything that he needed for his comfort. As a departing gesture, DuPont had the prison's allotment of coal increased, so Confederate prisoners spent the winter of 1864–65 in a warmer environment.[52]

In Virginia, the relentless combat of the spring and summer of 1864 had taken a horrific toll on the Charleston Light Dragoons, the 4th South Carolina Cavalry, and the rest of Butler's brigade. The dragoons had fought at each of Hampton's victories after their arrival in Virginia during the Richmond-Petersburg campaign of 1864. Following the battle of Ream's Station on June 28 and 29, during which Confederate cavalry thwarted a Union cavalry raid on the Weldon Railroad, the company received a break from continuous campaigning. On August 11, 1864, eleven dragoons were placed on horse detail for forty days and sent to South Carolina to replace the unit's animals that had been injured or killed since the unit's departure for Virginia.[53] By late September 1864, the dragoons were once again serving as a company, though one with barely enough men to form a squad. Third Lieutenant Edward Harleston Jr., the dragoons' officer who had been in Richmond during the unit's first three battles, commanded the survivors.[54] The company fought at every engagement in which Butler's brigade played a role, and it continued to suffer casualties. Eber R. Robertson had joined the dragoons at age sixteen in November 1863, after making the long trip to Charleston from Winnsboro, South Carolina. On September 25, 1864, four days after the dragoons returned from horse detail, he was accidentally killed by a Confederate sentinel near Petersburg.[55] Six days later, the forces of Union major general George G. Meade probed toward Petersburg. This movement led to a cavalry battle near McDowell's Farm, where Benjamin Bostick was mortally wounded and W. R. Davis was killed.[56]

By the end of September, Butler's brigade, under the command of Brigadier General John Dunovant, was badly depleted. Of the 2,845 men either present or absent from the brigade, only 479 were in the field. Of those, 171 were from the 4th South Carolina Cavalry. An inspecting officer described the unit as

"ragged," with its surgeon and chaplain both listed as sick, and its accommodations for the sick listed as "bad." Among the sick was Dragoon Captain
Richard H. Colcock.[57]

The dragoons also were in need of basic clothing and equipment to replace
those items that were worn out or had been lost during the actions of late May
and early June. Equipment losses included bridles, halters, spurs, pistols, rifles,
cartridge boxes, and sabers. Some dragoons had lost (or discarded) their
vaunted short Enfield rifles and had acquired Sharps and Springfield rifles,
which were plentiful in mid-1864. By September the dragoons also were in
need of clothing items to replace those that they had worn since coming north
from South Carolina. In small numbers, the quartermaster issued to the dragoons drawers, shoes (not boots), shirts, caps, and pants, but new clothing and
equipment could not compensate for all that the dragoons had lost since coming to Virginia.[58]

During October the dragoons regained some of their strength as wounded
men returned from furlough. Edward W. Nowell had been shot in the right
hand at Haw's Shop, and although the wounded hand would be of limited use
for the rest of his life, he returned to duty with the Charleston Light Dragoons.
Other wounded dragoons who rejoined their comrades included Timothy
O'Brien, who had been shot in the right thigh at Haw's Shop, and Edward L.
Wells, the New Yorker, who been hit in the back at Trevilian Station.[59]

With these additions, the dragoons participated in the battle of Burgess
Mill on October 27, 1864. There Confederate infantry and Hampton's cavalry
drove back a Union probe toward Boydton Plank Road and the Southside
Railroad below Petersburg, Virginia. During the fight the hard-luck O'Brien
was wounded for the second time—this time shot through the shoulder. In
leaving the firing line, he informed Harleston, "Lieutenant, I've got it again."[60]

By late October 1864, the dragoons, like much of the Army of Northern
Virginia, were reduced to scavenging for food and equipment among the
Union dead. After the battle of Burgess Mill, Wells wrote,

> Many were the spoils obtained by me, as canteens, coats, blankets, hats,
> &c., besides a countless number of rifles left behind by the enemy in his
> flight. The day after the fight, & during the pursuit, I was so fortunate,
> as to get from a knapsack a lot of nice crackers, & as I had eaten noth-
> ing, not a morsel, in forty-eight hours, you imagine I relished them, &
> blessed the provident spirit of the dead Yank, from whose corpse I got
> the knapsack.[61]

Inspections for October, November, and December revealed that the
4th South Carolina Cavalry, and the Charleston Light Dragoons especially,
continued to suffer privation. In late October an inspector rated the quality
of the unit's clothing as bad and commented that nearly all the regimental

and company books had been lost. There were no accommodations for the regiment's sick. Captain Colcock was still ill, and by the end of November, Lieutenant Edward Harleston Jr., the dragoon's only other officer, also was ailing. One inspector noted that the members of the 4th Cavalry were poorly fed. Many of the regiment's horses were unserviceable.[62]

In contrast to their large numbers and comfortable circumstances in South Carolina, the surviving dragoons occupied a single tent by December 1864, and the survivors were under the command of Sergeant Benjamin F. Huger, who had been shot in the leg at Haw's Shop, but who had returned to duty.[63] These men performed picket duty near Bellefield (Belfield), where news arrived that Union major general William T. Sherman had captured Savannah on December 21, 1864. Major General Wade Hampton pleaded with Lee for permission to rush his cavalry to the defense of South Carolina. Lee acceded to Hampton's request, and on January 19, 1865, the dragoons and the rest of Butler's brigade headed for home.[64]

Hampton's command traveled to Columbia by train and arrived there on February 1. They left their horses in Virginia and procured new ones upon their arrival in South Carolina. Their appearance in the city did much to raise the spirits of the residents.[65] While Hampton's cavalry was in transit from Virginia, Sherman's army had turned northward from Savannah into South Carolina, relentlessly foraging and destroying property as it moved deeper into the Palmetto State.[66]

A wave of refugees arrived in Columbia with tales of desolation and ruin.[67] Early in the war the city had grown accustomed to the influx of refugees, but it now could accommodate no more. When South Carolinians realized that Sherman was advancing toward the state capital, residents and refugees created a giant traffic jam in an attempt to escape.[68]

Rain and floods, however, slowed the Federal advance and allowed Butler to grant a brief furlough to many of his exhausted men. As Sherman slowly moved toward Columbia, the dragoons, now part of Brigadier General Thomas M. Logan's brigade, rode south from the city to reconnoiter and harass the Union army. Butler's cavalry, along with that of Major General Joseph Wheeler, remained on Columbia's outskirts, awaiting Sherman's forces. As the lead elements of the Yankee juggernaut approached, Butler retreated toward Columbia, burning a bridge over the Congaree River, while Wheeler's men burned a nearby bridge over the Saluda River.[69] The dragoons retreated with Logan's brigade through Columbia, and later claimed to have been the last Confederate soldiers there on February 16 and 17, when the city surrendered. Langdon Cheves, the son of a prominent St. Peter's Parish planter, later recalled that he saw the unit in Columbia on February 17. "There seemed about 20 men, as Gen. Hampton's body guard and couriers. I think Lionel Nowell; John O'Hear; Ben Huger; Jno Thurston, Johnny McPherson, Julius and Lynch Pringle; Edward and John Harleston; Mr. Wells." Although there were probably closer to twelve members, the dragoons served as part of the rear guard for the Confederate army. On February 17, 1865, the unit moved through the streets of Columbia, realizing that they were leaving many family members and friends to the mercy of the approaching Union soldiers, whom they were powerless to stop.[70]

The company camped eight miles outside of Columbia on the evening of February 17. Edward L. Wells received permission to return to the city to search for Madeira, twelve bottles of which he found, and to warn a friend about the approaching Union forces. He later claimed that he did not notice any Confederate stragglers or fires while in the city.[71] The next morning, the dragoons smelled smoke and realized that Columbia was burning. Some volunteered to return to the city in disguise to ascertain the plight of the city's residents, but permission was not granted.[72]

The dragoons, along with the rest of Butler's command, retreated northward, carrying with them Alfred Manigault, who had been on sick furlough since the company's departure for Virginia. Though still ill, he had rejoined the unit on February 7, 1865, after it arrived in Columbia. Manigault had been with the dragoons on February 16, less than two weeks later, when they had been forced to swim their horses through a creek three miles below Columbia. Exposure and exhaustion intensified his illness, and the dragoons took him by ambulance to Winnsboro, South Carolina, after Columbia's evacuation. By the time he arrived in the town, he was delirious. He died at the Winnsboro Hospital on February 20, 1865, of "Cerebro Spinal Meningitis."[73]

Manigault's decision to rejoin the dragoons despite his illness was undoubtedly influenced by the events that had transpired since the unit's departure the previous spring. He had missed the deadly battles in Virginia, where his brother had been captured. Perhaps he feared that further absence from the unit would impugn his honor, or perhaps he felt that he had to overcome his illness to protect his state. Regardless, his service and death signify a deep devotion to his unit and its cause.[74]

After leaving Winnsboro, the dragoons, who received little special treatment in Virginia, again benefited from their reputation and status in the lowcountry. Butler detached the company from the 4th Cavalry to serve as couriers. This detail allowed the troops to partake in whatever food or drink was available at division headquarters, a substantial benefit during a continuing period of reduced rations.[75]

Their new position within the division, however, did not shield them from combat. As a commander, Butler was always close to the action, and the Charleston Light Dragoons accompanied him wherever he went. As Butler's division retreated northward from Winnsboro, it attacked Sherman's "bummers," or foraging parties. Butler and his men were incensed at the behavior of

Sherman's troops as they moved across South Carolina, and they offered no quarter to Yankee foragers. Butler set the precedent when he questioned why his troops bothered to bring in prisoners. In one action, Butler's command attacked a party of Union foragers, perhaps numbering two hundred, at Cantey's Plantation on February 26, and killed most of them.[76]

The dragoons' behavior (and that of Butler's men generally) had much to do with contemporary concepts regarding the limits of warfare. Revenge was a common motivating factor for Southern men, who felt that the barbaric Yankees had violated rules that protected noncombatants, especially women and children, and their property.[77] In this case, their hatred focused on the Union soldiers who had devastated the South Carolina countryside. Filled with anger and outrage at the perceived barbarity of their enemy, the dragoons came to enjoy this new type of warfare. After the war, Wells fondly recalled stalking and killing Sherman's foragers, claiming that "there is probably no other kind of warfare that contains such a source of sport." Wells believed that "bummer-running," as it was called, combined "the delight of the sportsman and the devotion and fervor of the Crusader."[78]

As Butler's command retreated, its soldiers attempted to move around Sherman's right flank, but they soon discovered that instead of heading due north, Sherman's men had turned northeast toward Cheraw, South Carolina. On March 1, 1864, Butler led his division into Cheraw, where he conferred with General William J. Hardee, who held the town with ten thousand men who had retreated there from Charleston. Butler advised Hardee to abandon Cheraw and move his men across the Pee Dee River as soon as possible. Hardee agreed and ordered Butler's division to serve as a rearguard for the retreating Confederates.[79]

As the last of Hardee's men were crossing the Pee Dee, Sherman's advance guard reached the edge of Cheraw. The dragoons quickly formed a column of twos and turned to retreat through the town. Edward L. Wells arrived after having delivered a message, and he took up a position at the end of the dragoons' column. As the dragoons rode away from the advancing Federals, Union artillery found its range. A rifled shell hit Wells's horse from behind and passed through the animal without wounding its rider. Wells quickly freed himself from the dead animal and grabbed his personal effects before attempting to retreat. Butler was nearby and realized that Wells was going to abandon his saddle and bridle. "'Don't you think you will have further use for those things?'" Butler inquired. Wells hurriedly began to remove the items, when another Union artillery shell careened down the street into a house. Wells quickly grabbed the saddle and bridle and explained to Butler that he would not need the halter. He then scampered around a corner and followed his comrades to the covered bridge spanning the Pee Dee River.[80]

Soon after abandoning Cheraw, Butler led his men into North Carolina and arrived in Rockingham on March 5, 1865; Sherman's men entered the state two days later. Hampton divided his cavalry into two wings, with Butler taking the south column. This placed him in the path of Union cavalry commanded by Major General Judson Kilpatrick, who was looting along one wing of Sherman's advancing forces. On the night of March 9, Butler captured a large party of Kilpatrick's pickets and led his command into position to surprise the Union commander on the morning of March 10. As the sun rose, the Confederates swooped down upon Kilpatrick's command, driving his scattered troopers before them. The dragoons were with Butler, following the initial wave of cavalry that swarmed into Kilpatrick's camp. One dragoon, William Fishburne, carried a message to one of Butler's subordinates and then fell in with the charging column. The Union cavalry initially fled from its camp, which Butler's troops then stopped to plunder.[81] As Confederates swarmed around Kilpatrick's headquarters in the Charles Monroe House, the Union general emerged, dressed in only a shirt, underwear, and slippers. Butler had assigned Confederate captain Samuel D. Bostwick of Cobb's Legion with capturing Kilpatrick, so Bostwick, not realizing to whom he was talking, asked the half-dressed Union soldier the whereabouts of the Union commander. The general pointed at a fleeing Union cavalryman, then mounted a horse and dashed away. None of the Confederates recognized Kilpatrick, so no one pursued him.[82]

The Confederate advantage was short lived. Union cavalry that initially fled into the woods quickly returned and attempted to recapture the camp. The Monroe House was caught in the crossfire of Confederate and Union cavalry. One of two South Carolina women with whom Kilpatrick was traveling emerged from the house and attempted to reach her carriage. Dragoon Edward Wells escorted the woman, whom he later described as a "rather plain looking and not over young person," into a ditch. Kilpatrick's other companion, "a beautiful young Irish woman" dressed in a nightgown, soon emerged from the Monroe House. Captain Samuel Pegues of the 3rd Alabama Cavalry urged her to return to the house to avoid injury.[83]

As Butler attempted to rally his men near the Monroe House, artillerymen from the 10th Wisconsin Artillery made their way back to their two guns and began to fire at the Confederate cavalrymen, causing numerous casualties.[84] Shortly thereafter, Hampton ordered his men to withdraw.[85]

Following the failed assault on Kilpatrick's headquarters, Hampton moved his command toward Fayetteville, North Carolina. There they joined General Hardee and the rest of the Confederate troops under the command of General Joseph E. Johnston. Johnston ordered a general withdrawal across the Cape Fear River, and Hampton's men again served as a rear guard. On the morning of March 11, Hampton stopped at the Fayetteville Hotel for breakfast. As he dined, his scout Hugh Scott arrived and informed him that Union cavalry had arrived in the town and cut off the Confederates' escape route. Hampton quickly gathered as many men as he could find. Among those present were Scott, Hampton's two aides, a member of Wheeler's command, and three dragoons, W. H. Bellinger, William Fishburne, and Edward L. Wells. The Union scouts, numbering close to fifty, advanced toward Hampton and his entourage. Hampton immediately ordered a charge. The small party of Confederates rushed the Union troop, which quickly fired a volley, wheeled their horses, and fled. Attempting to escape, the Union cavalry crowded together as they rounded a corner, which caused Hampton and his escort to crash into their retreating opponents. Wells later bragged that he "had the pleasure of cleaving one fellow's head with my sabre, besides using my pistol freely." Hampton shot one man with his revolver, and then he killed another, who was five feet from Wells and aiming a rifle at him. In all, Hampton's tiny band killed eleven and captured twelve of the fleeing Union cavalry. Among the prisoners was Captain William Duncan, the detachment's commander, and David Day, a Union spy.[86]

Following this encounter, the dragoons joined Johnston's Confederate forces at Smithfield, North Carolina, where returning wounded veterans and new recruits suddenly swelled their numbers, so that Butler relieved them of courier duty and reassigned them as Company K, 4th South Carolina Cavalry.[87] The reorganized dragoons fought at Bentonville on March 19 through 21, 1865. By late March, however, there were few men in the regiment or brigade fit for duty. Lieutenant Colonel Stokes wrote that most of the 4th South Carolina Cavalry and the brigade were absent in South Carolina. In fact, prior to the battle of Bentonville, Colonel Rutledge had been ordered back to South Carolina to gather deserters from the brigade.[88]

After the engagement at Bentonville, a four-man detachment of dragoons under the command of Lieutenant Harleston departed for Nash County, North Carolina, in search of horses.[89] The detachment was there when they heard of Lee's surrender to Grant on April 9. Then on April 26, 1865, Johnston surrendered his army at James Bennett's farmhouse near Durham, North Carolina.[90] Contradictory evidence suggests that the other dragoons were either present at the surrender or were disbanded at Asheboro, North Carolina, on the same day.[91] Harleston and his detachment of dragoons did not surrender for many weeks. Vowing never to capitulate, they slipped through Union lines and headed for Mexico but, like many former Confederates, never completed the journey. The dragoons swam their horses across four rivers, because the bridges were burned and all crossings were guarded by Union troops. Wells, still not having surrendered, wrote to his mother and sister from Cheraw about heading to the Trans-Mississippi Department (that is, the Confederate territory west of the Mississippi River), to continue fight-ing. Many friends also wished to go there, too, "so that we can get along very comfortably, & happy, & and will not be cut off entirely from refined society."[92]

At the time of Johnston's surrender, a number of men from Butler's brigade were gathered in Chester, South Carolina, including "perhaps a dozen Charles-ton Light Dragoons." Many of these had been unhorsed during the previous campaign and were waiting for new mounts. At Chester they joined brigade members who had been imprisoned at Fort Delaware following the battles of late May and early June 1864, and who were exchanged in early spring 1865. Gabriel Manigault and other returning dragoons soon learned that their comrades no longer fought like gentlemen. Manigault "had a long talk" with three dragoons and "was surprised to hear them tell how many Yankee bum-mers they had killed in cold blood." He later wrote that one dragoon, Philip Hutchinson, who had been wounded at Haw's Shop, had "killed about a dozen." When he asked Hutchinson how he could do such a thing, he replied that he gave to the bummers what he considered to be "the punishment they so richly deserved" for their depredations against women and children.[93] This statement might well serve as a fitting epitaph for the dragoons' sense of honor.

At the war's end, the Charleston Light Dragoons' transformation was com-plete. They had begun the conflict as men who believed that their duty was to serve their state and the Confederacy. They had attempted, with much success, to maintain their independence and their unique position. The war's final year, however, had transformed the unit dramatically. In appearance, they looked like other Confederate cavalry units. Their uniforms were ragged, and the men were malnourished as was much of the Confederate army. The mate-rial losses of the dragoons and their families had been far greater than any could have imagined at the beginning of the war. Many once-proud planters' sons were as destitute as the poorest Southerners. Most of their wealth had been invested in slaves and land. With the end of the war and with emancipa-tion, slaves acquired independence and the ability to exercise free will, and simply walked away. To make matters worse for lowcountrymen, Union troops had destroyed many plantations as they swept through the state, and the dra-goons were left without labor or capital to rebuild their homes and plant crops.

The dragoons, however, suffered even heavier psychological losses. By the war's final days, in both behavior and deportment, the members of the Charleston Light Dragoons were no different than the troops of any other Confederate cavalry command. Indeed, they hardly seemed better than the Yankee invaders. As gentlemen, they had subscribed to a code of honor that became increasingly irrelevant as the war progressed. From all accounts, they took great pleasure in killing Union foragers, granting them no quarter. They had come to emulate the supposedly barbaric behavior of their foes. They began the war with the intention of serving and setting an example for men of lesser means and social standing. By war's end, they were mimicking those whom they had once scorned. Early in the conflict, the dragoons had operated as fortunate sons of privilege. By 1865 this pretense had not only dissipated in the minds of the unit's commanders, but it had faded from the minds of the dragoons themselves. Noblesse oblige was no longer a viable philosophy in combat. Peace, and the return of survivors to Charleston, however, would once again establish the company and its members as a group set apart from the common folk, but whether such privilege would amount to anything remained to be seen.

Chapter 6

BEGINNING AGAIN

The one thing, the only thing, they cannot descend to, these men of the stamp of the chivalrous Dragoons . . . is to profess a contrition that could not be sincere.

Charleston News and Courier

For the Charleston Light Dragoons, as for most returning veterans, the years following the Civil War were a time for adapting to a world that had undergone frightening changes. They began the conflict as a social organization made up of the city's financial and social elite. Garrison duty had slowly changed them, and combat had intensified this transformation. During a brief time in Virginia, the war had whittled them down to a small, battle-hardened group of veterans shorn of the trappings of privilege. By April 1865 homespun rags had replaced custom-tailored uniforms, and the brutal reality of combat had wiped away most vestiges of cavalier behavior and chivalric courage. The dragoons were left with little more than memories mixed with feelings of uncertainty and despair.

Combat had transformed antebellum notions of the unit's elite nature. Before the war, the dragoons' military reputation had been based upon members' social origins. With few opportunities to prove their efficiency or skill, they were viewed by the public as an elite unit because of the surnames and backgrounds of those who filled the company's ranks. Warfare, however, provided a new gauge by which to judge the Charleston Light Dragoons. The company's sacrifices in Virginia reinforced popular perceptions of its elite nature. In fact, the public became so cognizant of the company's wartime record that they came to disregard the unit's social origins. The postwar writings of one of the company's proudest and least typical members, however, reversed this trend. Edward L. Wells shaped the unit's postwar image, highlighting its social superiority to further distance the dragoons from their foes while creating, through association, an aura of knightliness for himself, a young Yankee who had chosen the South over his native New York.

In April and May 1865 the survivors of the Charleston Light Dragoons returned to a ruined and desolate landscape. As individuals and as a unit alike, their future remained uncertain. Charleston was garrisoned by Union troops, who would not likely tolerate the drilling of a militia company made up of former Confederates. Instead, the Federal occupiers offered assistance to the area's freedmen; however limited and innocuous that assistance might have been, it spread fears among lowcountry white residents. Rumors circulated of supposedly rapacious freedmen who were seeking retribution for past injustices, and these rumors further fueled planters' apprehensions.[1]

To address this supposed threat, many of the state's white residents proposed protecting themselves in a way reminiscent of the heyday of the old regime. On July 20, 1865, provisional South Carolina governor Benjamin Franklin Perry called for the formation of white volunteer militia companies to prevent lawlessness, and in response, an organization calling itself the Charleston Light Dragoons formed in Charleston.[2] Little is known about the new group's composition or operations during its first decade. The existence of these new Charleston Light Dragoons as an unofficial militia company may have ended with passage of the Reconstruction Acts of 1867, which abolished all Southern militia companies formed under the conservative state governments. Afterward these units became "social clubs," and the members of the Charleston Light Dragoons might have followed suit.[3]

For a variety of reasons, few wartime veterans of the original unit joined the new company. For those dragoons who had survived the war, service in the reconstituted company was hardly an attractive proposition. The events of the previous four years had been seared into their minds. Like most combat veterans, they looked forward to rebuilding their lives and did not wish to relive the struggle, or even drill or march. Consequently, there was little initial interest in forming or participating in militia or veterans' organizations.[4]

This aversion to recalling the war eventually waned, however, and veterans of the wartime Charleston Light Dragoons gathered on November 1, 1870, to form the Survivors Association. This organization's goals were "to preserve, by continued personal association, the friendships existing between the men, to dispense charity, as far as practicable, to the families of comrades, and eventually to erect a Monument to their fallen fellow soldiers."[5] Robert Adams, a veteran dragoon who had been wounded at Matadequin Creek and imprisoned at Elmira, New York, delivered to the survivors an address that utilized classical references and flowery prose to praise the dragoons' wartime sacrifices and to remind the survivors to live honorable lives and to pass to future generations "the heritage of a pure character."[6]

For a time, the Survivors Association and the new militia company existed as separate but affiliated bodies. Like its antebellum counterpart, the new company recruited members from the city's oldest and most prominent families. Although being a member of a leading family would always matter a great deal in Charleston, the new company did not seem especially noteworthy. Only when the survivors of the old dragoons joined with the new members did the company acquire an aura of noble sacrifice and military prowess. To lowcountry residents, the dragoons' wartime service became a source of considerable pride. This was especially true because so many of the soldiers faced serious hardships after the war. Their reduced circumstances left little room for aristocratic pretension, so they were forced to take satisfaction in past accomplishments. In 1861 a terrible fire had burned a large swath across Charleston's center; the city also had withstood Union shelling for nearly eighteen months before the Confederates abandoned it on February 18, 1865. The fire and the shelling had left the lower half of the city, where many dragoons lived, in ruins.[7] One postwar traveler from the North wrote, "The proud city lies humbled in its ashes, too poor to rise again without the help of Northern capital."[8]

Not surprisingly, the postwar mood of the dragoons and the rest of Charleston's elite was somber. A visiting Englishman commented that "young men were bent on going to seek their fortunes elsewhere, the elders having ceased to take interest in the future."[9] The weight of outmoded tradition and shattered dreams lay heavily on Charleston and its people. In the eighteenth century, the city's first families had established a system of privilege based upon genealogy, wealth, and political position. At war's end, these families were left with not much more than memories of a heritage that now carried little weight. Their material wealth had nearly vanished, and the city's prewar elite wielded little power in a city now controlled by Republicans.

No longer could members of prominent families live on deference and accumulated wealth. How to make a living became the question of the hour. The dragoons and their families reestablished prewar businesses in order to rebuild their fortunes.[10] Before the war most dragoons had been employed as cotton and rice factors despite the decline of agriculture in the lowcountry. In 1866, of those dragoons who were employed, at least half returned to their prewar occupations working as partners or clerks in commission merchant houses. Of the fifteen dragoons listed in the *City Directory* in 1867, seven worked as factors or clerks for factors. The New Yorker Wells, who would later write the first history of the unit's wartime exploits, initially moved to his family's farm in New Jersey after the war.[11] He did not stay there long. By 1867 he had returned to Charleston and, like so many of his comrades, joined a commission merchant firm. Four other veterans listed their profession as clerk without listing an employer, and of the remaining four in the directory, two did not list their occupation and two worked in other fields. None of the surviving dragoons listed in the *City Directory* referred to themselves as planters (table 5).[12]

For dragoons who returned home to the surrounding districts and the midlands, trying to recreate an operational plantation using free labor became something of a necessary experiment. Without slaves, however, these former dragoons were forced to perform far more labor than in their previous experiences. James and English Hopkins, wartime dragoons from lower Richland, returned to Cabin Branch, the family's ruined plantation. Union soldiers had spared the house but had pillaged and destroyed most of its contents. A

Table 5—Survivors by occupation

Occupation	Number	Percentage
Clerks/Factors	7	46.67
Clerks/Employer not listed	4	26.67
Other	2	13.33
Employer not listed	2	13.33

Source: Charleston City Directory for 1867–68 . . . (Charleston, S.C.: Jno. Orvin Lea Publishers, 1868).

Note: Those dragoons accounted for in this survey include only those listed on the company's rolls at the cessation of hostilities.

descendant wrote of the family's plight that "there were no provisions, no work animals, and the slaves were irresponsible and uncontrollable in their new freedom . . . there was no one to till the fields." The freedmen, she argued, "refused to work at all. Burglary and theft were rampant throughout the community."[13]

The Hopkins family was not alone in its postwar desperation. For its neighbors, the families of wartime dragoons Joel R. and Robert Adams, the kindness of a Union officer had preserved most of the family homes, but they too were faced with the prospect of planting with little labor to assist them. Through the generosity of fellow dragoon English Hopkins, Robert Adams, a Latin scholar who led a prewar "rebellion" at South Carolina College, became the first teacher at the Hopkins School, which was established by that family to serve planters' children of lower Richland.[14]

For some dragoons, the war's destruction forever erased their pretensions of social and economic superiority. William Bell returned from the conflict with few prospects for regaining his prewar wealth. With dreams of planting cash crops in other countries, he and a group of friends embarked on a cotton-growing venture in La Guaria, Venezuela. The business failed, and Bell returned to the United States, where he worked as a Pullman conductor on a train that ran from New Orleans to New York City. Evidently blessed with a good singing voice, he also performed as a solo tenor in concerts featuring railroad workers. He later served as a railroad station agent in Alabama before he purchased a small farm near Anniston, Alabama. He remained in Alabama, forsaking Charleston and memories of all that he had lost.[15]

For the slaves who had accompanied the dragoons to war, and who had nearly outnumbered the soldiers, emancipation and the postwar world provided a new set of challenges. Unfortunately, we know little about their activities following emancipation. Of all the servants who accompanied the dragoons during the war, only one, Peter Poinsett, applied for a Confederate pension in 1923. During that year, he received a pension for his wartime service as Captain Benjamin H. Rutledge's servant.[16]

At least one dragoon's servant prospered after the conflict. Quash Stevens, the mulatto servant of Lewis Vanderhorst, returned to South Carolina after Vanderhorst's death at the battle of Haw's Shop. Shortly thereafter, Lewis's mother willed Quash to Arnoldus Vanderhorst, Lewis's brother. Stevens continued to work for the Vanderhorst family after the war as a plantation manager on Kiawah Island. For the rest of his life he remained closely tied to the Vanderhorst family, although in 1900, Arnoldus Vanderhorst V, son of Arnoldus IV and nephew of Dragoon Lewis Vanderhorst, threatened Stevens with legal action regarding his lease of land belonging to Arnoldus's mother, Adele Allston Vanderhorst. With great tact and restraint, Stevens insisted that he would adhere to the terms of the lease and tried to remain on friendly terms with Adele Vanderhorst. In 1901 Stevens and his son William F. Stevens purchased Seven Oaks, a 839-acre plantation on Johns Island, which they owned until slightly before the elder Stevens's death in 1910.[17]

For white veterans of the Charleston Light Dragoons, membership in the Survivors Association allowed them to keep alive the memory of the unit's valor and commemorate those dragoons who had died in service. Edward L. Wells believed that the association accomplished these goals but also intimated that their most difficult task was bearing the cost for a monument. With some effort, former dragoons and the relatives of the fallen successfully raised the money, and for the remainder of its existence, the Survivors Association was largely a social and philanthropic organization.[18]

The reconstituted Charleston Light Dragoons, organized in 1870, found themselves caught up in the racial politics of the Reconstruction era. After being outlawed along with other white Democratic militias, the dragoons became a "saber club," the mounted version of a rifle club. White Democrats formed rifle clubs, gun clubs, and saber clubs as early as 1869 to circumvent federal laws proscribing the formation of militias. These organizations were self-professed social clubs, but in reality they provided Southern Democrats with a paramilitary force that could counter black militias and protect Democratic political interests. Undoubtedly, they also served as a tool for intimidating the state's large black majority.[19]

Few veterans joined their ranks. In May 1875 only three members of the new company had served with the dragoons during the war. First and foremost of these was Benjamin H. Rutledge. Fifteen years after leading the dragoons into the Civil War, he was once again their captain. Surgeon H. W. DeSaussure Jr. and Color Bearer Lawrence W. O'Hear also joined the postwar dragoons. Although the personnel had changed, the unit's new rank and file mirrored the social composition of the old dragoons. Of the fifty-nine members whose occupations were known, thirty-three were clerks or accountants for commission merchants (factors) or retail merchants. At least nine were partners in factor houses and two were practicing attorneys, and there was a scattering of other occupations represented (table 6). A significant number of these men were related to wartime dragoons. In 1875, twenty-nine of seventy-one members carried the same surname as had wartime members.[20]

On August 4, 1876, as campaigning for the 1876 gubernatorial election intensified and tensions escalated between Democrats seeking power and Republicans unwilling to part with it, Dragoon 1st Lieutenant Zimmerman Davis, wartime colonel of the 5th South Carolina Cavalry, called an extra meeting of the new dragoons "for the purpose of deciding what action should be taken by the Co. in case of any trouble arising between the blacks & whites." General James Conner, commander of the Charleston militia, had expressed full confidence that the dragoons would muster if he asked them to quell any disturbance. After listening to remarks from Davis, members resolved that "in case of an emergency [they] should come out on foot & the men as far as possible should arm themselves with double barreled shotguns and pistols." Three days later Davis called another meeting to announce that twenty-five members of the unit would gather on horseback at the corner of Charleston's King and Wentworth streets, while the dismounted dragoons would assemble at Holmes' Lyceum. The company also adopted two resolutions, one to ensure that all able-bodied members answered any muster call and the other offering the unit's services to General Conner for whatever purpose he deemed necessary.[21]

The dragoons' mobilization plans were closely tied to the upheaval that occurred in and around Charleston prior to the 1876 gubernatorial election. On September 6, 1876, a large number of black Republicans rioted in Charleston as a result of Democrat intimidation tactics during the campaign. Charleston Democrats and their rifle clubs did not intervene, hoping that the riot would paint the Republicans as the party of violence.[22] On the day following the riot, the Charleston Light Dragoons met to inform members that all of the city's militia companies planned to gather that evening at the Charleston Hotel "to assist in preserving the peace." Expectations for a racial clash were running high. At this same meeting, one member, just as concerned with the value of his horse as had been prewar members, made a motion that any horse killed or injured "should a fight occur between the whites & blacks" would be paid for by the members of the club.[23]

The atmosphere in Charleston in some ways recalled the heyday of secession, as the city became an armed camp. Gun clubs patrolled the streets at night and, amazingly, managed to acquire artillery. They even outfitted a gunboat to patrol the rivers around the city in case black militias tried to enter by water.[24]

Table 6—New militia company members by profession

Occupation	Number	Percentage
Clerks/Accountants	33	55.93
Partners/Factors	9	15.25
Attorneys	2	3.39
Other	15	25.42

Source: Charleston Light Dragoon Records, SCHS; Charleston City Directory, 1875–76 (Charleston, S.C.: Walker, Evans, and Cogswell, 1875).

As tensions mounted, officers of the Charleston Light Dragoons called a meeting to change the place of rendezvous for mounted members. The former location, the corner of King and Wentworth streets, was too close to "Military Hall," the headquarters of the black militias. Furthermore, leaders of the dragoons decided that shotguns and pistols were insufficient for quelling disturbances and so formed a committee to solicit either the purchase or donation of rifles by local citizens, but given the compromised economic circumstances of most Charlestonians, little assistance was forthcoming.[25]

The dragoons were far more interested in the state than in the presidential election, and they were especially interested in electing Wade Hampton governor. General Hampton held a special place in the heart of the dragoons, especially of those who had served during the war. Hampton belonged to one of the state's oldest and wealthiest families. He had led the Army of Northern Virginia's cavalry, and the dragoons were part of his command in Virginia, South Carolina, and North Carolina. Unlike Matthew C. Butler, their former brigade commander with whom Rutledge had clashed, Hampton understood and valued the fact that gentlemen filled the dragoons' ranks. After the bloodbath at Haw's Shop, he had shown concern for the unit's survivors; now in the fall of 1876, he promised to "redeem" the state from the hated Republicans.

As the election approached, however, leading Democrats remained divided over the possible use of force in the campaign. Hampton argued, at least publicly, that unity and peaceful demonstrations of power were enough to deter blacks from going to the polls and might even persuade some to vote Democrat. Yet while Hampton ostensibly preached peace and reconciliation, nearly three hundred rifle clubs numbering some fifteen thousand men stood ready to adopt a more forcible policy.[26] Their efforts at intimidation (including the occasional murder) were so effective that on October 7, 1876, Governor Daniel H. Chamberlain declared all rifle clubs illegal and ordered them to disband.[27] But unlike previous gubernatorial proclamations during Reconstruction, this edict had little effect on the military arm of the state's Democratic Party.[28]

Throughout South Carolina, the existence of rifle and saber clubs such as the Charleston Light Dragoons greatly alarmed Republicans. Their presence in

Charleston and the lowcountry was particularly inflammatory. On October 15, 1876, a little over a month after the Charleston riots, black Republicans rallied at St. Thomas and St. Denis Church in Cainhoy, on the Wando River. A large number of white Democrats traveled from Charleston to hear the speeches. As a precaution against violence, Republican militias attended and hid weapons around the church. Soon after the rally began, a fight broke out between two men, one of each party. The Republicans retrieved their weapons and fired into the Democrats, who attempted to defend themselves. During what came to be known as the Cainhoy Riot or Cainhoy Massacre, six whites and one black were killed. White rifle clubs arrived later that day to seek vengeance, but the black militia had dispersed.[29]

To preclude further violence and restore the peace, President Ulysses S. Grant sent more than 1,100 federal troops to South Carolina. These soldiers, however, served as little more than observers, while Hampton and his supporters were neither cowed nor alarmed. The dragoons may have tried to intimidate Republican voters, although the heavy Republican presence in Charleston and the lowcountry likely limited overt militia activity. Regardless of their success in helping to secure Hampton's election, the dragoons' participation on the side of the Redeemers further enhanced their reputation as defenders of the state's white population.

The concept of privilege in the lowcountry did not die with the end of the Civil War. Charleston's prewar social elite soon recovered some of its former luster as the Charleston Club reopened almost immediately after the war. Many dragoons who had not been members of this exclusive group before the Civil War joined during Reconstruction. The St. Cecilia Society quickly recovered and held its first meeting in November 1866 and revived its annual balls.[30] The city's social elite used these and other antebellum social organizations as a bulwark against Yankee influence, separating themselves from Northerners and other outsiders who had flocked to Charleston after the war.[31]

The Charleston Light Dragoons became part of this reestablished social order. Although only three members of the new company had served in the unit during the war, Charleston residents and wartime veterans continued to believe that the dragoons were something special. On April 4, 1877, at the company's anniversary meeting, Captain Rutledge, the longtime commander of the Charleston Light Dragoons, declared that he would not accept the nomination to serve as captain for another term, spoke briefly of the company's battlefield exploits, and expressed great fondness for his comrades.[32] With Rutledge's departure, H. W. DeSaussure Jr. was left as the sole wartime veteran of the unit.

Thus the dragoons lost the leader who had best embodied what the unit had been and what it had become. The ultimate dragoon, Rutledge represented the prewar militia unit and its pretensions of privilege. He had commanded the unit as it went to war and had overseen its transformation into a military force on active duty. His light-handed leadership had created a pattern of loose command and control that had had disastrous consequences in Virginia. Yet his postwar service as captain of the new Charleston Light Dragoons had provided continuity. He had supervised the transformation of this militia unit into a weapon of political intimidation and gained the appreciation of South Carolina's Redeemers. Rutledge's resignation, therefore, severed the unit's strongest tie to its past.

In one of his first acts, the newly elected captain, Zimmerman Davis, quickly dispelled any concern that Rutledge's departure would fundamentally alter the dragoons. On April 16, 1877, Davis called an extra meeting to express "his desire to have the Dragoons remain an independent & separate organization from the other militia organizations in the state." Without hesitation, members voted to maintain the unit's independence.[33] This action reaffirmed the traditional belief in the social superiority of its members. As with the old company, state officials reinforced the dragoons' prestige. In 1878 the General Assembly passed an act that reestablished the 4th Brigade of South Carolina Volunteers. The act dictated that no more than two cavalry companies could exist in the brigade, and one of those two was the Charleston Light Dragoons. If the dragoons could raise two companies of cavalry, then no other cavalry company would be authorized. In essence, the General Assembly granted the unit a monopoly over cavalry operations in the lowcountry's Fourth Brigade.[34]

Eight years after the State General Assembly reconfirmed the new dragoons' elite status, the Survivors Association of the original Charleston Light Dragoons raised the funds necessary to purchase a monument to be placed in Magnolia Cemetery. Magnolia was Charleston's largest Civil War burial site, a place where families coped with the war's devastating losses by honoring their dead.[35]

The proceedings of the monument's unveiling revealed a great deal about how time had transformed or, perhaps more accurately, suppressed the memories of those men who had served. The monument to the Charleston Light Dragoons was dedicated on Decoration Day (later called Confederate Memorial Day), May 10, 1886. General Benjamin H. Rutledge, always the quintessential dragoon, fittingly presided. The guest speaker, surprisingly enough, was General Matthew C. Butler, who had commanded the brigade and division to which the Charleston Light Dragoons had belonged. Twenty-one years earlier he had demeaned and provoked Rutledge on numerous occasions during the campaigns in Virginia. Lowcountry planters had accused him of insulting the dragoons and, worse still, they had blamed him for the deaths of their friends and neighbors and for the destruction of "that favored command."[36] And yet two decades later, he ascended the podium on an early spring evening to honor those whom he had supposedly done so much to destroy.

Time and subsequent events had apparently healed old wounds. Rutledge had been appointed a general in the state militia, and Butler was a U.S. Senator. Both men had found common cause in the struggle to redeem the state from the supposed horrors of Reconstruction. Each man therefore took more interest in winning the second struggle to determine who would govern South Carolina than they had in the first.[37]

At 5:00 P.M. the dedication service began at the Charleston Light Dragoons' monument. The stage was filled with company survivors who had taken their places as city leaders. General Rutledge began by delivering an address in which he recounted the company's first battle, at Pocotaligo, and the unit's steadfastness under fire. Later Butler took the stage, referring to Rutledge as "my distinguished friend . . . who has been so conspicuously identified with this organization." He praised the dragoons' bravery and recalled how he had grieved over their losses. Butler cited numerous accounts from Union reports to demonstrate how his brigade, the 4th South Carolina Cavalry, and the dragoons had struck fear into the Yankees. Finally, he spoke of the company's sacrifice and invoked, as was popular by the 1880s, the imagery of Robert E. Lee and Jefferson Davis as examples to the unit's survivors and those who would follow in their footsteps.[38]

After Butler's speech, Rutledge summoned Captain Samuel G. Stoney, commander of the new Charleston Light Dragoons, to the stage for the presentation of wartime colors. Rutledge extolled Stoney to "cherish it, and let it be in your hands and in those of your successors forever, what it has been, the symbol of gallantry, fortitude and patriotism." Captain Stoney received the flag and promised that "when the bugle sound to duty was heard, the Charleston Light Dragoons would not cause their forebears to blush, nor the fair women to be ashamed of them."[39]

The Survivors Association's final task was the completion of a unit history. Edward L. Wells undertook this project, and in 1888, two years after dedicating the memorial, the association published *A Sketch of the Charleston Light Dragoons from the Earliest Formation of the Corps.*

Wells's history of the dragoons presented an important record of the company's activities, but it was more than a chronicle of marches and battles. Filled with "Lost Cause" rhetoric and flowery prose, it extolled the bravery of Confederate soldiers in the face of overwhelming odds. More important, Wells used *A Sketch of the Charleston Light Dragoons* as a tool with which to craft his vision of how future generations should regard him and other unit members. He composed the history in the 1880s, at a time when there was a strong movement toward sectional reconciliation, especially between Union and Confederate veterans. Wells, who had lived in the North for a time after the war, understood that Northerners celebrated the "*democratic* nature of the war." Northern Memorial Day ceremonies created a language of service that praised the ethnic, religious, and social diversity of all those who had fought in defense of the Union.[40]

In contrast, Wells downplayed diversity and instead suggested that all Confederates "were representative in a marked degree of the influences which made the Confederate army a grand body of citizen-soldiers." More surprisingly, and unlike many Lost Cause writers, he did not shy away from slavery. On the first page of text, he asserted that slavery had made "yeomanry, as well as gentry, at the South quasi-aristocrats, the outcome of which was a brave people devotedly attached to civil liberty." In defense of the idea of service by an elite group, he recalled how the Duke of Wellington preferred aristocratic officers. Wells even recounted the story of the French household cavalry at the battle of Steinkirk, "dandies" who had saved the retreating French army. It was in that passage that he first referred to the dragoons as the "kid gloved company."[41] Wells's remarkably candid description, however, never mentioned how the company had received special dispensation from commanders based upon its members' origins. Nor did he wrestle with his own envy for a way of life that his comrades enjoyed.

Of all of the veteran dragoons, Wells, as an outsider, was most anxious to bind himself to his wartime comrades and their home. He had first entered this world of privilege on a prewar Christmas trip to a lowcountry plantation. While there he had become so enamored of the region, its traditions, its institutions, and its people that he later abandoned his home, his friends, and much of his family in order to embrace the South. His wartime actions demonstrated his willingness to give everything for the unit, and his effort to pen a history of the dragoons marked a continuation of this quest for complete acceptance.

The Civil War exploits of the Charleston Light Dragoons had established a legacy that blotted out a large part of the company's history as a haven for the indulged sons of the elite, who had before 1864 largely only played at war. Once noteworthy for the surnames of its members, it was thereafter known for its members' wartime sacrifices. The words printed on the monument spelled out what the survivors wanted succeeding generations to know about the company. Engraved in large letters on three sides of the obelisk were the names of the unit's most famous battles: Haw's Shop, Virginia; Pocotaligo, South Carolina; and Trevilian Station, Virginia. On the fourth side were the words "To the Heroic Dead." These inscriptions were road signs for future dragoons, who attempted to pattern their actions after the wartime exploits of their predecessors.

The death of so many wealthy young men during the Civil War provided the dragoons with an aura of military elitism and valor that had not been part of the company's history before the war. Service in the Charleston Light Dragoons acquired a seriousness unimaginable during the unit's antebellum days.

When Captain Stoney received the unit colors at the dedication of the unit's monument, he received a legacy that was hardly typical of Southern militia units. General Rutledge cautioned him to be ever protective of the company's banner, as though the new unit embodied the old dragoons. And although much had changed by 1886, the concept of privilege continued to follow the new dragoons. Members continued to originate from Charleston and the lowcountry elite, such as it was after the war. Men with prominent surnames continued to wear the distinctive uniforms and separate themselves from outsiders, perhaps dreaming of emulating (at least in part) the deeds of their forefathers. As before, outsiders recognized the Charleston Light Dragoons and extended certain privileges to its members. In 1916 the unit traveled to Texas as part of General John "Blackjack" Pershing's expedition in pursuit of Pancho Villa. One year later, at the beginning of the United States' entry into World War I, the unit was designated Headquarters Company for the 30th Division. It arrived in France and participated in World War I's final campaign. At war's end, the unit was disbanded due to budget cuts, ending a military tradition that had begun in the eighteenth century, although veterans of the dragoons would continue to meet well into the twentieth century.

Nearly one hundred and twenty years after its dedication, the stone obelisk commemorating the Civil War deeds of the Charleston Light Dragoons stands nearly unnoticed in Magnolia Cemetery. Today few remember the dragoons or their legacy, though many descendants of its members still inhabit the lowcountry. Privilege, long the centerpiece of the dragoons' social, political, and military identity, still plays a role in the lives of old Charleston families, many of whom continue to reside in the city's grand homes and belong to its most exclusive clubs and societies.

The military application of privilege, however, has diminished dramatically. The days of the city's militia companies have nearly passed. Those that remain serve only as social clubs and to remind the city of its martial tradition. The creation of the National Guard and Reserve system, the rise of military professionalism, and corresponding societal changes have created today's armed forces, which are representative of all elements of American society. Membership in an elite unit is no longer dependent on one's social, political, or economic status, but it is predicated upon one's ability. For the dragoons, such circumstances would have been both deplorable and incomprehensible.

APPENDIX
Rosters

Note: The following information is found in the Compiled Service Records for the Charleston Light Dragoons located at the National Archives. The author has added information in brackets for explication and to correct obvious errors.

Charleston Light Dragoons Militia Company (Captain Rutledge's Company of Cavalry, South Carolina Militia). Entered state service at Coosawhatchie, S.C., November 7, 1861; left state service on February 10, 1862

Alston, R. A. Enlisted as a private 11/15/61.

Ball, E. W. [E. N. or Elias]. Enlisted as a private 11/7/61; detached by order of General Ripley 11/22/61.

Beck, A. [Augustus], Sgt. Enlisted as a corporal on 11/14/61; promoted from corporal to sergeant 1/25/62; detached by General Evans as a guide 2/2/62.

Bee, James. Enlisted 1/1/62.

Bell, W. [William]. Enlisted 11/7/61; detached by General Ripley 1/7/62.

Bickly, J. C. [John]. Enlisted 11/7/61.

Brailsford, R. M. Enlisted 1/3/62; practicing physician, returned to Charleston 1/27/62.

Brown, Alfred. Colored.

Brown, William. Colored.

Chisolm, J. M. Enlisted 11/7/61.

Clarkson, Rob. Enlisted 11/9/61; left the unit 2/7/62, term of service having expired.

Clarkson, T. B. Enlisted 11/22/61; left the unit 2/7/62, term of service having expired.

Colcock, R. H. [Richard], 1st Lt. Enlisted 11/7/61.

Covert, H. C. Discharged by physician's certificate 11/27/61.

Creighton, James. Enlisted 11/8/61.

Creigton, J. M. P. Enlisted 11/7/61; detached by order of General Evans 2/7/62.

Desel, Charles. Enlisted 11/7/61.

Desel, J. B. Enlisted 12/21/61.

Drayton, C. E. R. Enlisted 11/12/61; left the unit 2/7/62, term of service having expired.

Elliott, T. O. Enlisted 11/13/61.

Fishburn, E. [Edward]. Enlisted 11/21/61; detached by General Evans as a guide 2/2/62.

Forreston, T. P. [Thomas]. Enlisted 11/7/61; discharged by physician's certificate 11/26/61.

Furguson, D. G. [David]. Enlisted 11/12/61; detached for special duty 2/2/62.

Gordon, A. B. [Alex]. Enlisted 11/7/61.

Happoldt, J. P. [John]. Enlisted 12/7/61; discharged by physician's certificate 12/21/61.

Harleston, E. [Edward]. Enlisted 11/7/61.

Heyward, T. S. Enlisted 11/7/61; left the unit 2/7/62, term of service having expired.

Holland, E. C. [Edwin]. Enlisted 11/7/61.

Holmes, P. G. Enlisted 11/7/61; detached to join former company, Carolina Light Infantry, 11/30/61.

Holmes, T. G. Enlisted 11/7/61.

Huger, B. F. [Benjamin]. Enlisted 11/7/61.

Legare, E. T. [Edward], Sgt. Enlisted 11/7/61; transferred to Rebel Troop 1/25/62.

Linning, Thomas. Enlisted 12/11/61.

Livingston, William. Enlisted 11/7/61; left the unit on 2/7/62, term of service having expired.

Lowndes, Ed. Enlisted 11/15/61; promoted to lieutenant 1/5/62.

Lowndes, William. Enlisted 11/7/61; detached by General Ripley 11/30/61.

Magwood, H. M. Enlisted 11/7/61; furloughed, physician's certificate, 11/24/61.

Manigault, A. [Alfred]. Enlisted 1/1/62.

Manigault, G. [Gabriel]. Enlisted 1/1/62.

Marshall, J. C. Enlisted 11/7/61; detached by General Ripley 11/26/61.

Marshall, R. M. Enlisted 11/7/61; detached to join White's Battalion as commissary.

Martin, George. Enlisted 11/7/61; left the unit 2/7/62, term of service having expired.

McPherson, J. J. Enlisted 11/29/61; left the unit 2/7/62, term of service having expired.

McTureous, B. W., Sgt. Enlisted 11/7/61; detached by General Ripley 2/7/62.

McTureous, J. C. Enlisted 11/7/61.

McTureous, Joseph. Enlisted 11/7/61.

Meyer, L. Enlisted 11/7/61; exempt as practicing physician 12/1/61.

Middleton, F. K. [Francis Kinloch]. Enlisted 11/7/61; on furlough and not expired.

Miller, J. B. Enlisted 11/7/61.

Mordecai, J. Enlisted 11/7/61; discharged by physician's certificate 11/27/61.

Nowell, E. W. [Edward]. Enlisted 11/7/61.

Nowell, L. C. [Lionel], 2nd Lt. Enlisted 11/7/61.

O'Brien, Tim, Sgt. Enlisted 11/7/61.

O'Hear, J. W. [James], Bvt. 2nd Lt. Enlisted 11/7/61; returned to city on sick furlough 2/7/62.

O'Hear, L. W. [Lawrence]. Enlisted 11/7/61; exempt by act of legislature exempting schoolboys 12/7/61.

O'Neill, J. J. Enlisted 11/7/61.

Owens, Alex. Enlisted 11/7/61.

Poincett, Paul. Colored, musician.

Prioleau, C. E. [Charles], Cpl. Enlisted 11/7/61.

Prioleau, J. M. Enlisted 11/7/61.

Purcell, James. Enlisted 11/7/61; furlough, death in family, 2/6/62.

Rhett, B. S. Enlisted 11/7/61; left the unit 2/7/62, term of service expired.

Rhett, Roland. Enlisted 11/7/61; detached by General Ripley 11/28/61.

Robertson, Alex. Enlisted 11/7/61.

Robinson, John. Enlisted 11/7/61.

Roddin, B. Enlisted 11/7/61; detached by General Ripley 11/28/61.

Roddin, William. Colored.

Rose, Alex. Enlisted 11/7/61.

Rutledge, B. H. [Benjamin], Capt. Enlisted 11/7/61.

Simmons, S. W. Enlisted 11/7/61; on furlough at time of disbanding.

Smith, T. A., Sgt. Enlisted 11/7/61; transferred to South Carolina Rangers 1/6/62.

Thurston, John. Enlisted 1/1/62.

Toomer, F. S. Enlisted 11/7/61; on furlough at time of disbanding.

Vanderhorst, L. [Lewis]. Enlisted 11/7/61.

Wagner, A. C., Sgt. Enlisted 11/7/61; promoted from corporal 1/6/62; left the unit 2/7/62, term of service having expired.

Walpole, H. Enlisted 11/7/61; exempt by act of legislature, bank teller.

Whaley, M. Enlisted 11/15/61; in receipt of commission 1/14/62.

White, J. D. Enlisted 11/7/61; detached by General Ripley 12/24/61.

White, W. W., 1st Sgt. Enlisted 11/7/61; detached special duty 2/2/62 [Engineering Service]; listed as acquainted with "management of Negroes."

Wilson, John, Sgt. Enlisted 11/11/61; promoted from corporal on 1/25/62; on furlough and did not return [sick].

Charleston Light Dragoons, later Company K, 4th South Carolina Cavalry, Enlisted in Confederate Service at Grahamville, S.C., March 25, 1862

Adams, Joel R. Enlisted as a private 1/1/63 at Pocotaligo, age 18; absent, on home detail for 40 days from 8/11/64; present 9–10/64; daily duty, bugler.

Adams, Robert, Cpl. Enlisted as a private 7/6/62 at McPhersonville; on daily duty "undug shells" 3–4/63; promoted to 3rd corporal 7–8/63; absent, detached for 10 days from 10/24/63; absent, furlough for 20 days from 2/15/64; wounded and captured 5/30/64 at Cold Harbor [Matadequin Creek]; admitted to Lincoln General Hospital USA, Washington, D.C., 6/8/64, gunshot wound illiar region, age 31; admitted to Old Capitol Prison USA Hospital in Washington, D.C., 6/13/64; returned to duty 6/27/64; sent to Elmira, N.Y., transferred for exchange 2/13/65; admitted to General Hospital No. 9, Receiving and Wayside Hospital, Richmond, Va., 2/21/65, then to Jackson Hospital in Richmond, Va., 2/22/65; transferred to Camp Lee 3/7/65; admitted to Pettigrew General Hospital No. 13, Raleigh, N.C., 3/20/65; returned to duty, diarrhea, 3/27/65.

Adger, James, Jr. Enlisted as a private 3/1/63 at Pocotaligo, $50 bounty due; appears on register of payments descriptive list, paid $144, horse included; absent, wounded, Haw's Shop, 5/28/64; admitted to General Hospital No. 9, Receiving and Wayside Hospital Richmond, Va., 5/29/64; admitted to Jackson Hospital 5/30/64; wounded and on furlough from 6/9/64 for 30 days; applied for position of sgt. major of Maj. Martin's Battalion of Artillery, Hardee's Corps, Army of Tennessee on grounds that position is open and he is suffering from a wound.

Bailey, John [A.]. Enlisted as a private 5/12/62 at Grahamville; detached by Col. Walker for 10 days 8/20/62; out with guide corps 2/63; absent, detached special order of General Walker to Signal Corps 3–4/63; absent detached 3/29/63; absent detached 7–8/63; absent sick 9–10/63; absent AWOL 11–12/63; absent on sick furlough from 11/15/63; dropped from rolls 4/9/64 by order for reduction of the company.

Ball, E. N. [Elias]. Enlisted as a private 3/25/62 at Grahamville, age 28; appointed sergeant 3/25/62; absent 3/25–6/30/62; absent, detached by order of General Pemberton 4/28/62; resigned position as sergeant 6/7/62; absent detached through 10/63; absent on furlough for 15 days from 12/20/63; absent on furlough from 2/18/64 for 20 days; absent AWOL 3/1/64–8/31/64; dropped from company rolls 9–10/64; transferred to Company H, 1st South Carolina Artillery 3/24/64; returned to company, special order no. 204–8 revoked.

Bates, John. Enlisted as a private 10/18/62 at McPhersonville; due bounty money 11–12/62; transferred to Company D, 4th South Carolina Cavalry, Captain Pinckney, 6/30/63.

Beck, A. [Augustus]. Enlisted as a private 7/10/62 at McPhersonville; detached by General Beauregard 11/03/62; absent, detached through 7–8/63; sick in camp 11–12/63; absent, dropped from the rolls 4/9/64 by order for reduction of company; paid $48.40; ordered to report to company special order no. 174–8.

Bedon, Josiah. Enlisted as a private 4/11/63 at Pocotaligo; absent, detached by special order of General Walker 6/3/63; absent, detached through 12/63; present until killed 5/28/64 at Haw's Shop.

Bee, J. L. [James]. Enlisted as a private 3/25/62 at Grahamville, age 17; pay due from enlistment 3/25–6/30/63; absent on sick furlough from 6/24/63 for 10 days; surgeon's certificate furnished until 12/63; captured at Old Church [Matadequin Creek] 5/30/64; admitted to Lincoln General Hospital USA, "gunshot wound, fracture tibia lower third, ball entered just above articulations anteriorly and passing out on inner side shattering tibia extensively. Oval flap dissected back as in circular operations, at leg middle third, 5 ligatures used. Result June 30 very low; of field, gunshot fracture of tibia lower third, missile, conical" [Record of death enclosed. List cause of death "Pyanmia"]; Died of exhaustion from wounds 7/8/64.

Bell, William. Enlisted as a private 3/25/62 at Grahamville, age 25; absent, due pay from enlistment 3/25–6/30/62; absent, detached by order of Gen. Pemberton 3/24/62; absent, detached through 2/63; transferred to Engineer Corps 4/4/63, descriptive roll furnished; absent, captured 5/30/64 at Cold Harbor [Matadequin Creek]; admitted to Lincoln General Hospital USA, Washington, D.C., gunshot wound, Olecranon process flesh right buttock, age 27; roll of POW's received at Elmira, N.Y., 8/12/64 from Old Capitol Prison, D.C.; transferred for exchange 10/11/64; roll of prisoners at Point Lookout, Md., 10/14/64, exchanged 10/29/64; on roll of Jackson Hospital for "disenteria" 12/18/64; returned to duty 1/30/65.

Bellinger, W. H. Enlisted as a private 7/14/63 at Green Pond, age 18; present, bounty money due $50 7–8/63; present until appears on register of General Hospital, Howard's Grove, Richmond, Va., May 30, 1864; returned to duty 6/26/64; present through 10/64.

Bickley, J. C. [John], 1st Sgt. Enlisted as sergeant 3/25/62 at Grahamville; on sick furlough in Charleston 3/25/62; present to 1/15/63 when appointed 1st Sgt.; present until 12/17/63 when absent on furlough for 15 days; present until 10/22/64 when on sick duty.

Blake, W. See Blake, Walter.

Blake, Walter. Enlisted as a private 10/8/62 at McPhersonville; present until detached by order of Gen. Walker 12/17/62 for 15 days; present until detached by special order of General Walker 4/28/63; present 5–6/63 until absent by special order no. 221 of General Beauregard for 30 days 9–10/63; present until absent on horse detail 8/11/64 for 40 days; present 10–11/64.

Boone, J. W. [Waring]. Enlisted as a private 1/16/63 at Pocotaligo; present until killed at Trevilian Station 6/11/64.

Bostick, Benjamin. Enlisted as a private 7/10/62 at McPhersonville; present until sick in camp 9–10/62, due bounty pay; present until absent, detached by order of General Walker 12/23/62 for 10 days; absent on sick furlough for 1/4/63; present 1–2/63 until absent on horse detail 8/11/64 for 40 days; mortally wounded 10/1/64, died 10/5/64; listed in a consolidated report of sick and wounded in the Hospitals of North Carolina 10/64, Station Wilson General Hospital.

Bostick, Edw. Enlisted as a private 3/25/62 at Grahamville, age 33; present until absent on furlough 6/26/62 for 4 days; present 7–8/62; sick in camp 9–10/62; discharged 12/17/62, being appointed lieutenant of 21st Regiment.

Bostick, L. R. [Luther], Sgt. Enlisted as 4th corporal 3/25/62 at Grahamville, age 18; present until 1/23/63, detached by special order of General Walker for 15 days; detached by special order of General Walker 12/26/62 for 10 days; present and appointed 5th sergeant 1/1/63; present until 3–4/63, absent on furlough for 24 hours; present sick in camp 9–10/63 until absent on furlough from 12/17/63 for 15 days; present until captured 5/30/64 at Cold Harbor [Matadequin Creek]; on roll of prisoners at Point Lookout, Md.; exchanged at Aikens Landing 3/14/65; later denotes that he was captured at Haw's Shop.

Bostick, R. F. [Richard]. Enlisted as a private 5/15/62 at Grahamville; transferred to Beaufort Volunteer Artillery, Captain Elliott commanding, on 9/15/62.

Boyles, W. A. [William]. Enlisted as a private 2/10/63 at Pocotaligo; appears on muster roll of officers and men paroled at Greensboro from Johnston's army 4/22/65.

Brisbane, J. L. Enlisted as a private 1/15/63 at Pocotaligo; absent on sick furlough from 9/4/63; absent on horse detail from 8/11/64 for 40 days; discharged on 2/22/65 by special order and appointed 2nd lieutenant, Company I, Foreign Battalion.

Bulow, T. L. [Lionet]. Enlisted as a private 12/12/63 at Charleston; absent on furlough for 20 days from 2/27/64; dropped from the rolls 4/9/64 by order for reduction of company.

Burnet, B. R. Enlisted as a private 3/25/62 at Grahamville, age 17; AWOL 11–12/63; absent on horse detail for 40 days from 8/11/64; AWOL from 9/31/64; applied for appointment as 2nd lieutenant in 1st South Carolina Artillery.

Burnet, H. D. Enlisted as a private 3/25/62 at Grahamville, age 22; sick in camp 9–10/62; detached by order of General Walker 12/17/62; absent on furlough from 1/30/63; transferred to Company C, Rutledge's regiment 3/7/63; detached from Company C, 4th South Carolina Cavalry on 12/1/63 by special order.

Carson, I. P. [James]. Enlisted as a private 8/21/62 for war; on roll of Medical Officers, Stewards, Attendants and patients at Wayside Hospital No. 2 at Greensboro, 4/29/65 [parole date]; on muster roll from Johnston's army.

Chisolm, J. M. [John]. Enlisted as a private 3/25/62 at Grahamville, age 22; absent on furlough from 8/23/62 for 10 days; absent on sick furlough from 10/1/62; sick in camp 9–10/63; detached to report to General Hoke 3/1–8/31/64; absent 9–10/64; moved on furlough from 9/64.

Clark, J. M., Cpl. Enlisted as a private 3/25/62 at Grahamville, age 35; value of horse, $325, equipment, $100; pay due from enlistment 3/25–6/30/62; absent on furlough 1/15/63 for 20 days; promoted to 3rd corporal 5–6/63 and to 2nd corporal 7–8/63; absent detached by order of General Beauregard 9/5/63 until 1/31/64; absent on horse detail on 8/11/64 for 40 days.

Colclough, J. H. Enlisted as a private 2/8/64 at Charleston; present until 4/9/64 when dropped from the rolls by order for reduction of the company.

Colcock, R. H. [Richard]. Enlisted as 1st lieutenant 3/25/62 at Grahamville, age 39; present, pay due; signs certificate as Inspection and Enlisting Officer; present through 12/62 [signs roll as commanding officer]; on furlough for 18 days from 1/16/63; present and sick in camp 1–2/63; on furlough 4/28/63 for 10 days; detailed to inspect troops at McPhersonville 5–6/63; present through

12/63; furlough for 10 days from 12/22/63; present through 2/64; absent 3/1–8/31/64; sent to hospital 8/9/64; sick furlough 10/21/64 for 30 days; sick in Limestone Springs, S.C., 8/22/64; absent for Medical Examiners Board 11/30/64; returned to duty 7/14/64.

Colcock, T. H. Enlisted as private 3/25/62 at Grahamville, age 25; present through 6/30/62 [pay due from enlistment]; present through 1/31/63 [on daily duty secretary]; detached by special order no. 30 of General Walker 2/16/63; detached through 4/63; discharged and appointed adjutant of the 3rd South Carolina Cavalry Regiment 5/1/63.

Creighton, James. Enlisted as private 3/25/62 at Grahamville, age 36; absent on furlough from 6/28/62 for four days; present until died of disease on 9/13/62.

Darby, E. [Edward]. Enlisted as a private 1/23/64 at Charleston; absent on furlough for 40 days beginning 2/25/64; dropped from the rolls 4/9/64 by order for reduction of the company.

Darby, J. B. [John]. Enlisted as a private in Captain Joseph Treyevants Company of South Carolina Cavalry, later Company E, 1st South Carolina Cavalry 10/26/61; transferred to Charleston Light Dragoons; enlists 6/1/63 at McPhersonville; absent on sick furlough from 3/5/64, certificate furnished and descriptive roll given; sick furlough from 8/12/63 for 20 days, certificate furnished; bounty money [$50] due in June 1863; sick in camp 2/64; requested detail 5/13/64 on medical certificate to Glover Army Hospital, Orangeburg, S.C.; to act as stock keeper for Tax in Kind Quartermaster in Orangeburg because of "ulcular of the Borrets and Tuburcula deposit in apex of right lung."

Davant, Charles. Enlisted as a private 4/23/63 at Pocotaligo, $50 due; present until detached by special order no. 120 by General Walker on 6/15/63; detached by special order no. 217 by General Beauregard until 12/31/63; detached by special order no. 283 by General Beauregard on 12/24/63; appointed Assistant Surgeon in May 1864; listed as detached in hospital in Grahamville; request to be detached acting assistant surgeon; letter from Samuel Logan, chief surgeon of the division, Pocotaligo, 12/27/63 claiming that Davant's services are *"absolutely essential"* to him.

Davant, Frank. Enlisted as a private 6/7/62 at Grahamville; present until 10/63; sick furlough from 10/22/63, certificate furnished; present until 2/64, sick furlough from 2/28/64; transferred to 2nd South Carolina Cavalry Regiment in Beaufort District in March 1864.

Davis, W. R. Enlisted as a private 3/25/62 at Grahamville, age 37, pay due from enlistment; present through 10/62; absent on furlough 10/27/62 for 12 days; present 1/1/63; appointed corporal 1/1/63; detached by special order no. 66 of General Beauregard 3/17/63 without pay; on roster of Jackson Hospital in Richmond with dysentery 6/9–7/17/64; 7/4/64 in private quarters; returned to duty 7/17/64; letter from citizens to General Beauregard informing him that Davis had been chartered by the South Carolina Legislature to reestablish ferry service for residents along the Santee River; present 9–10/64.

DeSaussure, H. W. [Jr., Dr.]. Enlisted as a private 5/1/63 at Pocotaligo, bounty due $50; present until 7/17/63, detached by special order no. 7 of Lieutenant Colonel Stokes; detached by special order no. 217 of General Beauregard until December 31, 1863; discharged, being appointed assistant surgeon, Confederate States Army between January and February 1864.

Desel, C. M. [Charles]. Enlisted as a private 3/25/62 at Grahamville, age 32; present until 11–12/62; sick in camp 11–12/62; detached by special order no. 20 of General Beauregard 1/20/63 as clerk in arsenal in Charleston; 3–4/63 detached without pay; dropped from the rolls 4/9/64 by order for reduction of the company; paroled 7/12/65 in the Trans-Mississippi when the theater was surrendered by General E. Kirby Smith.

Desel, J. B. [John]. Enlisted as a private 3/25/62 at Grahamville, age 22; present until 6/18/62 when on furlough for 15 days; present until 8/15/62 when on furlough for 20 days; sick in camp 9–10/62; present until 1–2/64 when sick in camp; present until 5/30/64 when captured at Old Church [Matadequin Creek]; admitted to Lincoln General Hospital [USA], Washington, D.C., with a gunshot wound right of the median line; transferred 7/20/64; arrived in Elmira, N.Y. 8/12/64; transferred for exchange 10/11/64; exchanged 10/29/64.

DuBose, J. E. [Julius Edward]. Enlisted as a private 7/25/62 at McPhersonville; present until 12/29/62 when on furlough for 12 days; present until 2/22/62 when detached by special order of General Beauregard; present until 3–4/63; transferred to Company D., 4th South Carolina Cavalry, Captain Pinckney, 5/22/63.

DuPont, B. C. [Bohna]. Enlisted as a private 3/25/62 at Grahamville, age 18; present until 2/28/64 when on furlough for 10 days; present through 9/20/64; detailed as brigade mail carrier on extra or daily duty 9/20/64.

DuPont, T. D. [Theodore]. Enlisted as a private 5/12/62 at Grahamville; present until 10/2/62 when detached by order of Colonel Walker; present 11–12/62; detached 1/20/63 by special order no. 18 of General Walker; detached, courier to court martial 1–2/63; present 3–4/63 through 7–8/63; on sick furlough from 8/25/63, certificate furnished; present 9–10/63 through 4/9/64; dropped from the rolls by order for reduction of the company 4/9/64.

Durant, T. M. [Thomas]. Enlisted as a private 2/13/63 at Pocotaligo; present on daily duty guarding shells 3–4/63; present 5–6/63 through 10/1/63; on sick furlough through 2/64; present 3–10/64.

Elliott, R. E. [Ralph]. Enlisted as a private 10/23/63 at Charleston; present until 12/26/63; detached by special order no. 285 of General Beauregard 12/26/63 for 15 days; dropped from the rolls on 4/9/64, by order for the reduction of the company; volunteer ADC to Generals Evans and Hagood, chief of guides and couriers, courier in Charleston 2/1–2/29/64.

Elliott, T. O. [Thomas]. Enlisted as a private 3/25/62 at Grahamville, age 26; present until 10/28/62 when on furlough for 15 days; present 11–12/62; sick in camp 1–2/63; present 3–4/63; on sick furlough from 6/22/63 for 20 days, certificate furnished; on sick furlough until 10/64.

Elmore, A. R. [Alfred Rhett]. Enlisted as a private 8/1/63 at Green Pond; present through 2/24/64 when on sick furlough for 20 days; present 3–8/64; on horse detail for 40 days beginning 8/11/64; present 9–10/64.

Evans, J. W. [Jonathon]. Enlisted as a private 1/17/64 at Charleston; present until 5/28/64 when captured at Haw's Shop; arrived at Point Lookout, Md., 6/8/64; exchanged 3/15/65.

Fairly, W. H. [William]. Enlisted as a private 3/25/62 at Grahamville, age 25; present until 8/29/62 when on furlough for 2 days; present until 1–2/63 when out with the Guide Corps; present on daily duty as a guide 3–4/63; on furlough from 6/22/63 for 15 days; present 7–8/63 through 2/19/64 when detached by special order no. 36 of General Beauregard [to serve as clerk to Col. Rhett]; present until 6/11/64 when killed at Trevilian Station.

Fishburne, E. B. [Edward]. Enlisted as a private 1/19/64 at Charleston; dropped from the rolls on 4/9/64 by order for reduction of the company.

Fishburne, W. H. [William]. Enlisted as a private 11/1/63 at Charleston; present through 10/64.

Fitzsimons, P. G. [Paul]. Enlisted as a private 3/25/62 at Grahamville, age 34; detached 3/24/62 by special order no. 5 of General Pemberton; detached through 12/8/62 when discharged by surgeon's certificate.

Flud, Daniel [Dr.]. Enlisted as a private 3/25/62 at Grahamville, age 43; present until 10/7/62 when detached by order of Colonel Walker; on daily duty as a surgeon 11–12/62; present on daily duty as a surgeon through 6/63; discharged on 7/1/63, terms of enlistment having expired and being over age.

Foreter, William W. See Forster, W. W.

Forster, W. W. Enlisted as a private 12/1/63 at Charleston; present until 2/24/64 when transferred to Santee Light Artillery [Captain Gaillard].

Freer, J. H. [James]. Enlisted as a private 3/25/62 at Grahamville, age 30; present until 8/26/62 when on sick furlough for 10 days; present 9–10/62 until 3/4/63 when sick in camp; detached by special order no. 117 of General Walker; detached as a sutler through 10/64.

Frierson, Augustus C. [Converse]. Enlisted as a private 4/1/63 at Pocotaligo, $50 bounty money due; present until 9–10/63 when sick in camp; sick in camp through 12/63; on sick furlough 1/1/64, certificate furnished; captured 5/30/64 at Old Church [Matadequin Creek] and sent to Point Lookout, Md.; died in hands of the enemy on 7/30/64.

Frierson, J. J. Enlisted as a private 3/25/62 at Grahamville, age 31; present until 9/25/62 when detached by special order no. 174 of General Beauregard; detached through 9/63 for duty in the Adjutant General Office; present 9–10/63 through 4/9/64 when dropped from the rolls by order for reduction of the company.

Fuller, H. M. [Henry], Jr. Enlisted as a private 3/25/62 at Grahamville, age 26; present until 1/1/63 when transferred to the 11th South Carolina Regiment.

Gaillard, E. T. Enlisted as a private 3/25/62 at Grahamville, age 22; on furlough, absent sick 5/15/62; discharged for disability on certificate of surgeon of the post 7/24/62.

Gordon, A. B. [Burgess]. Enlisted as a private 3/25/62 at Grahamville, age 28; present until 4/27/63 when on furlough for 15 days; present 5–10/27/63 when detached for 15 days by order of Colonel Rhett; present from 11/63 until 2/25/64 when on furlough for 40 days; captured 6/11/64 at Trevilian Station; arrived at Fortress Monroe 6/20/64, then sent to Point Lookout, Md.; exchanged 3/11/65 at Aikens Landing, Va.

Gregorie, A. F. [Fraser]. Enlisted as a private 3/25/62 at Grahamville, age 37; present until 11–12/62 when on daily duty as commissary; on daily duty as quartermaster on 3/4/63; listed as AWOL 11–12/63; on daily duty as a quartermaster 1–2/64; on horse detail from 8/11/64 for 40 days; on sick furlough for 30 days from 10/4/64.

Gregorie, J. McP. [Isaac], Maj. Enlisted as a private 3/25/62 at Grahamville, age 36; present until 11–12/62 when sick in camp; present 12/31/62–2/13/63 when appointed surgeon of Rutledge's Regiment of Cavalry; discharged, being appointed surgeon of the 4th South Carolina Cavalry 3/1/63; present, stationed at McPhersonville 10/63; present 9/1–12/31/63 in Pocotaligo; present 9–10/64, ranks as major.

Gregorie, W. D., Jr. Enlisted as a private 3/25/62 at Grahamville, age 36; present until 8/5/62 when transferred by Colonel Walker to Lieutenant Colonel Colcock's staff of the 8th Battalion South Carolina Cavalry.

Happoldt, John. Enlisted as a private 3/25/62 at Grahamville, age 28; present until 12/6/62 when detached by order of General Walker; present 12/31/62 through 2/22/63 when on sick furlough for chronic hepatitis; detached by order of General Beauregard 6/11/63 [railroad workshops]; transferred 4/15/64 to Kunspaugh's Battery of Light Artillery.

Harleston, Edward, Jr., 3rd Lt. Enlisted as 1st sergeant 3/25/62 at Grahamville, age 26; present until 12/62; elected 3rd lieutenant 1/15/63 and present from 12/31/62 until 1/31/63; present, acting 2nd lieutenant 3–4/63; detailed acting adjutant to Lieutenant Colonel Stokes in Green Pond, 5–6/63; present until 2/23/64 when on leave of absence for 20 days; present 3/1/64–8/31/64; signs roll commanding squadron 2/29–8/31/64; present 9–10/64; on register of CSA General Hospital in Danville, Va., 11/29/64 with Splinitis, returned to duty 12/30/64; extension by medical board; sick and before a medical examining board 11/28/64.

Harleston, John. Enlisted as a private 12/1/62 at Pocotaligo; present until 9/63; present on daily duty as a secretary 9–10/63; discharged, appointed 2nd lieutenant, 1st Regiment South Carolina Artillery, age 30.

Henry, Charles [or C. W. or Charles M.]. Enlisted as a private 1/27/64 at Charleston; dropped from the rolls 4/9/64 by order for reduction of the company.

Heyward, B. Enlisted as a private 1/20/64 at Charleston, age 24; dropped from the rolls 4/9/64 by order for reduction of the company.

Heyward, J. K. [Keith]. Enlisted as a private 3/25/62 at Grahamville, age 22; present to 8/28/62 when detached by order of Colonel Walker for 12 days; detached by special order no. 199 of General Beauregard 10/20/62; detached until 1/64; present 1/64 until dropped from the rolls 4/9/64 by order for reduction of the company.

Holland, E. C. Sgt., [Edwin]. Enlisted as a private 3/25/62 at Grahamville, age 37; sick in camp 7–8/62; wounded at Pocotaligo 10/22/62; on report of casualties of Pocotaligo and Yemassee, wounded slightly in the head; on sick furlough 9–10/62; sick in camp 11–12/62; elected corporal 1/1/63; elected 5th sergeant 5–6/63; in hospital for chronic diarrhea, cholera 6/23–7/13/64; present until detached by General Butler 7/18/64; detailed brigade quartermaster 10/15/64.

Holmes, E. G. [Edmund]. Enlisted as a private 3/25/62 at Grahamville, age 38; present until 3/24/62 when detached by special order no. 5 of General Pemberton; detached until 12/31/63; on sick furlough from 1/1/64 [chronic dysentery] until dropped from the rolls; appointed Commissioner of Claims, 2nd Congressional District.

Holmes, T. G. Enlisted as a private 3/25/62 at Grahamville, age 25; present until detached by special order no. 45 of General Pemberton 5/15/62 [Government Stables as an assistant clerk]; detached until 2/26/64 when detached by special order no. 55 of General Beauregard [Engineer on Torpedo bearing Steamers belonging to Southern Torpedo Company]; missing 5/28/64 [Haw's Shop]; killed 5/28/64 [Haw's Shop].

Hopkins, E. [English]. Enlisted as a private 2/6/64 at Charleston; absent on furlough for 40 days from 2/21/64; dropped from the rolls 4/9/64 by general order for reduction of the company.

Hopkins, James. Enlisted as a private 7/6/62 at Grahamville; wounded 10/22/62 at Pocotaligo; on report of casualties from the Charleston Light Dragoons for Pocotaligo and Yemassee, wounded seriously in the left shoulder; on sick furlough 11/62–4/63; on furlough for 20 days 2/21/64; captured 5/30/64 at Cold Harbor, Old Church Road [Matadequin Creek]; arrived at Point Lookout, Md., 6/8/64; exchanged 3/11/65.

Howell, J. M. Enlisted as a private 1/14/64 at Charleston; absent on furlough for 40 days from 2/25/64; captured 5/30/64 at Cold Harbor [Matadequin Creek]; transferred to Point Lookout, Md., 6/11/64; exchanged 11/1/64; listed as member of Logan's Brigade and paroled 4/26/65 at Greensboro, N.C.

Huger, B. F. [Benjamin], Sgt. Enlisted 3/25/62 at Grahamville as 4th sergeant, age 25; on sick furlough in Charleston 3/25/62; elected 3rd sergeant 3/25/62–6/30/62; elected 2nd sergeant 12/31/62–1/31/63; present until wounded at

Haw's Shop, 5/28/64, shot in the right thigh; on the role of Jackson Hospital in Richmond.

Huguenin, Abram. Enlisted as a private 4/5/62 at Grahamville, age 23; present until 8/16/62 when detached by order of Colonel Walker for 14 days; absent on sick furlough 10/2/62; transferred to Captain Gates's Company, 3rd South Carolina Cavalry 11/9/62.

Hutchinson, J. H. W. [Joseph], Sgt. Enlisted 3/25/62 at Grahamville as 1st corporal, age 28; elected to 4th sergeant 4/25/62; absent on sick furlough in Summerville 5/14/62; still sick 12/62; reduced to private, still absent sick 12/31/62–1/31/63; on sick furlough to 10/64.

Hutchinson, P. H. [Philip]. Enlisted as a private 7/10/62 at McPhersonville; present until 6/15/62 when placed on sick furlough for 10 days; present until 9/30/63 when on sick furlough, certificate furnished, General Hospital #1 in Summerville; present 11/63–12/63; sick in camp 1/64–2/64; absent wounded [Haw's Shop] 5/28/64; admitted Jackson Hospital, Richmond, Va., "U.S.R. Thigh" [gunshot wound right thigh]; General Hospital No. 9, Receiving and Wayside Hospital Richmond, Va.; transferred to Summerville 6/3/64 "U.S.R. Thigh, M.B."

Izard, R. S. [Ralph]. Enlisted as a private 1/14/63 at Pocotaligo; present 1–2/64, daily duty artificer; appointed 2nd Lieutenant of Engineers 3/64.

Jenkins, A. H., Jr. Enlisted as a private 3/25/62 at Grahamville, age 17; present until 8/28/62 when listed on sick furlough for 20 days; present 5–6/63 to 7/18/63 when placed on sick furlough; 9–10/63 on sick furlough for 48 hours; present until 8/11/64 when placed on horse detail for 40 days; sick furlough extended for 30 days from 10/17/64; on list of men surrendering from Logan's Brigade 4/26/65 in Greensboro, N.C.

Jones, Seaborn. Enlisted as a private 6/20/63 at Green Pond; present until 8/20/63 when placed on sick furlough; sick through 1–2/64 when present on duty as a farrier; detached by order of the secretary of war from 6/27/63–10/64.

Kirkland, W. L. [William]. Enlisted as a private 11/20/62 at Pocotaligo; present until 6/19/63 when detached for 20 days; present until 8/29/63 when given sick furlough through 10/63; present until 5/28/64 when wounded at Haw's Shop; admitted General Hospital #9 in Richmond, wounded minié ball in thigh, fracturing the bone, amputated May 30, 1864; transferred to private quarters on 5/31/64; died 6/17/64 from gangrene.

Lance, W. J. See Lance, W. S.

Lance, W. S. Enlisted as a private 5/16/62 at Grahamville; present until 10/20/62 when detached [Signal Corps] by special order no. 199 of General Beauregard; detached for service with the signal corps from 3/64–8/31/64; detached with signal corps through 10/64; appears on roll of enlisted men on extra duty to Lieutenant C. C. Memminger Jr., signal officer, Charleston, S.C., through 11/64; ordered 11/5/64 to rejoin his command.

Law, J. W. Enlisted as a private 12/12/63 at Charleston; present through 5/30/64 when captured at Cold Harbor [Matadequin Creek]; transferred to Point Lookout, Md.; exchanged 10/30/64.

Lawton, J. M. [Joseph]. Enlisted as a private 5/1/64 at Pocotaligo; captured 6/11/64 at Trevilian Station; exchanged 2/10/65.

Lewis, F. P. Enlisted as a private 1/1/64 at Charleston; present until absent on horse detail 8/11/64 for 40 days; AWOL from 9/21/64.

Lewis, J. Enlisted as a private 1/3/64 at Charleston; dropped from the rolls 4/9/64 by order for the reduction of the company.

Lewis, John W. Enlisted as a private 9/1/63 at Charleston; detached by special order no. 178 of General Beauregard 9/9/63; detached by special order no. 283 of General Beauregard 12/24/63; dropped from the rolls 4/9/64 by order for reduction of the company; two sons, F. P. Lewis and J. Lewis; aged 44; detailed as engineer and assistant superintendent of Negro labor on James Island and St. Andrews; letter to Secretary of War James Seddon.

Lining, Arthur [P.], Commissary. Enlisted as a private 3/25/62 at Grahamville; present 3/25/62–6/30/62, listed as musician; present through 9–10/62 when absent by consent of captain on special business for 48 hours; present 11–12/62 until 1/2/63 when detailed by order of Colonel Rutledge; detached by order of Colonel Rutledge on his staff, listed as private 1/25/63; detached through 7/1/63 when discharged and appointed commissary for the 4th South Carolina Cavalry; furloughed for 20 days 6/22/63; declined appointment as 2nd lieutenant in 1st Regiment South Carolina Artillery 6/62; letter to William Porcher Miles asking for a commission.

Lining, Thomas, Jr. Enlisted as a private 3/25/62 at Grahamville, age 32; present until 1–2/63 when listed as sick in camp; present 3–4/63 until 8/13/63 when detached by special order no. 112 of Captain Rutledge through 1–2/64 [color sergeant, 4th South Carolina Cavalry]; killed 6/11/64 at Trevilian Station.

Lynah, Edward. Enlisted as a private on 9/3/63 in Charleston; detailed by special order no. 185 of General Beauregard on 9/17/63; detailed until dropped from the rolls 4/9/64 by order for reduction of the company; detailed as an engineer, Special Order 180/12; Captain volunteer aide to General Drayton commanding the 3rd Military District, Department of South Carolina; letter asking for extension of detail from Confederate States Engineering Office, Savannah, November 4, 1863 to Brigadier General Thomas Jordan, chief of staff to Gen. Beauregard [Dept. of S.C., Ga. and Florida from Captain John McCrady].

Manigault, A. [Alfred], Cpl. Enlisted as a private 3/25/62 at Grahamville, age 21; present until 1/29/63 when on furlough for 4 days and listed as 4th corporal; 1–2/63, listed as on guard in camp; elected corporal 1/1/63; on sick furlough from 4/23/63, certificate furnished [for 5 days]; on sick furlough from 6/14/63 and listed as 2nd corporal; present 7–8/63 listed as 1st corporal; present until 3/20/64 when on sick furlough; 9–10/64 on sick furlough in hospital in Charleston.

Manigault, G. E. [Gabriel], 2nd Lt., Adj. Enlisted as a private 3/25/62 at Grahamville; wounded slightly in the head at Pocotaligo 10/22/62; on sick furlough 11–12/62, on daily duty as quartermaster; on sick furlough until 1/4/63; detached on the staff of Colonel Rutledge 1/25/63–6/63; present 7/63–11/63; sick in camp 11–12/63; on sick furlough from 2/1/64; 3/64 appointed adjutant, 4th South Carolina Cavalry; captured 6/11/64 at Trevilian Station; transferred to Fortress Monroe 6/20/64; transferred to Fort Delaware, Del., 6/25/64; exchanged 3/65.

Manning, W. H. [Wade Hampton]. Enlisted as a private 11/19/63 at Charleston, age 18; on furlough for 20 days from 2/18/64; present until detached as a courier to General Hampton 5/27/64; listed on roll of Jackson Hospital, Richmond, Va., 7/18/64 for 30 days for chronic diarrhea; listed among those paroled on 4/26/65 in Greensboro, N.C.; application endorsed by numerous officers for cadetship from the 6th Congressional District of South Carolina; letter to William Porcher Miles about a brevet 2nd lieutenant in Lucas Battalion of Artillery, in which he refers to Miles as "our representative and a friend of my father" and writes that he would like to apply for a cadetship if no one else has applied.

Marion, B. P. Enlisted as a private 4/11/62 at Grahamville; present until absent on furlough for 15 days from 6/18/62; present until 12/29/62 when absent on furlough for 13 days; present 12/31/62–1/31/63, listed as 2nd corporal on 1/1/63; present until 2/26/63 when detached by special order no. 53 of General Walker; on sick furlough from 4/26/63 until 11–12/63 when sick in camp; on sick furlough from 1/1/64; demoted 7–8/63 because sick; on light duty by board of surgeons; dropped from the roles, appointed assessor in kind of 2nd Congressional District of South Carolina 9–10/64.

Marion, T. S. [Theodore]. Enlisted as a private 9/26/63 at Charleston; on sick furlough from 10/2/63; present 11–12/63 until 1/15/64 when detached by special order no. 9 of General Beauregard; died 3/1/64.

Marion, Theodore S. See Marion, T. S.

Martin, Edward [H.]. Enlisted as a private 3/25/62 at Grahamville, age 20; present until 11/25/62 when detached by special order of General Walker; 1/5/63 on sick furlough, certificate furnished; detached to the signal corps through 10/64 as a signal operator, Signal Station Charleston; 10/28/64 ordered to Wilmington, N.C., by Major General Whiting; ordered to rejoin his command 11/5/64; furloughed by special order no. 238 when appointed Special Clerk of the Senate; letter [to Samuel Cooper] from J. H. Brooks, captain commanding a battalion asking if Martin could serve as a 2nd lieutenant in his battalion.

Martin, G. G. [George]. Enlisted as a private 7/30/62 at McPhersonville; detached by special order no. 83 of Colonel Walker 8/3/62; detached until 10–11/63 when present; present until dropped from the rolls 4/9/64 by orders for reduction of the company.

Martin, J. M. [John McL.]. Enlisted as a private 3/25/62 at Grahamville, age 35; discharged per conscript law as being over 35 years of age 6/3/62; dispatched per special order no. 154 of Colonel Walker from 9/27/62; absent on sick furlough 9/30/62, certificate furnished; on light duty 4/7/64 as per medical board; detached 3/64–8/31/64, hospital duty at McPhersonville as clerk for medical examining board; copy of certificate of disability for "constant hemorrhaging piles."

Martin, J. N. See Martin, J. M.

Martin, R. H. [Richard]. Enlisted as a private 1/27/64 at Charleston by Captain Colcock; present until 8/11/64 when placed on horse detail for 40 days; sent to Pettigrew General Hospital #13, in Raleigh, N.C., with pelvis remittus.

Martin, Vincent. Enlisted as a private 3/25/62 at Grahamville, age 18; present until wounded accidentally 6/24/62 and thereafter sick in camp; 7–8/62 absent on sick furlough from accidental wound; absent until discharged 11–12/62, being appointed 2nd lieutenant in 1st Regiment South Carolina Regulars.

Martin, W. A. [William]. Enlisted as a private 3/25/62 at Grahamville, age 29; present until absent on furlough from 6/27/62 for 10 days; present until transferred by General Pemberton to Martin's Company of Artillery, 8/5/62.

Maxwell, P. J. [Dr.]. Enlisted as a private 3/25/62 at Grahamville; present until 7–8/62; present 9–10/62 until 12/31/62–1/31/62 when listed as sick in camp; present 1–2/63–9/10/63 when on daily duty as a musician; present until 12/19/63 when on sick furlough; discharged 1–2/64, appointed assistant surgeon, 24th South Carolina Volunteers.

McCleod, W. W. Enlisted as a private 3/25/62 at Grahamville, age 42; present until detached by order of Colonel Walker on 8/22/62 for 15 days; present until 12/31/62–1/31/63 when listed as on daily duty as quartermaster; present until 2/18/64 when on furlough for 15 days; present until 7/17/64 when detached at regimental headquarters as assistant commissary; detailed as assistant regimental commissary until detached for light duty [orderly] by Medical Board 10/10/64.

McPherson, J. J. [John]. Enlisted as a private 3/25/62 at Grahamville, age 25; present until discharged by General Pemberton, being appointed paymaster in Confederate States Navy 5/10/62.

Metz, J. Y. Enlisted as a private 3/25/62 at Grahamville, age 30; present until detached by order of General Pemberton 3/24/62; detached until 9–10/62 when present; present until 2/14/63 when detached by special order no. 32 of General Beauregard; detached until 3/31–8/31/64 when listed as detached for light duty, recommended by the board of surgeons 3/11/64; detached by the secretary of war at Charleston, S.C., for 6 months from 2/11/64; name appears on parole at Charlotte, N.C., 5/4/65; listed as assistant wagon master in Charleston while detached.

Middleton, F. K. [Francis Kinloch]. Enlisted as a private 3/25/62 at Grahamville, age 25; present until 5–6/63 when sick in camp; present until detached by special order no. 336 of General Ripley 10/12/63 without pay; present 11–12/63 until 5/28/64 when mortally wounded at Haw's Shop; appears on list of Confederate wounded at Hanovertown; wound to back, severe, bullet, 3rd Division, 5th Army Corps, Army of the Potomac; died 5/30/64 and buried on farm of Mrs. Newton near Pamunkey River, Va.; request [to Rutledge] for leave of absence to tend to father's plantation on 11/18/62 since father is 70 and is ill and living on a rice plantation with 300 slaves on Pee Dee River near Georgetown; Yankees have made raids and F. Middleton is the only near relative; large family dependent on plantation for support; his mother sends the same letter.

Middleton, O. H. [Oliver Hering, Jr.]. Enlisted as a private 1/4/63 at Pocotaligo; present until 1/28/63 when detached by special order of Colonel Rutledge to serve on his staff [private secretary]; bounty due, $50; detached until 9–10/63 when present; present until 5/30/64, killed at Cold Harbor [Matadequin Creek].

Middleton, T. A. [Thomas Alston]. Enlisted as a private 5/17/62 at Grahamville, age 26; present until detached [Signal Corps] by special order no. 199 of General Beauregard; discharged 11–12/62 being appointed 3rd lieutenant of the 1st Artillery Regiment.

Mikell, E. W. [Edward Wilkinson]. Enlisted as a private 10/1/63 at Green Pond; detailed by special order no. 181 of Colonel Colcock 10/9/63 as commissary agent at District Headquarters; AWOL 1–2/63; 3/1–8/31/64 transferred to Company K; detailed with Brigade Commissary, extra or daily duty 6/1/64; paroled at Greensboro, N.C., 5/2/65.

Miles, J. A. [James Allen]. Enlisted as 3rd corporal 3/25/62 at Grahamville, age 27; present until 3/25–6/30/62 when appears on rolls as 1st corporal; present until 1–2/63 when elected 4th sergeant; present until 3–4/63 when sick in camp; present 5–6/63, listed as 3rd sergeant; present until 5/28/64 when missing [Haw's Shop]; killed 5/28/64 at Haw's Shop; listed as casualty at battle of Pocotaligo and Yemassee 10/22/62, "wounded slight in the posterior."

Miles, J. J. [Jeremiah]. Enlisted as a private 3/25/62 at Grahamville, age 26; sick in camp 3/25/62–6/30/62; present until detached as courier for Garrison Court Martial; present 9–10/62 until 3/27/63 when on furlough for 10 days; present 5–6/63 until 9–10/64 when sent with dismounted men to Stoney Creek on 10/12/64; captured at Stoney Creek 12/2/64, taken to City Point, Va., 12/5/64; taken to Point Lookout, Md.; released 6/19/65; signed oath of allegiance at Point Lookout, Md., 6/29/65.

Moore, J. B. [John Burchell]. Enlisted as a private 12/14/62 at Pocotaligo; sick in camp 11–12/62 and 12/31/62–1/31/63; detached by special order of General Beauregard 2/22/63; present 3–4/63 through 10/15/63 when detached by special order no. 24 of General Beauregard; detached until appointed adjutant of the Shiloh Battalion of Artillery 3/64; detached as clerk for the state of

South Carolina; denoted as an intelligent planter of education and position; held position in Camden; letter from agent to General Jordan asking for extension of the detail dated 12/25/63 from William M. Shannon.

Neyle, H. M. Enlisted as a private 3/25/62 at Grahamville, age 20; present until 9–10/62 when present, sick in camp; present until 8/11/64 when on horse detail for 40 days; 9–10/64 absent on sick furlough, 9/23/64.

Nowell, E. W. [Edward]. Enlisted as a private 3/25/62 at Grahamville; present until 10/9/62 when detached by special order no. 186 of General Beauregard; detached until 1/14/63 when listed as on sick furlough, certificate furnished; detached [Signal Corps] until present 5–6/63; present 7–8/63 to 9–10/63 when sick in hospital; present until 5/28/64 when wounded at Haw's Shop; on register of Jackson Hospital in Richmond, Va.; "U.S. right hand," admitted 5/29/64; furloughed 6/15/64 for 30 days; appears on roll of 3rd N.C. Hospital in Charleston 8/31/64; absent wounded furlough 9–10/64; appears on register of Invalid Corps 12/30/64; sent to the Army of Northern Virginia 3/2/65; paroled in Greensboro 4/26/65, Logan's Brigade; other correspondence.

Nowell, Lionel C., 1st Lt. Enlisted as a 2nd lieutenant 3/25/62 at Grahamville, age 26; present until detached by Colonel Walker 8/23/62 for garrison court martial; present 9–10/62 until detached by special order of Colonel Walker 1/5/63; detached until 5–6/63 when detached on court martial at McPhersonville; 7–8/63 not stated; present from 9–10/63 until 1–2/64 when absent on leave of 20 days from 2/26/64; present until captured 5/30/64 at Cold Harbor [Matadequin Creek]; 9–10/64 captured; on roll of prisoners at Point Lookout, Md., arriving 6/8/64; transferred to Fort Delaware, Del., 6/23/64; signed oath of allegiance at Fort Delaware and released 6/12/65; listed as complexion dark, hair dark, eyes gray, height 6'1", residence Charleston, S.C.; record of request to General Thomas Jordan, chief of staff, for leave of absence [30 days] to be married 1/12/64; copy of letter from Accabee 12/28/63 by Nowell asking that 15 men be returned to Charleston Light Dragoons from details to General Jordan.

O'Brien, T. [Timothy]. Enlisted as a private 3/25/62 at Grahamville, age 28; present until 11–12/62 when on daily duty as nurse to wounded man in hospital; on sick furlough from 1/4/63, certificate furnished; on roll of Jackson Hospital, "U.S. R. Thigh," 5/30/64 [admitted 5/29/64, wounded at Haw's Shop]; present until wounded and in hospital, 10/27/64; on roll of Jackson Hospital, "U.S. L. shoulder," 10/30/64; returned to duty 11/1/64; transferred to Charlotte, N.C.; on muster roll of employees at the Ordnance Works, Charlotte, N.C., paroled 5/3/65 according to terms listed.

O'Hear, James W., 2nd Lt. Enlisted as a 3rd lieutenant 3/25/62 at Grahamville, age 26; present until detached by general order no. 62 of General Beauregard 9/30/62 on court martial duty; present until 1/27/63 when on furlough for 10 days, as 2nd lieutenant; detached by special order no. 56 of General Walker

2/27/63; present 3–4/63 until 9–10/63 when detached by special order no. 221 of General Beauregard 10/25/63 for 30 days; present 11–12/63 until 5/28/64 when missing [Haw's Shop]; killed 5/28/64 at Haw's Shop.

O'Hear, L. W. [Lawrence]. Enlisted as a private 11/17/63 at Charleston; present until 8/11/64 when on horse detail for 40 days; AWOL from 9/21/64; on roster of those paroled at Greensboro, N.C., from Logan's Brigade 4/26/65.

O'Neal, J. J. A. See O'Neille, J. J. A.

O'Neille, J. J. A. Enlisted as a private 3/25/62 at Grahamville, age 23; present until 10/22/62 when wounded at Pocotaligo; sick in hospital through 12/62; on sick furlough through 10/64; on muster roll of employees at Ordnance Works, Charlotte, N.C.; on list of men paroled; on list of casualties from Pocotaligo and Yemassee, wounded, seriously in the left leg [fracture].

Palfrey, A. C. See Palfrey, Alfred C.

Palfrey, Alfred C. Enlisted as a private 3/25/62 at Grahamville, age 23; present until 7/16/62 when detached by special order no. 109 of General Pemberton; detached until 9–10/63 when detached by special order no. 214 of General Beauregard 10/23/63 for 15 days; present 11–12/63 until 8/8/64 when sent to hospital; 9–10/64 kept in Columbia, S.C., by order of Governor Bonham; application for commission in Confederate service received by Major Roland Rhett and others dated 10/26/63; Major Rhett gives recommendation; James Tupper, Auditor of South Carolina, letter to Secretary of War James Seddon mentions Palfrey and service in Quartermaster Corps in Columbia, calls him "an experienced accountant and man of the highest business qualities, attentive, assured and laborious"; asks for Palfrey, his son in law, to be his private secretary; calls him "gentleman of the highest character, sober, industrious."

Phillips, O. B. [Otis]. Enlisted as a private 7/27/63 at Green Pond; bounty money due, $50; present until 6/15/64 when on sick furlough; on morning report of Jackson Hospital, Richmond, Va., admitted 6/2/64; trampled by horses [cystitis] [ambush following Matadequin Creek]; transferred 7/14/64 to Charlotte, N.C., CSA General Hospital No. 11, chronic cystitis, returned to duty 9/23/64; sent to hospital 10/14/64; admitted 10/28/64; returned to duty 11/1/64; admitted to Pettigrew General Hospital No. 13 in Raleigh, N.C., paralysis of bladder 10/9/64; transferred to Charlotte, N.C., 10/25/64; paroled at Charlotte, N.C., 5/4/65.

Porcher, J. D. [Dubose]. Enlisted as a private 7/26/62 at McPhersonville; wounded at Pocotaligo 10/22/62; on sick furlough 11–12/62; present 12/31/62–1/31/62; discharged 7/1/63, appointed war tax collector; appears on Report of Casualties at Pocotaligo and Yemassee 10/22/62, report dated 12/12/62; wounded slightly right hip.

Porcher, P. R. See Porcher, Percival.

Porcher, Percival [R]. Enlisted as a private 7/26/62 at McPhersonville; wounded in leg at Haw's Shop 5/28/64; died 6/3/64; bayonet wound left thigh [incorrect]; died in hospital in Richmond [gangrene].

Porcher, W. E. [William Edward]. Enlisted as a private 11/5/63 at Charleston; dropped from the rolls 4/9/64 by order for reduction of the company.

Pringle, D. L. [Dominick Lynch]. Enlisted as a private 5/1/64 at Columbia; present until 10/22/64; seeks appointment as lieutenant in 1st South Carolina Artillery, Alfred Rhett Commanding; AWOL 10/22/64 to get commission in 1st South Carolina Artillery; listed on roll of those paroled at Greensboro, N.C., 4/26/65 as member of Logan's Brigade; recommendation for appointment as 2nd lieutenant, 1st South Carolina Artillery sent to Secretary of War James Seddon.

Pringle, J. J. [John Julius]. Enlisted as a private 9/14/62 for war; detached 12/16/62 for 15 days by order of General Walker; sick in camp 12/31/62–1/31/63; present until 10/12/63 when detached by special order no. 336 of General Ripley for 20 days; present 11–12/63 until 8/11/64 when on horse detail for 40 days; present 9–10/64; applied for appointment in 1st South Carolina Artillery 10/28/64; letter from Alfred Rhett, requesting Pringle for the unit; letter from William Porcher Miles to Secretary of War James Seddon concerning Pringle.

Pringle, J. R. P. [Joel Roberts Poinsett]. Enlisted as a private 2/19/63; present until 6/25/63 when on furlough for 15 days; present 7–8/63 until mortally wounded at Matadequin Creek; died in the hands of the enemy 5/31/64.

Pringle, Julius J. See Pringle, J. J.

Pringle, M. B. [Miles Brewton]. Enlisted as a private 3/25/62 at Grahamville, age 26; wounded at Pocotaligo 10/22/62; on list of casualties for Pocotaligo and Yemassee; wounded left foot, slight; letters of recommendation for appointment as quartermaster; on sick furlough 11–12/62; present 12/31/62–8/8/64; sent to hospital 8/8/64; detached 9–10/64 as quartermaster officer; read by medical board for light duty; paroled Charlotte, N.C., 5/3/65; employed in supply train in charge of Captain J. W. Wallace; parole describes him as light complexion, blue eyes, 5'10", age 30.

Pringle, Poinsett. See Pringle, J. R. P.

Prioleau, C. E. [Charles]. Enlisted as a private 3/25/62 at Grahamville, age 22; sick in camp 3/25/62 to 6/30/62; absent on furlough for 10 days from 8/29/62; present 9–10/62 until on sick furlough from 9/22/63; present 1–12/63 until killed 5/28/64 at Haw's Shop.

Prioleau, J. M. [James]. Enlisted as a private 9/23/62 for war; sick in hospital, wounded 10/22/62 at battles of Pocotaligo and Yemassee; on report of casualties from Pocotaligo and Yemassee; wounded seriously in the right thigh; on sick furlough 11–12/62; present 12/31/62–1/31/63; detached over next year periodically [General Walker, special order no. 47] 2/22/63; 6/3/64 detailed as brigade mail courier; reported 9/13/64 as unfit for field duty, services as a clerk are indispensable [medical purveyor, Macon, Ga.], age 27; clerk 3/9/64 through 3/65.

Pritchett, G. E. See Pritchett, George E.

Pritchett, George E. Enlisted as a private 3/25/62 at Grahamville; present until on sick furlough from 11/5/63 until 3/1–8/31/64 when on light duty in Wilmington by recommendation of the board of surgeons, 1/64; hospital steward; 4/27/64 on furlough for 24 hours.

Purcell, James. Enlisted as a private 3/25/62 at Grahamville; absent on sick furlough 6/10/62; present 7–8/62 until 12/14/62 when on sick furlough until 1–2/63; present until 7–8/63 when detached by special order of General Beauregard for 20 days; discharged, being appointed assistant surgeon PACS 10/1/63.

Ravenel, T. P. See Ravenel, Thomas P.

Ravenel, Thomas P. Enlisted as a private 10/18/63 at Charleston; present until 11–12/63 when sick in camp; present 1–2/64 until dropped from the rolls 4/9/64 by order for reduction of the company.

Rhett, B. S. [Benjamin], Jr. Enlisted as a private 3/25/62 at Grahamville, age 27; present, elected 4th corporal 6/7/62; present until absent on furlough for 10 days from 8/28/62; present until detached by special order no. 242 [clerk in office of the inspector general] by General Beauregard 12/4/62; ordered to report to his command 5/26/64; detached until 3/31–8/31/64 at regimental headquarters; light duty until 9–10/64; list of men paroled, Burn's House, N.C., 4/20/65.

Rice, H. W. [Waring]. Enlisted 1/1/62 in Purrysburg; on list of officers and men paroled in Greensboro on May 2, 1865.

Richardson, H. W. Enlisted as a private 7/21/62 at McPhersonville; absent detached by order of Colonel Walker 8/28/62 for 3 days; present until 1–2/63 when present on guard duty in camp; present until 3–4/63 when absent by order of General Walker to buy forage; detached until 9–10/63 when on sick furlough; on sick furlough from 12/17/63; present 1–2/64 until captured 5/30/64 at Cold Harbor [Matadequin Creek]; on roll of prisoners paroled at Point Lookout, Md., and transferred to Aikens Landing, Va., on 3/14/65 for exchange; captured at Haw's Shop [incorrect] 5/30/64; exchanged 3/14/65.

Richardson, J. B. [James]. Enlisted as a private 3/25/62 at Grahamville, age 28; absent on furlough from 6/28/62 for 10 days; attached by order of Colonel Walker, 9/20/62; on sick furlough for 7 days, 8/29/62; on furlough for 30 days from 12/28/63; relieved of detached duty to rejoin company 4/8/64; sick in camp, 9–10/64; on roll of CSA General Hospital in Danville, Va., 11/18/64 for nephritis; furloughed for 60 days, 12/8/64.

Richardson, J. M. Enlisted as a private 3/25/62 at Grahamville; detached by order of Colonel Walker for 15 days, sick at home, 8/8/62; detached by order of General Walker 12/28/62 for 10 days; on sick furlough 7/13/63; dropped from the rolls 4/9/64 by order for reduction of the company.

Richardson, James B. See Richardson, J. B.

Richardson, R. C. Enlisted as a private 7/26/62 at McPhersonville; sick in camp 9–10/62; on furlough for 10 days from 4/24/63; on sick furlough for 7 days

8/28/63; on sick furlough from 9/30/63; sent to hospital 8/10/64; on sick furlough for 60 days from 9/29/64.

Robertson, Alex. Enlisted as a private 3/25/62 at Grahamville, age 22; detached by order of General Walker 12/10/62 for 30 days; detached by special order of General Ripley 10/18/63 for 15 days; killed 5/28/64 at Haw's Shop; letter from his father, Alexander Robertson Sr., dated 12/2/62 to General Thomas Jordan asking for 30 day leave of absence for his son to remove "Negroes from St. Thomas Parish Plantation to his residence in Buncombe County, NC"; also needs help because he must move Colonel Ward's "Negroes at Waccamaw" to Marlborough when he purchased a plantation.

Robertson, E. R. [Eber]. Enlisted as a private 11/5/63 at Charleston; present until detailed as a courier to General Butler from 3/1/64–8/31/64; killed by friendly fire on 9/25/64.

Robinson, John. Enlisted as a private 3/25/62 at Grahamville, age 29; detached by order of Colonel Walker 10/25/62; detached by order of Colonel Rutledge 3/26/63 as a courier; detached until transferred to Company C of the 4th South Carolina Cavalry 11/29/63; transferred from Company C, 4th South Carolina Cavalry 10/22/64; on list of paroled from Logan's Brigade serving at HQ, Cavalry, Army of Tennessee, 4/29/65 at Greensboro, N.C.

Rose, Alex. Enlisted as a private 3/25/62 at Grahamville, age 24; present elected 3rd corporal 3/25/62; detached by order of Colonel Walker 9/22/62; detached by special order of General Beauregard 11/7/62; discharged 12/31/62, being appointed aide to Brigadier General Gannan, PACS.

Rutledge, B. H. [Benjamin Huger], Col. Enlisted as captain 3/25/62 at Grahamville, age 33; absent on furlough for 10 days from 8/21/62; detached by special order of Colonel Walker 10/28/62 to muster and inspect Captains Franklin Heyward and Kinds Company; discharged 12/17/62, being appointed colonel of Rutledge's Regiment; detached, commanding brigade by General Lee, 11/17/64; date of Confederate appointment 4/2/64, confirmed 6/10/64 to take rank 12/16/62; detached for board 12/8/62; detailed for court 9/22/63; detailed for council 3/5/64; detailed president of court 3/26/63; request to Thomas Jordan to move his family from Columbia to Darlington [only absent 7 days in 8 months]; letter explaining promotion from Beauregard to Secretary of War James Seddon, notes Rutledge "has no superior as a volunteer cavalry officer."

Sass, G. H. Enlisted as a private 10/1/63; absent, detached by special order of General Beauregard 10/27/63; detached until dropped from the rolls 4/9/64 by order for reduction of the company; appears on roll for HQ Department of South Carolina, Georgia, Florida, 7/1/64, clerk; certificate from medical examiner board 9/1–9/30/64; 8/64, 1st class clerk.

Seabrook, G. H. See Seabrook, H. [Henry].

Seabrook, H. [Henry]. Enlisted as a private 5/21/62 at Grahamville; transferred to Marion Artillery in exchange for J. M. Prioleau 9/13/62.

Seabrook, Joseph. Enlisted as a private 5/21/62 at Grahamville; transferred to Marion Artillery, Captain Parker commanding, 9/13/62 in exchange for J. M. Prioleau.

Shedd, J. N. Enlisted as a private 9/18/63 at Charleston; detached by order of General Ripley for 15 days from 10/17/63; on furlough for 20 days from 2/11/64; dropped from the rolls 4/9/64 by order for reduction of the company.

Simons, Ion, Cpl. Enlisted as a private 3/25/62 at Grahamville, age 22; on furlough from 1/29/63 for 10 days; elected 4th corporal 5–6/63; appointed lieutenant in Ferguson's Battery of Artillery 7/1/63; appointed, but not on register until date appointed 12/8/64, confirmed same day to stand on 11/12/64, accepted 1/1/65; request to Samuel Cooper for commission, acting as officer by order of Beauregard without CSA acknowledgment; will have to return to rank unless commissioned; more letters concerning confusion over his rank.

Simons, Lewis. Enlisted as a private 9/1/63; detached by special order of General Beauregard 8/28/63; volunteered to "Help collect Negroes from near Charleston for work on fortifications"; noted as "gentleman of the highest character" and "sends his hands at every call"; "will recruit Negroes from plantations on the Cooper River"; two letters about Captain Read not sending any slaves; dropped from the rolls 4/9/64 by order for reduction of the company.

Simons, S. W. [Samuel Wragg], Cpl. Enlisted as corporal on 3/25/62 at Grahamville, age 24; elected sergeant 6/7/62; accidentally shot in the neck by a pistol 10/24/62; absent, sick furlough 10/26/62; detached by special order of General Beauregard 6/22/63; demoted to private 7–8/63; detached for light duty in Columbia, recommendation of the board of surgeons, 3/1–8/31/64; on light duty in Columbia for six months from 1/28/64; on roll of detailed men in the Quartermaster Department in Columbia; board finds Simons "suffering from neck wound, tiny ball lodged between carotid artery and tonsil of right side, occasioning great discomfort to any atmospheric changes" [ball passed through face and lodged in the back of the throat].

Sinkler, W. [William]. Enlisted as a private 11/1/63 at Charleston; present until 1–2/64.

Stoney, J. S. [John, Dr.], Sgt. Enlisted as 2nd sergeant 3/25/62 at Grahamville, age 29; transferred, appointed assistant surgeon of Colonel Hagood's regiment 4/25/62.

Tate, P. J. [Pinckney]. Enlisted as a private 1/18/63 at Pocotaligo; present, sick in camp 3–4/63; on furlough for 20 days from 3/27/64; dropped from the rolls 4/9/64 by order for reduction of the company.

Taylor, A. R. Enlisted as a private 8/24/63 in Charleston, bounty money due; absent 5/64, detached as orderly to General Butler; absent on horse detail from 8/11/64 for 40 days.

Taylor, Thomas. Enlisted as a private 4/23/63 at Pocotaligo; $50 bounty due; discharged 9/24/63, being appointed aide-de-camp to General Hampton.

Thompson, J. S. Enlisted as a private 11/10/63 at Charleston; dropped from the rolls 4/9/64 by order for reduction of the company.

Thurston, J. G. [John]. Enlisted as a private 3/25/62 at Grahamville, age 23; absent on sick furlough 6/63; on sick furlough 12/17/63.

Trenholm, E. D. [Edward]. Enlisted as a private 1/17/64 at Charleston; on register of Jackson Hospital, Richmond, Va., 6/23/64; absent on horse detail from 8/11/64 for 40 days; in hospital at Columbia from 9/22/64; listed as deserted 10/16/64; listed as dead on 10/6/64; Februs Int. [contused wound]; trampled [rolled on by his horse at Matadequin Creek].

Tupper, W. T. [William]. Enlisted as a private 1/21/64 at Charleston; sick in camp; dropped from the rolls 4/9/64 by order for reduction of the company.

Vanderhorst, Lewis. Enlisted as a private 3/25/62 at Grahamville, age 35; sick in camp April 1863; granted a furlough for 5 days 12/63; killed 5/28/64 at Haw's Shop.

Vincent, W. E. See Vincent, Wm. E.

Vincent, Wm. E. Enlisted as a private 3/25/62 at Grahamville, age 18; sick in camp 3/25/62–6/30/62; detached by order of General Pemberton 7/30/62 as assistant engineer; detached until 11–12/63; AWOL 1–2/64; on horse detail 8/11/64 for 40 days; in hospital in Columbia from 9/22/64; asked Colcock for a transfer and was refused.

Wagner, A. C. Enlisted as a private 3/25/62 at Grahamville, age 35; absent on sick furlough from 3/25/62; on sick furlough until discharged on surgeon's certificate of disability 7/1/63.

Waring, J. H. [Joseph]. Enlisted as a private 8/30/63, $50 bounty money due; present on daily duty at commissary 1–2/64; discharged 12/22/64, elected to civil office.

Waring, J. R. [John Rhodes]. Enlisted as a private 3/25/62 at Grahamville, age 29; present until 10/21/62 when absent on furlough; on sick furlough until discharged on surgeon's certificate 3/1/63; present 1–2/64; dropped from the rolls 4/9/64 by order for reduction of the company; brother of Dragoon Morton Nathaniel Waring.

Waring, M. N. [Morton Nathaniel, Dr.]. Enlisted as a private 8/12/63 at McPhersonville; detached by special order of General Beauregard 5/22/63 without pay and allowances [physician to St. John's, Berkeley, and St. Stephen's parish]; sick in camp 9–10/63; detached 10/3/63; on furlough 1/8/64; relieved from detached duty to rejoin company on 4/8/64; detailed with unserviceable horses at Lynchburg from 8/18/64; sent with disabled horses to Gordonville 9–10/64; brother of Dragoon John Rhodes Waring.

Wells, E. L. [Edward]. Enlisted as a private 12/30/63 at Charleston, bounty due; absent wounded 6/11/64 at Trevilian Station; CSA hospital, Farmville, Va.,

6/20/64; deserted 6/27/64 [incorrect]; Jackson Hospital, Richmond, Va., 7/13/64, pistol shot in the back; furloughed 7/18/64 for 30 days; appears on register of Pettigrew General Hospital in Raleigh 10/9/64 with chronic diarrhea; returned to duty 10/24/64.

Weston, R. A. Enlisted as a private 11/21/63 at Charleston; on sick furlough 1/18/64; detached with division quartermaster 8/11/64; detached for light duty with brigade headquarters 9/16/64; on roll of prisoners paroled at Augusta, Ga., 5/22/65.

White, J. D. [James]. Enlisted as a private 3/25/62 at Grahamville, age 28; detached by order of General Pemberton 3/24/62; discharged on surgeon's certificate 12/8/62.

White, W. W. [William]. Enlisted as a private 3/25/62 at Grahamville, age 31; detached by special order of General Beauregard 11/28/62 to act as assistant commissary on James Island; captured at Haw's Shop 5/28/64; list of wounded at the 2nd Division USA General Hospital at Alexandria, Va., "gunshot wound, right leg, just below knee"; on register of prisoners at Old Capital Prison, Washington, D.C.; sent to Elmira, N.Y., 8/12/64 from Old Capital Prison; paroled at Elmira, N.Y., 2/25/65, sent to James River for exchange.

Wilkins, Governeur M. Enlisted as a private 3/25/62 at Grahamville, age 33; detached by order of Colonel Walker for 20 days from 8/24/62; on furlough for 4 days from 12/30/64; detached by Colonel Walker 2/6/63; detached by special order of General Beauregard 2/26/64; detached by Secretary of War 3/64; detached 9–10/64.

Withers, W. R. Enlisted as private 11/21/63 at Charleston; on roll of Jackson Hospital, Va., with contusions [trampled by horse in ambush following Matadequin Creek]; discharged from hospital 6/7/64; on roll of Jackson Hospital, Va., 6/27/64, returned to duty same day; absent on horse detail from 8/11/64 for 40 days.

Witsell, E. [Dr.]. Enlisted as a private 3/25/62 at Grahamville, age 40; detached by order of Colonel Walker 8/25/62; detached by order of General Pemberton 8/25/62; transferred to 11th South Carolina Regiment 11/18/62; on daily duty as a surgeon 7–8/63; dropped from the rolls 4/9/64 by order for reduction of the company.

Witsell, F. [Frederick]. Enlisted as a private on 1/31/64 in Charleston; dropped from the rolls 4/9/64 by order for reduction of the company.

Witsell, W. H. [Walter]. Enlisted as a private 3/25/62 at Grahamville, age 37; absent on sick furlough 10/1/62; on sick furlough until dropped from the rolls 4/9/64 by order for reduction of the company.

Wragg, A. McD. Enlisted as a private 3/25/62 at Grahamville, age 23; absent 7–8/62 [not stated]; detached by order of Colonel Walker 10/13/62; on daily duty as secretary [bookkeeper] 1–2/64; absent wounded on 5/28/64 at Haw's Shop; on register of Jackson Hospital, Richmond, Va., wound, right thigh, admitted 5/30/64, furloughed June 4 for 60 days; register of First Georgia Hospital until 8/31/64; detailed for light duty for 30 days at regimental headquarters 10/17/64; on muster roll of officers and men paroled at Greensboro, N.C., 5/2/65.

NOTES

Introduction

1. *Proceedings at the Unveiling of the Monument to the Charleston Light Dragoons,* . . . (Charleston, S.C.: Walker, Evans, Cogswell, 1889), 4–5; Edward L. Wells, *A Sketch of the Charleston Light Dragoons, from the Earliest Formation of the Corps* (Charleston, S.C.: Lucas, Richardson and Co., 1888), 4–6. Wells's wartime history of the dragoons provides unique details regarding a number of aspects of the dragoons' service. Until recently, it was the only history of the unit during the Civil War.

2. William Kauffman Scarborough addresses this issue at length and speculates that "many of the large slaveholders supported the Confederate cause with unremitting devotion . . . but many of them could have contributed more to the war effort." William Kauffman Scarborough, *Masters of the Big House: Elite Slaveholders of the Mid-Nineteenth-Century South* (Baton Rouge: Louisiana State University Press, 2003), 317. The "rich man's war, poor man's fight" thesis is defended by David Williams in *Rich Man's War: Class, Caste, and Confederate Defeat in the Lower Chattahoochee Valley* (Athens: University of Georgia Press, 1998).

3. Most studies of lowcountry slavery are concerned with the institution during the colonial era. See Peter H. Woods, *Black Majority: Negroes in Colonial South Carolina from 1670 through the Stono Rebellion* (New York: Alfred A. Knopf, 1974); and Daniel C. Littlefield, *Rice and Slaves: Ethnicity and the Slave Trade in Colonial South Carolina* (Baton Rouge: Louisiana State University Press, 1981). For a study of nineteenth-century lowcountry slavery, see William Dusinberre, *Them Dark Days: Slavery in the American Rice Swamps* (New York: Oxford University Press, 1996).

4. See Edmund Morgan, *Inventing the People: The Rise of Popular Sovereignty in England and America* (New York: W. W. Norton, 1988), 288–306. On the rejection of privilege and ideas of social superiority, see Gordon S. Wood, *The Radicalism of the American Revolution* (New York: Alfred A. Knopf, 1992).

5. James M. Banner Jr., "The Problem of South Carolina," in *The Hofstadter Aegis: A Memorial,* ed. Stanley Elkins and Eric McKitrick (New York, Alfred A. Knopf, 1974), 68.

6. Morgan, *Inventing the People,* 293.

7. For a brief and insightful look at the hierarchical world created by the elite of the South Carolina lowcountry, see George C. Rogers Jr., *Charleston in the Age of the Pinckneys* (Norman: University of Oklahoma Press, 1969).

8. Banner, "The Problem of South Carolina," 71, 73–74.

9. For an assessment of the concept of "liberty" and how it was used to draw rich and poor Southerners together, see J. Mills Thornton III, *Politics and Power in a Slave Society: Alabama, 1800–1860* (Baton Rouge: Louisiana State University Press, 1978).

10. Bertram Wyatt-Brown, *Southern Honor: Ethics and Behavior in the Old South* (New York: Oxford University Press, 1982), 88. For the dragoons, as with others who aspired to gentility, the appearance of moral uprightness was more common than the virtue itself.

11. A brother of Dragoon Lewis Vanderhorst was involved in one duel prior to the war and one during the conflict. Arnoldus Vanderhorst Dueling Papers, 1862–1868, South Carolina Historical Society, Charleston, S.C. (hereafter SCHS). For more on the defense of honor, see Wyatt-Brown, *Southern Honor.*

12. This idea conflicts directly with the assertions made by David Williams in *Rich Man's War.*

13. For an important assessment of the role of courage in Civil War combat, see Gerald F. Linderman, *Embattled Courage: The Experience of Combat in the American Civil War* (New York: Free Press, 1987).

14. James M. McPherson, *For Cause and Comrades: Why Men Fought in the Civil War* (New York: Oxford University Press, 1997), 100–101.

15. Don H. Doyle, *New Men, New Cities, New South: Atlanta, Nashville, Charleston, Mobile, 1860–1910* (Chapel Hill: University of North Carolina Press, 1990), 237–45. Doyle's book provides an insightful understanding of Charleston society after the Civil War.

16. Most notably in Wells's *Sketch of the Charleston Light Dragoons,* esp. 1–7.

1. Origins in Privilege

1. *City Gazette* (Charleston, S.C.), July 10, 1792; Wells, *Sketch of the Charleston Light Dragoons,* 5; Revised Constitution, January 8, 1844, Charleston Light Dragoons Records, 1835–1948, 11/510, SCHS. According to Wells, the unit traced its origins to the Charleston Horse Guards, which was founded in 1733.

2. Wells, *Sketch of the Charleston Light Dragoons,* 5–7.

3. Rogers, *Charleston in the Age of the Pinckneys,* 3.

4. Wood, *Black Majority,* 144. For more on lowcountry slavery, see Robert Olwell, *Masters, Slaves and Subjects: The Culture of Power in the South Carolina Low Country, 1740–1790* (Ithaca: Cornell University Press, 1998); and Philip D. Morgan, *Slave Counterpoint: Black Culture in the Eighteenth Century Chesapeake and Lowcountry* (Chapel Hill: Published by the Omohundro Institute of Early American History and Culture, Williamsburg, Va., by the University of North Carolina Press, 1998).

5. Rogers, *Charleston in the Age of the Pinckeys,* 11–15. For more on the concept of "gentlemen-planters," see Maurie D. McInnis, *In Pursuit of Refinement: Charlestonians Abroad, 1740–1860* (Columbia: University of South Carolina Press, 1999). For more on the development of a planter class in the South Carolina lowcountry, see Jack P. Greene, Rosemary Brana-Shute, and Randy J. Sparks, eds., *Money, Trade, and Power: The Evolution of Colonial South Carolina's Plantation Society* (Columbia: University of South Carolina Press, 2001).

6. Rogers, *Charleston in the Age of the Pinckeys,* 23; Scarborough, *Masters of the Big House,* 24.

7. Nell S. Graydon, *Tales of Edisto* (Columbia, S.C.: R. L. Bryan, 1955).

8. Lawrence S. Rowland, Alexander Moore, and George Rogers Jr., *The History of Beaufort County, South Carolina,* vol. 1, *1514–1861* (Columbia: University of South Carolina Press, 1996), 277, 313–14.

9. J. H. Easterby, ed., *The South Carolina Rice Plantation as Revealed in the Papers of Robert F. W. Allston* (Chicago: University of Chicago Press, 1945), 7.

10. George C. Rogers Jr., *The History of Georgetown County, South Carolina* (Columbia: University of South Carolina Press, 1970), 269.

11. Ibid.

12. Peter A. Coclanis, *The Shadow of a Dream: Economic Life and Death in the South Carolina Lowcountry, 1670–1920* (New York: Oxford University Press, 1989), 111, 115, 120.

13. Ibid., 135.

14. Ibid., 121, 127.

15. William W. Freehling, *The Road to Disunion*, vol. 1, *Secessionists at Bay* (Oxford: Oxford University Press, 1990), 217–19, 224–25. Freehling contends that "Charleston epitomized waning upper-class wealth."

16. In a letter to Alfred Huger, Charles Manigault commented that he had seen between forty and fifty plantations sold by established families because they had not been prudent in the management of their holdings. Manigault obviously found this idea appalling, being from a prominent French Huguenot family (as was Huger) that arrived in the lowcountry in the late seventeenth century. Charles I. Manigault to Alfred Huger, April 1, 1847, Charles Izard Manigault Family Papers, 1807–ca. 1869, SCHS.

17. Wood, *Black Majority*, 144.

18. United States Bureau of the Census, *Fifth Census of the United States (South Carolina), 1830* (Washington, D.C.: Government Printing Office, 1835), 94–95.

19. Sally E. Hadden, *Slave Patrols: Law and Violence in Virginia and the Carolinas* (Cambridge, Mass.: Harvard University Press, 2001), 145–48; and David P. Geggus, ed., *The Impact of the Haitian Revolution in the Atlantic World* (Columbia: University of South Carolina Press, 2002), 232. For more on the Denmark Vesey slave revolt, see Douglas R. Egerton, *He Shall Go Out Free: The Lives of Denmark Vesey* (Madison, Wis.: Madison House, 1999); and David Robertson, *Denmark Vesey* (New York: Alfred A. Knopf, 1999). There has been a heated debate over the past few years regarding Vesey and whether a slave conspiracy actually existed. For more information on this controversy, see Michael P. Johnson, "Denmark Vesey and His Co-Conspirators," *William and Mary Quarterly* 58 (October 2001): 915–76; Johnson, "Reading Evidence," *William and Mary Quarterly* 59 (January 2002): 201; "Forum: The Making of a Slave Conspiracy, Part 2," *William and Mary Quarterly* 59 (January 2002): 135–202; and Robert L. Paquette and Douglas R. Egerton, "Of Facts and Fables: New Light on the Denmark Vesey Affair," *South Carolina Historical Magazine* (hereafter *SCHM*) 105 (January 2004): 18–35. For more on the Nat Turner Rebellion, see Stephen B. Oates, *The Fires of Jubilee: Nat Turner's Fierce Rebellion* (New York: HarperPerennial, 1990).

20. *State Papers on Nullification. . . .* (Boston: Dutton and Wentworth, 1834), 28–33.

21. Freehling, *Road to Disunion*, 279–86.

22. Jean Martin Flynn, "South Carolina's Compliance with the Militia Act of 1792," *SCHM* 69 (January 1968): 27, 29.

23. Jean Martin Flynn, *The Militia in Antebellum South Carolina Society* (Spartanburg, S.C.: Reprint Company, 1991), 62–63, 69.

24. Section 9 of the state's 1794 Militia Act dictated that each company would muster twice a year. Companies in Charleston, Camden, and Georgetown, however, were required to train every month. The areas around these cities had large concentrations of slaves, so extra musters would provide local militia units more training time while perhaps deterring slave plots. Flynn, "South Carolina's Compliance with the Militia Act," 37.

25. Ibid., 39. The cost of joining these outfits contributed to their elitism. Members not only had to provide their own equipment, as in line units, but they also had to buy their own uniforms, which could be quite elaborate and expensive (uniforms of Charleston militia units ranged as high as $50 in 1849, or $1,119 in 2000 dollars). Report from the Adjutant General, 1849, South Carolina Department of Archives and History, Columbia, S.C. (hereafter SCDAH).

26. Michael Stauffer, "Volunteer or Uniformed Companies in Antebellum Militia: A Checklist of Identified Companies, 1790–1859," *South Carolina Historical Magazine* 88 (April 1987): 112–13.

27. Ibid., 112.

28. Revised Constitution, Charleston Light Dragoons Records, SCHS.

29. Records of the General Assembly, Petitions, 1831, No. 170, SCDAH.

30. John Hope Franklin, *The Militant South, 1800–1861* (Cambridge, Mass.: Harvard University Press, 1956), 73, 178; Hadden, *Slave Patrols,* 19–21.

31. *Charleston Mercury,* February 23, 1853.

32. Meeting Minutes, February 6, 1854, Charleston Light Dragoons Records, SCHS; Flynn, *Militia in Antebellum South Carolina,* 17.

33. Meeting Minutes, February 20, 1854, Charleston Light Dragoons Records, SCHS. Thirty-eight members signed the petition.

34. *Charleston Daily Courier,* March 18, 1854.

35. Meeting Minutes, March 6, 1854, Charleston Light Dragoons Records, SCHS.

36. Meeting Minutes, January 9, 1854, Charleston Light Dragoons Records, SCHS; Thomas Cooper and David J. McCord, eds., *The Statutes at Large of South Carolina,* 26 vols. (Columbia, S.C.: A. S. Johnston, 1836–1876), 8:492; Flynn, *Militia in Antebellum South Carolina,* 108.

37. Revised Constitution, Charleston Light Dragoons Records, SCHS.

38. Specialists included a saddler, a farrier (a person who shoes horses), and a trumpeter. Flynn, "South Carolina's Compliance with the Militia Act," 28.

39. Revised Constitution, Charleston Light Dragoon Records, SCHS.

40. Chalmers Gaston Davidson, *The Last Foray; The South Carolina Planters of 1860: A Sociological Study* (Columbia: Published for the South Carolina Tricentennial Commission by the University of South Carolina Press, 1970), 83–109, esp. 85.

41. The best source of information regarding the Middleton families and Benjamin H. Rutledge are found at the South Carolina Historical Society See, in particular, the Harriott K. Middleton Family Correspondence, the Oliver Hering Middleton Family Correspondence, and the Benjamin Huger Rutledge Letterbook. See also Richard N. Cote, *Mary's World: Love, War, and Family Ties in Nineteenth-Century Charleston* (Charleston, S.C.: Corinthian Books, 2000), 114–19.

42. Cote, *Mary's World,* 118.

43. Rogers, *Charleston in the Age of the Pinckneys,* 23; William W. Freehling, *Prelude to Civil War: The Nullification Controversy in South Carolina, 1816–1836* (New York: Harper & Row, 1965), 11–17.

44. Jospeh Bell Hyde, *Union Kilwinning Lodge, No. 4, Ancient Free Masons of South Carolina* (Charleston, S.C., 1930); *Proceedings of the Most Worshipful Grand Lodge of Ancient Freemasons of South Carolina at the Annual Communication, November 5859* (Charleston, S.C.: A. J. Burke, 1859), 57–58. Other Civil War veterans of the dragoons, like Edward L. Wells and Lawrence W. O'Hear, would join Union Kilwinning No. 4 after the war.

45. *Proceedings of the Grand Lodge of South Carolina, November 5859,* 103–4.

46. *The Charleston Club, Chartered 1852,* 367–1938, pp. 8–10, 30–41, SCHS.

47. Ibid.; C. Vann Woodward, ed., *Mary Chesnut's Civil War* (New Haven, Conn.: Yale University Press, 1981), 5. Kirkland married Chesnut's first cousin, Mary Miles Withers.

48. St. Cecilia Society Records, 11/554/1, SCHS.

49. Ibid.; *South Carolina Genealogies: Articles from the South Carolina Historical (and Genealogical) Magazine,* 5 vols. (Spartanburg, S.C.: Reprint Company, 1983), 3:341.

50. List of Members Joining the Organization, Charleston Light Dragoons Records, SCHS.

51. Revised Constitution, Charleston Light Dragoon Records, SCHS. For the conversion of this and other monetary amounts in this book into their 2000 equivalents, I have used John J. McCusker, *How Much Is That in Real Money? A Historical Commodity Price Index for Use as a Deflator of Money Values in the Economy of the United States,* 2nd ed., rev. and enlarged (Worcester, Mass.: American Antiquarian Society, 2001), 55, 59.

52. Meeting Minutes, August 5, 1839, November 1, 1839, December 20, 1839, and February 13, 1840, Charleston Light Dragoons Records, SCHS.

53. Meeting Minutes, April 14, 1840, Charleston Light Dragoons Records, SCHS.

54. Meeting Minutes, Charleston Light Dragoons Records, SCHS 1835–1861. Those members removed from the unit roles averaged five years of service prior to their expulsion. The company expected former members to return their uniforms and equipment to the troop when they resigned or were expelled. Furthermore, the troop passed a resolution that allowed it to collect uniforms from previous members by purchasing them at a fair price. This committee was also required to report at each meeting on its activities. In one report the committee reported that it had purchased two uniforms at $35 ($720 in 2000 dollars) each, and collected three sets of pistols, holsters, and sabers valued at $70 ($1440) combined. These were sold to members or nonmembers. The uniforms could also have been sold to new members or given to unit musicians.

55. Ibid.

56. Ibid. The phrases "rule suspended," "laid over," "redrawn," and "notice repealed" appear in the result column of the list of "Members notified according to

Article 6th" regarding delinquent dues or fees. The unit's treasurer, therefore, was unwilling to suspend certain members based on their individual circumstances, while expelling other members who owed money in dues and fees.

57. *Charleston Directory and Stranger's Guide for 1840 and 1841 . . .* (Charleston, S.C.: T. C. Fay, 1840), 105.

58. List of Members Joining the Organization, Charleston Light Dragoon Records, SCHS. Prior to expulsion or resignation the unit had to clear a member's account. The troop would send a member to collect his outstanding dues or fines first. If he were unsuccessful, the troop would enlist an attorney to take legal action against the member for the amount due. Upon the payment of outstanding fees, the individual was removed from the unit roster.

59. An example of this is listed in the unit meeting minutes for February 6, 1854. In that record the secretary-treasurer recorded the comment "Lieut. Ryan, 1st Young —a dragoon—all well," meaning that Lieutenant Ryan had missed a meeting for the birth of his first child, a boy, and the mother and child were doing well. In many cases, members resigned immediately after a life-changing event like marriage or parenthood as a gesture that they were acquiescing to their newfound responsibilities. Meeting Minutes, February 6, 1854, Charleston Light Dragoons Records, SCHS.

60. Ibid.; Junior League of Charleston, *Charleston Receipts* (Charleston, S.C.: Wimmer Brothers, 1950), 14.

61. List of Difficulties, Charleston Light Dragoons Records, SCHS. In consecutive entries the difficulties denote "paid in Champagne" and "drank in Champagne." This last punishment appears on numerous occasions.

62. Ibid.

63. Ibid.; Meeting Minutes, March 6, 1854, Charleston Light Dragoons Records, SCHS. The "List of Difficulties" does not include all mishaps suffered by unit members. During Governor Manning's inspection visit to Charleston in 1853, the *Charleston Mercury* records that one member of the troop, H. C. Tobias, was thrown from his horse and knocked unconscious for several hours. This incident does not appear on the unit's list, perhaps for some extenuating circumstances or perhaps not to further the member's embarrassment. *Charleston Mercury,* February 23, 1853.

64. Revised Constitution, Charleston Light Dragoons Records, SCHS.

65. The business and social relationships between planters and factors in nineteenth-century Charleston are not topics that have received much attention from historians. The best sources remain work done on the Allston Family Papers at the South Carolina Historical Society by J. H. Easterby. See Easterby, "The South Carolina Rice Factor as Revealed in the Papers of Robert F. W. Allston," *Journal of Southern History* 7 (May 1941): 160–72; and Easterby, ed., *South Carolina Rice Plantation in the Papers of Robert F. W. Allston.*

66. Easterby, "South Carolina Rice Factor," 166–67.

67. Charles Kershaw to Charlotte Ann Allston, March 12, 1818, Allston Family Papers, SCHS.

68. National Archives, War Department Collection of Confederate Records, RG 109, Compiled Service Records of Confederate Soldiers Who Served in Organizations

from the State of South Carolina (hereafter Compiled Service Records), microcopy 267, 4th South Carolina Cavalry, rolls 24–30; Janet B. Hewett, *South Carolina Confederate Soldiers, 1861–1865*, vol 2, *Unit Roster* (Wilmington, N.C.: Broadfoot Publishing, 1998), 35–36; *Directory of the City of Charleston. . . . 1860. Vol. 1.* (Charleston, S.C.: W. Eugene Ferslew, 1860), microfilm 291, pp. 33–145, SCHS.

69. National Archives, Compiled Service Records, microcopy 267, 4th South Carolina Cavalry, rolls 24–30; Hewitt, *South Carolina Confederate Soldiers*, 35–36; *Directory of the City of Charleston*, microfilm 291, pp. 33–145

70. William H. Pease and Jane H. Pease, *The Web of Progress: Private Values and Public Styles in Boston and Charleston, 1828–1843* (New York: Oxford University Press, 1985), 14–15.

71. In sharp contrast to these planters were men who had traveled outside the South and the country prior to joining the dragoons. Many planters took at least one "grand tour" of Europe, but John Julius Izard Pringle, father of three dragoons, and others lived there for extended periods prior to the war.

72. Davidson, *Last Foray,* 170–267.

73. National Archives, Compiled Service Records, microcopy 267, 4th South Carolina Cavalry, rolls 24–30; Hewett, *South Carolina Confederate Soldiers*, 2:35–36; *Directory of the City of Charleston 1860;* Davidson, *Last Foray,* 170–267; United States Bureau of the Census, *Eighth Census of the United States (South Carolina), 1860,* Beaufort, Charleston, Colleton, Georgetown, Richland, and Sumter Districts; *South Carolina Genealogies,* vols. 1–3.

74. Hewett, *South Carolina Confederate Soldiers*, 2:35; *Eighth Census, 1860,* Richland District, 92; Laura Jervey Hopkins, *Lower Richland Planters: Hopkins, Adams, Weston and Related Families of South Carolina* (Columbia, S.C.: R. L. Bryan, 1976), 307. James U. Adams listed his assets as $125,000 ($2.57 million in 2000) in real estate and $340,000 ($7 million) in personal property in the 1860 census.

75. Hewett, *South Carolina Confederate Soldiers*, 2:35; *Eighth Census, 1860,* Beaufort District, 97; Davidson, *Last Foray,* 179. The elder Walter Blake listed $100,000 ($2.06 million) in real estate and $200,000 ($4.12 million) in personal property on the census. The elder Blake had managed 545 slaves for his father, Joseph Blake, and 75 in his own name. The younger Blake resided at his father's Bonny Hall Plantation on the Combahee River in Beaufort District.

76. National Archives, Compiled Service Records, microcopy 267, 4th South Carolina Cavalry, roll 24; Hewett, *South Carolina Confederate Soldiers*, 2:35; *Eighth Census, 1860,* Beaufort District, 25; Davidson, *Last Foray,* 194. Charles C. DuPont listed his holdings in the 1860 census as $45,000 ($926,550) in real estate and $160,000 ($3.29 million) in personal property. He owned 181 slaves at Hap Hazard Plantation near Grahamville. Theodore lived nearby at his own plantation, where he listed his worth in 1860 as $9,000 ($185,310) in real estate and $43,000 ($885,370) in personal property.

77. Hewett, *South Carolina Confederate Soldiers*, 2:35; *Eighth Census, 1860,* Colleton District, 312; Davidson, *Last Foray,* 182. Andrew William Burnet owned 176 slaves at his plantation in St. Bartholomew's Parish, Colleton District.

78. Hewett, *South Carolina Confederate Soldiers*, 2:35–36; *Eighth Census, 1860*, Charleston District, 120; Davidson, *Last Foray*, 178. Bell owned real estate valued at $25,000 ($515,750) and personal property valued at $117,000 ($2.41 million), most of it in the 160 slaves that he owned at his plantation in St. James Parish, Goose Creek, Charleston District.

79. National Archives, Compiled Service Records, microcopy 267, 4th South Carolina Cavalry, roll 26; Hewett, *South Carolina Confederate Soldiers*, 2:35; *Eighth Census, 1860*, Beaufort District, 1; Davidson, *Last Foray*, 195. William Elliott owned Oak Lawn Plantation on the Edisto River, Farniente at Flat Rock, North Carolina, and a home in Beaufort. He also owned 216 slaves in Colleton and Beaufort Districts.

80. National Archives, Compiled Service Records, microcopy 267, 4th South Carolina Cavalry, roll 26; Hewett, *South Carolina Confederate Soldiers*, 2:36; *Eighth Census, 1860*, Georgetown District, 315; Davidson, *Last Foray*, 228. William Rivers was worth $50,000 ($1.03 million) in real estate and $70,000 ($1.44 million) in personal property, much of which was invested in 125 slaves in Prince George, Winyah Parish, in Georgetown District.

81. Hewett, *South Carolina Confederate Soldiers*, 2:35–36; *Eighth Census, 1860*, Charleston District, 230; *Directory of the City of Charleston 1860*, 121.

82. *Directory of the City of Charleston 1860*, 121; *Eighth Census, 1860*, Colleton District, 331. R. S. Bedon claimed $14,600 ($300,614) in real estate and $54,000 ($1.11 million) in personal property.

83. Hewett, *South Carolina Confederate Soldiers*, 2:35–36; *Directory of the City of Charleston 1860*. Only a few of the dragoons were involved in other professional pursuits. Sergeant E. C. Holland and A. C. Wagner were both wharfingers (owners or operators of wharves), and Alex Robertson was an assistant harbor master.

84. Hewett, *South Carolina Confederate Soldiers*, 2:35–36; *Eighth Census, 1860*, Charleston District, 230; *Directory of the City of Charleston 1860*, 121; *Cyclopedia of Eminent and Representative Men of the Carolinas*, vol. 1, *South Carolina* (Madison, Wis.: Brant & Fuller, 1892), 148–50.

85. Jervey, *Lower Richland Planters*, 193.

86. *South Carolina Genealogies*, 3:143–44.

2. Service and Change

1. James M. McPherson, *Battle Cry of Freedom: The Civil War Era* (New York: Oxford University Press, 1988), 213–33; Walter Edgar, *South Carolina: A History* (Columbia: University of South Carolina Press, 1998), 351.

2. Edgar, *South Carolina: A History*, 351–53. The convention adjourned to Charleston because the city was more amenable to secession.

3. Charles H. Lesser, *Relic of the Lost Cause: The Story of South Carolina's Ordinance of Secession* (Columbia: South Carolina Department of Archives and History, 1990), 8–9; *Charleston Mercury*, December 21, 1860; *Charleston Daily Courier*, December 21, 1860.

4. *Charleston Mercury*, December 22, 1860; *Charleston Daily Courier*, December 22, 1860.

5. Cooper and McCord, *Statutes at Large,* 12:726–32. One surprising stipulation in the legislation was that the governor could draft men from militia units to form volunteer units if existing militia units were unable to fill vacancies in their own ranks as stipulated in the statute.

6. List of Members Joining the Organization, Charleston Light Dragoons Records, SCHS.

7. Stephen Z. Starr, *The Union Cavalry in the Civil War,* vol. 1, *From Fort Sumter to Gettysburg, 1861–1863* (Baton Rouge: Louisiana State University Press, 1979), xi, 90.

8. *Charleston Mercury,* December 27, 1860; *Charleston Daily Courier,* December 27, 1860.

9. McPherson, *Battle Cry of Freedom,* 266; Edgar, *South Carolina: A History,* 357–58.

10. *War of the Rebellion: The Official Records of the Union and Confederate Armies* (Washington, D.C.: Government Printing Office, 1880–1909) (hereafter *Official Records*) Series I, 1:35–37; Maury Klein, *Days of Defiance: Sumter, Secession, and the Coming of the Civil War* (New York: Alfred A. Knopf, 1997), 408–18; Wells, *Sketch of the Charleston Light Dragoons,* 7.

11. Col. L. B. Northrop to Hon. L. P. Walker, August 10, 1861, National Archives, War Department Collection of Confederate Records, RG 109, Letters Received by the Confederate Secretary of War (hereafter Secretary of War Letters), microcopy 437, 3129–1861, 136–G-1863, rolls 6 and 93.

12. John F. Marszalek, ed., *The Diary of Miss Emma Holmes, 1861–1866* (Baton Rouge: Louisiana State University Press, 1979), 69–70; *Charleston Mercury,* July 27, 1861.

13. Marszalek, *Diary of Miss Emma Holmes,* 89; *Charleston Mercury,* September 14, 1861.

14. Gabriel Edward Manigault Autobiography, unpublished typescript, South Caroliniana Library (hereafter SCL), University of South Carolina, Columbia, p. 296.

15. Rowland, Moore, and Rogers, *History of Beaufort County,* 1:448; Wells, *A Sketch of the Charleston Light Dragoons,* 7.

16. Rowland, Moore, and Rogers, *History of Beaufort County,* 1:448–50.

17. Ibid., 448–55; Richard B. McCaslin, *Portraits of Conflict: A Photographic History of South Carolina in the Civil War* (Fayetteville: University of Arkansas Press, 1994), 127; *Confederate Military History: Extended Edition,* 17 vols. (Wilmington, N.C.: Broadfoot Publishing, 1987) 6:469–70.

18. *Confederate Military History,* 6:448–55.

19. Ibid., 6:455–56; N. B. De Saussure, *Old Plantation Days: Being Recollections of Southern Life before the Civil War* (New York: Duffield, 1909), 6–68; Mary Elizabeth Massey, *Refugee Life in the Confederacy* (Baton Rouge: Louisiana State University Press, 1964), 13, 80–83.

20. Davidson, *Last Foray,* 170–267; Hewett, *South Carolina Confederate Soldiers,* 2:36; *Eighth Census, 1860,* Beaufort District, 1, 17, 21, 23–25, 70, 74, 95, 97–98; Rowland, Moore, and Rogers, *History of Beaufort County,* 1:444, 450, 454, 456.

21. F. K. Middleton to Mrs. H. A. Middleton, November 16, 1861, Harriott K. Middleton Family Correspondence, SCHS; F. K. Middleton to Harriott Middleton, November 24, 1861, Harriott K. Middleton Family Correspondence, SCHS; Wells, *Sketch of the Charleston Light Dragoons,* 7–9.

22. Gabriel Edward Manigault Autobiography, SCL, 298; *Official Records,* Series I, 6:322–23.

23. Gabriel Edward Manigault Autobiography, SCL, 292–93, 295–97.

24. Ibid., 301.

25. Ibid.

26. Ibid., 303.

27. Ibid., 300, 307.

28. Susan M. Middleton to Harriott Middleton, June 26, 1863, and July 13, 1863, Harriott Middleton Family Papers, 1168.02.08, SCHS.

29. Ibid.

30. Gabriel Edward Manigault Autobiography, SCL, 300.

31. F. K. Middleton to Harriott Middleton, November, 24, 1861, Harriott K. Middleton Family Correspondence, SCHS.

32. Linderman, *Embattled Courage,* 84–85.

33. George C. Rable, *Civil Wars: Women and the Crisis of Southern Nationalism* (Urbana: University of Illinois Press, 1989), 57; Harriott Middleton to Susan M. Middleton, February 6, 1862, Harriott Middleton Family Papers, 1168.02.08, SCHS.

34. Wells, *Sketch of the Charleston Light Dragoons,* 22; Starr, *Union Cavalry in the Civil War,* 213.

35. F. K. Middleton to Harriott Middleton, November 24, 1861, Harriott K. Middleton Family Correspondence, SCHS.

36. Wells, *Sketch of the Charleston Light Dragoons,* 22.

37. Gabriel Edward Manigault Autobiography, SCL, 339; Starr, *Union Cavalry in the Civil War,* 212.

38. F. K. Middleton to Harriott Middleton, May 21, 1861, Harriott K. Middleton Family Correspondence, SCHS.

39. List of Difficulties, Charleston Light Dragoons Records, SCHS.

40. Gabriel Edward Manigault Autobiography, SCL, 305; F. K. Middleton to Harriott Middleton, May 21, 1861, Harriott K. Middleton Family Correspondence, SCHS.

41. Wells, *Sketch of the Charleston Light Dragoons,* 8; National Archives, Compiled Service Records, microcopy 267, Capt. Rutledge's Company, Cavalry Militia, roll 55.

42. Ibid.; Ervin L. Jordan Jr., *Black Confederates and Afro-Yankees in Civil War Virginia* (Charlottesville: University Press of Virginia, 1995), 185–86.

43. F. K. Middleton to Mrs. H. A. Middleton, November 16, 1861, Harriott K. Middleton Family Correspondence, SCHS.

44. F. K. Middleton to Mrs. H. A. Middleton, November 26, 1861, Harriott K. Middleton Family Correspondence, SCHS; F. K. Middleton to Mrs. C. M. Cheves, November 29, 1861, Harriott K. Middleton Family Correspondence, SCHS.

45. F. K. Middleton to Mrs. C. M. Cheves, December 29, 1861, Harriott K. Middleton Family Correspondence, SCHS.

46. Daniel E. Huger Smith, Alice R. Huger Smith, and Arney R. Childs, *Mason Smith Family Letters* (Columbia: University of South Carolina Press, 1950), 78.

47. Wells, *Sketch of the Charleston Light Dragoons,* 8.

48. F. K. Middleton to Harriott Middleton, August 15, 1863, Harriott K. Middleton Family Correspondence, SCHS.

49. Gabriel Edward Manigault Autobiography, SCL, 304.

50. F. K. Middleton to Harriott Middleton, August 10, 1862, Harriott K. Middleton Family Correspondence, SCHS.

51. O. H. Middleton Jr. to Mrs. O. H. Middleton Sr., January 15, 1864, Oliver Hering Middleton Family Correspondence, SCHS.

52. F. K. Middleton to Harriott Middleton, August 10, 1862, Harriott K. Middleton Family Correspondence, SCHS.

53. F. K. Middleton to Mrs. H. A. Middleton, February 22, 1863, Harriott K. Middleton Family Correspondence, SCHS.

54. Gabriel Edward Manigault Autobiography, SCL, 301–2.

55. F. K. Middleton to Harriott Middleton, November 24, 1861, Harriott K. Middleton Family Correspondence, SCHS.

56. F. K. Middleton to Mrs. H. A. Middleton, January 7, 1862, Harriott K. Middleton Family Correspondence, SCHS.

57. Jordan, *Black Confederates and Afro-Yankees,* 187.

58. F. K. Middleton to Harriott Middleton, August 10, 1863, Harriott K. Middleton Family Correspondence, SCHS.

59. Jordan, *Black Confederates and Afro-Yankees,* 186.

60. Gabriel Edward Manigault Autobiography, SCL, 304; F. K. Middleton to Harriott Middleton, December 28, 1861, Harriott K. Middleton Family Correspondence, SCHS.

61. Gabriel Edward Manigault Autobiography, SCL, 308; F. K. Middleton to Mrs. H. A. Middleton, February 22, 1863, Harriott K. Middleton Family Correspondence, SCHS.

62. Gabriel Edward Manigault Autobiography, SCL, 308; F. K. Middleton to Mrs. H. A. Middleton, February 22, 1863, Harriott K. Middleton Family Correspondence, SCHS.

63. *"Your Servant, Quash": Letters of a South Carolina Freedman* (Columbia, S.C.: Chicora Foundation, 1994), 4–13. For more information on Quash Stevens, see the Arnoldus Vanderhorst Papers, 12/312/15, SCHS.

64. Gabriel Edward Manigault Autobiography, SCL, 304.

65. Jordan, *Black Confederates and Afro-Yankees,* 186, 187; F. K. Middleton to Harriott Middleton, August 10, 1862, Harriott K. Middleton Family Correspondence, SCHS.

66. Gabriel Edward Manigault Autobiography, SCL, 304.

67. Wells, *Sketch of the Charleston Light Dragoons,* 8.

68. National Archives, Compiled Service Records, microcopy 267, Capt. Rutledge's Company, Cavalry Militia, roll 55.

69. Ibid.

70. *Official Records,* Series I, 6:350.

71. *Charleston Daily Courier,* January 6, 1862.

72. Cooper and McCord, *Statutes at Large,* 12:730–32, 13:63–64.

73. F. K. Middleton to Harriott Middleton, December 28, 1861, Harriott K. Middleton Family Correspondence, SCHS. Middleton relates the events of the meetings occurring between Lee and Rutledge in a letter to his sister. Whether they occurred as related is not known, since no official account of the meetings exists. There was evidently confusion in the unit regarding the terms of service, since Middleton seemed to think that the unit was eligible to volunteer for one year of service, an option that no longer existed after the passage of the most recent legislation.

74. F. K. Middleton to Mrs. H. A. Middleton, November 16, 1861, Harriott K. Middleton Family Correspondence, SCHS; F. K. Middleton to Harriott Middleton, November 24, 1861, Harriott K. Middleton Family Correspondence, SCHS; F. K. Middleton to Mrs. C. M. Cheves, November 29, 1861, Harriott K. Middleton Family Correspondence, SCHS; Wells, *Sketch of the Charleston Light Dragoons,* 7.

75. National Archives, Compiled Service Records, microcopy 267, Capt. Rutledge's Company, Cavalry Militia, roll 55.

76. *Charleston Daily Courier,* February 17, 1862.

77. Susan M. Middleton to Harriott Middleton, March 2, 1862, Harriott Middleton Family Papers, 1168.02.08, SCHS.

78. Susan M. Middleton to Harriott Middleton, March 10, 1862, Harriott Middleton Family Papers, 1168.02.08, SCHS.

79. National Archives, Compiled Service Records, microcopy 267, 4th South Carolina Cavalry, roll 24; Wells, *Sketch of the Charleston Light Dragoons,* 11–13.

80. Wells, *Sketch of the Charleston Light Dragoons,* 8.

81. Gabriel Edward Manigault Autobiography, SCL, 298, 301. The delays resulting from the dragoons' election of new members and officers lend credence to David Donald's argument that the South "died of democracy." See Donald, ed. *Why the North Won the Civil War* (Baton Rouge: Louisiana State University Press, 1960), 79–80.

82. James W. Matthews, ed., *The Statutes at Large of the Confederate States of America . . . First Session . . . First Congress* (Richmond, Va., 1862), 29.

83. The Middleton's oldest son, Cleland, was committed to an asylum prior to the war. *South Carolina Genealogies,* 3:258; Susan M. Middleton to Harriott Middleton, July 26, 1861, Harriott Middleton Family Papers, 1168.02.08, SCHS; Elizabeth W. Allston Pringle Diary, July 24, 25, 26, 31, 1861, Elizabeth W. Allston Pringle Family Papers, SCHS.

84. Susan M. Middleton to Harriott Middleton, July 26, 1861, Harriott Middleton Family Papers, 1168.02.08, SCHS.

85. Harriott Middleton to Susan M. Middleton, January 21, 1862, Harriott Middleton Family Papers, 1168.02.08, SCHS.

86. Harriott Middleton to Susan M. Middleton, February 6, 1862, Harriott Middleton Family Papers, 1168.02.08, SCHS.

87. *South Carolina Genealogies,* 3:258; Rable, *Civil Wars,* 57; Harriott Middleton to Susan M. Middleton, January 8, 1862, Harriott Middleton Family Papers, 1168.02.08, SCHS.

88. Susan M. Middleton to Harriott Middleton, September 3, 1861, and January 9, 1862, Harriott Middleton Family Papers, 1168.02.08, SCHS.

89. Harriott Middleton to Susan M. Middleton, January 21, 1862, Harriott Middleton Family Papers, 1168.02.08, SCHS.

90. Ibid.; Reid Mitchell, *The Vacant Chair: The Northern Soldier Leaves Home* (New York: Oxford University Press, 1993), 74–75.

91. Drew Gilpin Faust, *Mothers of Invention: Women of the Slaveholding South in the American Civil War* (Chapel Hill: University of North Carolina Press, 1996), 10. Therein, Faust notes that as war came to the South, Southern women attempted "to find a place for themselves in a culture increasingly preoccupied with the quintessentially male concerns of politics and battle" (10).

92. Susan M. Middleton to Harriott Middleton, August 6, 1861, Harriott Middleton Family Papers, 1168.02.08, SCHS; Faust, *Mothers of Invention,* 24–25.

93. Rable, *Civil Wars,* 54–56.

94. Susan M. Middleton to Harriott Midddleton, May 16, 1862, Harriott Middleton Family Papers, 1168.02.08, SCHS.

95. Faust, *Mothers of Invention,* 10.

96. Ibid., 238–44; Rable, *Civil Wars,* 72.

97. Faust, *Mothers of Inventions,* 59, 247.

98. *Charleston News and Courier,* February 16, 1881. This new company owned seven blockade-runners, which made over forty round trips into and out of Confederate ports supplying the government and individuals with rare goods.

99. William C. Bee to Valeria N. Bee, February 13, 1862, Bee-Chisolm Family Papers, SCHS.

100. William C. Bee to Valeria N. Bee, April 3, 1862, Bee-Chisolm Family Papers, SCHS.

101. H. A. Middleton to Mrs. H. A. Middleton, July 24, 1862, Henry A. Middleton Papers, SCHS; Rogers, *History of Georgetown County,* 317, 374, 427, 427n.

3. A Taste of War

1. John Harleston to R. E. Elliott, October 13, 1863, Elliott-Gonzalez Family Papers, Southern Historical Collection, University of North Carolina, Chapel Hill (hereafter SHC). In this letter, Harleston informs Elliott that he has been "elected" a member of the dragoons. Harleston, a lieutenant, lists himself as "Sec. C.L. Dragoons."

2. Hewett, *South Carolina Confederate Soldiers,* 2:36.

3. *South Carolina Genealogies,* 3:341. Several members of the Pringle family were either living in or visiting Europe at the war's outset in 1861.

4. Woodward, *Mary Chesnut's Civil War,* 386. A family friend in Philadelphia, Elizabeth Izard Middleton Fisher, cousin of Dragoon Frank Middleton, loaned money to the trio to make the journey through Union lines.

5. National Archives, Compiled Service Records, microcopy 267, 4th South Carolina Cavalry, roll 29. J. J. I. Pringle joined the dragoons in September 1862, followed by J. R. P. Pringle in February 1863 and Dominick Lynch Pringle in May 1864.

6. Woodward, *Mary Chesnut's Civil War,* 5. Kirkland married Chesnut's first cousin, Mary Miles Withers. Suzanne Cameron Linder, *Historical Atlas of the Rice Plantations of the ACE River Basin—1860* (Columbia: South Carolina Department of Archives and History Foundation, Ducks Unlimited, and the Nature Conservancy, 1995), 509–18.

7. Woodward, *Mary Chesnut's Civil War,* 5.

8. National Archives, Compiled Service Records, microcopy 267, 4th South Carolina Cavalry, roll 27; Stephen W. Sears, *Landscape Turned Red: The Battle of Antietam* (New York: Ticknor and Fields, 1983), 134; Woodward, *Mary Chesnut's Civil War,* 423; *Confederate Military History,* 6:710–11.

9. F. K. Middleton to Harriott Middleton, November 25, 1862, Harriott K. Middleton Family Correspondence, SCHS.

10. Frances Wallace Taylor, Catherine Taylor Matthews, and J. Tracy Power, eds., *The Leverett Letters: Correspondence of a South Carolina Family, 1851–1868* (Columbia: University of South Carolina Press, 2000), 315; National Archives, Compiled Service Records, microcopy 267, 4th South Carolina Cavalry, roll 27; *Eighth Census, 1860,* Colleton District, 331; Woodward, *Mary Chesnut's Civil War,* 766.

11. National Archives, Compiled Service Records, microcopy 267, 4th South Carolina Cavalry, roll 24; *Confederate Military History,* 8:474–75; "Wm. Bell, Co. K, 4th S.C. Cav.," August 25, 1913, p. 1, William Bell Alumni Undergraduate Records, Seeley G. Mudd Manuscript Library, Princeton University, Princeton, N.J.

12. Lt. Col. H. W. Fishburne to Capt. Ralph Elliott, March 16, 1861, Elliott-Gonzalez Family Papers, SHC; National Archives, Compiled Service Records, microcopy 267, 4th South Carolina Cavalry, roll 27; John Harleston to R. E. Elliott, Esq., October 13, 1863, Elliott-Gonzalez Family Papers, SHC.

13. John B. Irving, *A Day on Cooper River* (Columbia, S.C.: R. L. Bryan, 1969), 142; Marszalek, *Diary of Miss Emma Holmes,* 86; National Archives, Compiled Service Records, microcopy 267, 4th South Carolina Cavalry, roll 27.

14. Irving, *Day on Cooper River,* 142; National Archives, Compiled Service Records, microcopy 267, 4th South Carolina Cavalry, rolls 24–30.

15. National Archives, Compiled Service Records, microcopy 267, 4th South Carolina Cavalry, rolls 24–30.

16. Eric H. Walther, *The Fire-Eaters* (Baton Rouge: Louisiana State University Press, 1992), 270–96.

17. National Archives, Compiled Service Records, microcopy 267, 4th South Carolina Cavalry, rolls 24–30.

18. G. E. Manigault to William Porcher Miles, February 16, 1861; G. E. Manigault to W. H. Trescott, February 10, 1861; Thos. Middleton Jr. to William Porcher Miles, July 22, 1861; Arthur P. Lining to William Porcher Miles, April 17, 1862, William Porcher Miles Papers #508, Box 3, Folders 29–42, SHC.

19. National Archives, Compiled Service Records, microcopy 267, 4th South Carolina Cavalry, rolls 24–30.

20. Ibid.

21. Gabriel Edward Manigault Autobiography, SCL, 305.

22. *Official Records,* Series I, 14:20–27.

23. Gabriel Edward Manigault Autobiography, SCL, 306.

24. Ibid.; Lloyd Halliburton, *Saddle Soldiers: The Civil War Correspondence of General William Stokes of the 4th South Carolina Cavalry* (Orangeburg, S.C.: Sandlapper Publishing, 1993), 30–32; Wells, *Sketch of the Charleston Light Dragoons,* 13–14. The dragoons were armed with Colt army revolvers and sabers. *Charleston Daily Courier,* February 17, 1862.

25. Wells, *Sketch of the Charleston Light Dragoons,* 14.

26. Starr, *Union Cavalry in the Civil War,* 219–20; Bell Irvin Wiley, *The Life of Johnny Reb: The Common Soldier of the Confederacy* (New York: Bobbs Merrill, 1943), 296–97. For perhaps the most comprehensive assessment of cavalry tactics during the war, see Brent Nosworthy, *The Bloody Crucible of Courage: Fighting Methods and Combat Experience of the Civil War* (New York: Carol and Graf Publishers, 2003).

27. Nosworthy, *Bloody Crucible of Courage,* 286–87, 292.

28. Gabriel Edward Manigault Autobiography, SCL, 304.

29. Linderman, *Embattled Courage,* 15–16.

30. Halliburton, *Saddle Soldiers,* 53 (added emphasis). Hussars were units of light cavalry found in European armies and noted for their elaborate uniforms and élan. It is not clear why Rutledge used this designation, unless he was attempting to impress the letter's recipient. There is no record of the unit ever adopting the title.

31. National Archives, Compiled Service Records, microcopy 267, 4th South Carolina Cavalry, rolls 24–30.

32. Wiley, *Life of Johnny Reb,* 291–92.

33. Wells, *Sketch of the Charleston Light Dragoons,* 14.

34. F. K. Middleton to Harriott Middleton, August 10, 1862, Harriott K. Middleton Family Correspondence, SCHS.

35. Capt. B. H. Rutledge to Col. L. B. Northrop, September 3, 1862, National Archives, Secretary of War Letters, microcopy 437, 136-6-1863, roll 93.

36. Halliburton, *Saddle Soldiers,* 48.

37. Capt. B. H. Rutledge to Col. L. B. Northrop, September 3, 1862, National Archives, Secretary of War Letters, microcopy 437, 136-6-1863, roll 93.

38. Halliburton, *Saddle Soldiers,* 49, 53.

39. *Official Records,* Series, I, 14:643–44.

40. Halliburton, *Saddle Soldiers,* xi, 32, 41–42; *Directory of the City of Charleston 1860,* 43; *Eighth Census, 1860,* Charleston District, Ward 2, 232.

41. Halliburton, *Saddle Soldiers,* 32.

42. McCaslin, *Portraits of Conflict,* 195, 311; Dusinberre, *Them Dark Days,* 304; H. A. Middleton to Harriott Middleton, October 26, 1862, Harriott K. Middleton Family Correspondence, SCHS.

43. *Official Records,* Series I, 14:114–15, 13: 214.

44. Ibid., 14:145.

45. Ibid.

46. Ibid., 14:180–81.

47. Ibid., 14:145–46.

48. Ibid., 14:146–47, 150.

49. Ibid., 14:180–81.

50. F. K. Middleton to Harriott Middleton, October 24, 1862, Harriott K. Middleton Family Correspondence, SCHS; Wells, *Sketch of the Charleston Light Dragoons,* 16–17.

51. *Official Records,* Series I, 14:150.

52. Ibid., 151, 181; Wells, *Sketch of the Charleston Light Dragoons,* 16–17; F. K. Middleton to Harriott Middleton, October 24, 1862, Harriott K. Middleton Family Correspondence, SCHS.

53. Wells, *Sketch of the Charleston Light Dragoons,* 16–17; McPherson, *For Cause and Comrades,* 38.

54. McPherson, *For Cause and Comrades,* 151, 181; Wells, *Sketch of the Charleston Light Dragoons,* 16–17; F. K. Middleton to Harriott Middleton, October 24, 1862, Harriott K. Middleton Family Correspondence, SCHS.

55. F. K. Middleton to Harriott Middleton, October 24, 1862, Harriott K. Middleton Family Correspondence, SCHS.

56. *Official Records,* Series I, 14:181; F. K. Middleton to Harriott Middleton, October 24, 1862, Harriott K. Middleton Family Correspondence, SCHS.

57. Wells, *Sketch of the Charleston Light Dragoons,* 17; National Archives, Compiled Service Records, microcopy 267, 4th South Carolina Cavalry, rolls 24–29. Wells claims that Lt. Daniel P. Campbell, a recent Citadel graduate, was killed fighting alongside the Dragoons after borrowing a rifle from a horse holder. Both Charleston newspapers, the *Charleston Daily Courier* and the *Charleston Mercury,* claimed that Daniels, son of the Charleston City Treasurer, Archibald Campbell, had served with the Beaufort Volunteer Artillery. *Charleston Daily Courier,* October 24 and 25, 1862; *Charleston Mercury,* October 23, 25, and 27, 1862.

58. *Official Records,* Series I, 14:181; Wells, *Sketch of the Charleston Light Dragoons,* 18–19; F. K. Middleton to Harriott Middleton, October 24, 1862, Harriott K. Middleton Family Correspondence, SCHS.

59. *Official Records,* Series I, 14:181.

60. McPherson, *For Cause and Comrades,* 48–51.

61. Ibid., 182; F. K. Middleton to Harriott Middleton, October 24, 1862, Harriott K. Middleton Family Correspondence, SCHS.

62. McPherson, *For Cause and Comrades,* 38.

63. F. K. Middleton to Harriott Middleton, October 24, 1862, Harriott K. Middleton Family Correspondence, SCHS.

64. *Official Records,* Series I, 14:182; F. K. Middleton to Harriott Middleton, October 24, 1862, Harriott K. Middleton Family Correspondence, SCHS.

65. *Official Records,* Series I, 14:151–52.

66. Ibid., 14:181–87.

67. Ibid., 14:183; Wells, *Sketch of the Charleston Light Dragoons,* 19.

68. Linderman, *Embattled Courage,* 21–23; *Official Records,* Series I, 14:183; Wells, *Sketch of the Charleston Light Dragoons,* 19.

69. *Official Records,* Series I, 14:148, 180.

70. National Archives, Compiled Service Records, microcopy 267, 4th South Carolina Cavalry, rolls 27–30; Wells, *Sketch of the Charleston Light Dragoons*, 19. The Compiled Service Records do not authenticate Wells's assertion that Sgt. B. F. Huger and Lewis Vanderhorst received slight wounds during the engagement, although his estimate of unit casualties matches that in the *Official Records*. Wells later wrote of a dragoon (either Gabriel Manigault or E. C. Holland) being slightly wounded in the forehead, after which he began doing addition out loud to ensure that he had his faculties. Wells, *Sketch of the Charleston Light Dragoons*, 20.

71. Linderman, *Embattled Courage*, 30–31.

72. Terry Reimer, "Poisonous Techniques and Dressing," *North and South* 5, no. 1 (2001): 72–73.

73. National Archives, Compiled Service Records, microcopy 267, 4th South Carolina Cavalry, rolls 27–30.

74. Ibid., roll 29; Cote, *Mary's World*, 214–15, 228. *Mary's World* is a narrative genealogical study of one branch of the Pringle family. Cote's account of Pringle's service fails to record his family's efforts to acquire an appointment for him during April 1863.

75. Gabriel Edward Manigault Autobiography, SCL, 314.

76. F. K. Middleton to Mrs. H. A. Middleton, November 1, 1862, Harriott K. Middleton Family Correspondence, SCHS.

77. Ibid.

78. F. K. Middleton to Harriott Middleton, November 25, 1862, Harriott K. Middleton Family Correspondence, SCHS.

79. National Archives, Compiled Service Records, microcopy 267, 4th South Carolina Cavalry, roll 24. Several months would pass before the unit would be designated the 4th South Carolina Cavalry. Prior to that it was known simply as Rutledge's Regiment.

80. F. K. Middleton to Mrs. C. M. Cheves, January 6, 1863, Harriott K. Middleton Family Correspondence, SCHS. Middleton's impression of Emanuel was undoubtedly shaped by his father's experiences with him in Georgetown. The overt anti-Semitism of planters and dragoons toward Emanuel contradicts the assertions of Robert Rosen, whose book *The Jewish Confederates* (Columbia: University of South Carolina Press, 2000) argues that such attitudes were mostly a Northern phenomenon.

81. Dusinberre, *Them Dark Days*, 38–39.

82. Louis Manigault Scrapbook, box 1, p. 303, Louis Manigault Papers, 0177, SCHS; Gabriel Edward Manigault Autobiography, SCL, 315. Manigault lost the position because there was already a quartermaster in one of the regiment's battalions. Rutledge therefore offered to make him regimental adjutant, a position that Manigault occupied until Rutledge learned that regulations prevented the promotion because there was already an adjutant in one of the the the regiment's battalions.

83. *South Carolina Genealogies*, 3:248–49; Davidson, *Last Foray*, 230.

84. F. K. Middleton to Mrs. C. M. Cheves, January 6, 1863, Harriott K. Middleton Family Correspondence, SCHS; O. H. Middleton Jr. to O. H. Middleton, January 6,

1863, Oliver Hering Middleton Family Correspondence, SCHS; F. K. Middleton to Alicia Middleton, January 5, 1863, Harriott Middleton Family Papers, SCHS.

85. F. K. Middleton to Mrs. H. A. Middleton, February 22, 1863, Harriott K. Middleton Family Correspondence, SCHS; O. H. Middleton to O. H. Middleton Jr., February 9, 1863, Oliver Hering Middleton Family Correspondence, SCHS.

86. Wells, *Sketch of the Charleston Light Dragoons,* 9.

87. F. K. Middleton to Mrs. H. A. Middleton, February 22, 1863, Harriott K. Middleton Family Correspondence, SCHS.

88. Gabriel Edward Manigault Autobiography, SCL, 315, 317.

89. F. K. Middleton to Mrs. H. A. Middleton, May 10, 1863, Harriott K. Middleton Family Correspondence, SCHS.

90. Gabriel Edward Manigault Autobiography, SCL, 318.

91. F. K. Middleton to Mrs. H. A. Middleton, May 10, 1863, Harriott K. Middleton Family Correspondence, SCHS. A previous move had entailed borrowing two wagons from a local quartermaster to transport the unit's furniture to the railroad station. The unit's supplies included "tents, boxes, trunks, iron bedsteads, tables, chairs, and other things." Onlookers looked with amazement on the unit's extensive baggage as it was unloaded at their destination. Gabriel Edward Manigault Autobiography, SCL, 307.

92. Gabriel Edward Manigault Autobiography, SCL, 318.

93. "Reminiscences of the War and Reconstruction Times, ca. 1910," Thomas Pinckney Reminiscences, pp. 15–16, 34/0594, SCHS.

94. *Official Records,* Series I, 14:290–308. Walker was promoted to brigadier general soon after his victories at Pocotaligo and Coosawhatchie; Pinckney, "Reminiscences of the War," pp. 15–16, 34/0594, SCHS.

95. Pinckney, "Reminiscences of the War," p. 16, 34/0594, SCHS.

96. *Charleston Mercury,* June 3, 4, and 19, 1863.

97. F. K. Middleton to Mrs. C. M. Cheves, June 16, 1863, Harriott K. Middleton Family Correspondence, SCHS; O. H. Middleton Jr. to Mrs. O. H. Middleton Sr., June 4, 1862, Oliver Hering Middleton Family Correspondence, SCHS; Walter Lord, ed., *The Fremantle Diary: Being the Journal of Lieutenant Colonel James Arthur Lyon Fremantle, Coldstream Guards, on His Three Months in the Southern States* (Boston: Little, Brown, 1954), 158.

98. National Archives, Compiled Service Records, microcopy 267, 4th South Carolina Cavalry, roll 24; Halliburton, *Saddle Soldiers,* 92; F. K. Middleton to Mrs. C. M. Cheves, June 16, 1863, Harriott K. Middleton Family Correspondence, SCHS.

99. Halliburton, *Saddle Soldiers,* 89–92.

100. Ibid., 92; F. K. Middleton to Harriott Middleton, May 10, 1863, Harriott K. Middleton Family Correspondence, SCHS.

101. Halliburton, *Saddle Soldiers,* 93, 95.

102. E. Milby Burton, *The Siege of Charleston, 1861–1865* (Columbia: University of South Carolina Press, 1970), 151–54.

103. National Archives, Compiled Service Records, microcopy 267, 4th South Carolina Cavalry, roll 24; Gabriel Edward Manigault Autobiography, SCL, 328.

104. Wells, *Sketch of the Charleston Light Dragoons,* 24.

105. Ibid., 24–28; F. K. Middleton to Alicia Middleton, September 5, 1863, Harriott Middleton Family Papers, 0373, SCHS.

106. Wells, *Sketch of the Charleston Light Dragoons,* 23–28; F. K. Middleton to Alicia Middleton, September 5, 1863, Harriott Middleton Family Papers, 0373, SCHS.

107. John Harleston, "Battery Wagner on Morris Island," *South Carolina Historical Magazine* 57 (January 1956): 8–13. Wells, *Sketch of the Charleston Light Dragoons,* 23. The wounded dragoons included A. Burgess Gordon, W. H. Fairly, A. R. or Thomas Taylor, and Harleston.

108. C. P. Pelham, "The Last Days of Battery Wagner," *Columbia Daily Southern Guardian,* November 4, 1863.

109. Gabriel Edward Manigault Autobiography, SCL, 328; F. K. Middleton to Harriott Middleton, August 26, 1863, Harriott K. Middleton Family Correspondence, SCHS.

110. Gabriel Edward Manigault Autobiography, SCL, 328–29; Louis Manigault Scrapbook, box 1, p. 303, Louis Manigault Papers, 0177, SCHS.

111. Burton, *Siege of Charleston,* 251–60.

112. Ralph E. Elliott to Mrs. Anne H. Elliott, undated [late 1863], Elliott-Gonzalez Family Papers, SHC.

113. Gabriel Edward Manigault Autobiography, SCL, 335; Louis Manigault Scrapbook, box 1, p. 304, Louis Manigault Papers, SCHS.

114. Gabriel Edward Manigault Autobiography, SCL, 303, 334.

115. Ibid.

116. Ralph E. Elliott to Mrs. A. H. Elliott, undated [late 1863], December 8, 1863, and December 13, 1863, Elliott-Gonzalez Family Papers, SHC.

117. National Archives, Compiled Service Records, microcopy 267, 4th South Carolina Cavalry, roll 24.

118. O. H. Middleton Jr. to Mrs. O. H. Middleton Sr., June 24, 1863, Oliver Hering Middleton Family Correspondence, SCHS.

119. O. H. Middleton Jr. to Mrs. O. H. Middleton Sr., August 6, 1863, Oliver Hering Middleton Family Correspondence, SCHS.

120. Smith, Smith, and Childs, *Mason Smith Family Letters,* xxii–xxiii, 3–9.

121. Allen S. Izard to William Porcher Miles, April 29, 1861, William Porcher Miles Papers, SHC.

122. Smith, Smith, and Childs, *Mason Smith Family Letters,* 70.

123. O. H. Middleton Jr. to Susan M. Middleton, January 10, 1864, Oliver Hering Middleton Family Correspondence, SCHS; F. K. Middleton to Harriott Middleton, February 18, 1864, Harriott K. Middleton Family Correspondence, SCHS.

124. Smith, Smith, and Childs, *Mason Smith Family Letters,* 77–78.

125. *Official Records,* Series I, 14:290–308.

126. B. H. Rutledge to Barnwell Rhett, December 3, 1863, Benjamin Huger Rutledge Papers, 1863, Rare Book, Manuscript, and Special Collections Library, Duke University, Durham, N.C; *Official Records,* Series I, 18:745–46.

4. Cataclysm

1. *Year Book—1891. City of Charleston, So. Ca.* (Charleston, S.C.: Walker, Evans, and Cogswell, 1891), 143–53.

2. F. K. Middleton to Alicia Middleton, May 31, 1863, Harriott Middleton Family Papers, SCHS; *Official Records,* Series I, vol. 51, part II: 835–37; Special Orders No. 65, March 18, 1864, John Caldwell Calhoun Order Book, 1863–1864, SCL.

3. *Official Records,* Series IV, II:813–15.

4. B. H. Rutledge to M. C. Butler, undated, B. H. Rutledge Letterbook, 0142, pp. 304–5, SCHS.

5. Ibid. The 5th and 6th South Carolina Cavalry regiments faced a similar problem, but their response was different. The two regiments simply disregarded the order to reduce their numbers, claiming that the directive did not apply to units in the Army of Northern Virginia.

6. National Archives, Compiled Service Records, microcopy 267, 4th South Carolina Cavalry, rolls 24–30. Some dragoons were forced to leave the ranks. Capt. Richard H. Colcock claimed that he wanted to drop from the rolls those dragoons on permanent detail. Frank Middleton believed that Colcock used the reductions as a way to rid the unit of those with whom he had clashed. F. K. Middleton to Mrs. H. A. Middleton, March 10, 1864, Harriott K. Middleton Family Correspondence, SCHS.

7. Ralph E. Elliott to Mrs. A. H. Elliott, March 30, 1864, Elliott-Gonzalez Family Papers, SHC.

8. Gabriel Edward Manigault Autobiography, SCL, 344.

9. Mrs. O. H. Middleton Sr. to O. H. Middleton Jr., March 27, 1864, Oliver Hering Middleton Family Correspondence, SCHS; O. H. Middleton Jr. to Mrs. O. H. Middleton Sr., March 29, 1864, Oliver Hering Middleton Family Correspondence, SCHS.

10. B. H. Rutledge to O. H. Middleton Jr., March 26, 1864, Oliver Hering Middleton Family Correspondence, SCHS.

11. O. H. Middleton Jr. to B. H. Rutledge, March 31, 1864, Oliver Hering Middleton Family Correspondence, SCHS.

12. B. H. Rutledge to M. C. Butler, undated, B. H. Rutledge Letterbook, 305, SCHS.

13. Gabriel Edward Manigault Autobiography, SCL, 339.

14. O. H. Middleton Jr. to Mrs. O. H. Middleton Sr., March 21, 1864, Oliver Hering Middleton Family Correspondence, SCHS.

15. Mrs. O. H. Middleton Sr. to O. H. Middleton Jr., March 24, 1864, Oliver Hering Middleton Family Correspondence, SCHS.

16. Gabriel Edward Manigault Autobiography, SCL, 337.

17. Ibid., 340.

18. F. K. Middleton to Alicia Middleton, April 5, 1864, Harriott K. Middleton Family Correspondence, SCHS.

19. Gabriel Edward Manigault Autobiography, SCL, 342.

20. Ibid., 343.

21. Ibid., 344–46; Manly Wade Wellman, *Giant in Gray: A Biography of Wade Hampton of South Carolina* (New York: Charles Scribner's Sons, 1949), 4–8.

22. Gabriel Edward Manigault Autobiography, SCL, 347. The dragoons stopped in Camden for two days to have their horses shod before rejoining the regiment in

Charlotte. O. H. Middleton Jr. to Mrs. O. H. Middleton Sr., May 2, 1864, Oliver Hering Middleton Family Correspondence, SCHS.

23. Gabriel Edward Manigault Autobiography, SCL, 342, 351.

24. O. H. Middleton Jr. to Mrs. O. H. Middleton Sr., May 12, 1864, Oliver Hering
Middleton Family Correspondence, SCHS.

25. Gabriel Edward Manigault Autobiography, SCL, 352.

26. B. H. Rutledge to M. C. Butler, undated, B. H. Rutledge Letterbook, 306, SCHS.
The rest of the regiment was in a similar condition despite the fact that many men
were transported by rail to lighten the loads on their horses.

27. Gabriel Edward Manigault Autobiography, SCL, 355.

28. J. Tracy Power, *Lee's Miserables: Life in the Army of Northern Virginia from the
Wilderness to Appomattox* (Chapel Hill: University of North Carolina Press), 72–74.

29. Gabriel Edward Manigault Autobiography, SCL, 356.

30. O. H. Middleton Jr. to Mrs. O. H. Middleton Sr., May 24, 1864, Oliver Hering
Middleton Family Correspondence, SCHS.

31. Wells, *Sketch of the Charleston Light Dragoons,* 36.

32. Ibid., 37.

33. O. H. Middleton Jr. to Mrs. O. H. Middleton Sr., May 24, 1864, Oliver Hering
Middleton Family Correspondence, SCHS.

34. James L. Bee to William C. Bee, May 24, 1864, Bee-Chisolm Family Papers,
SCHS; O. H. Middleton Jr. to Mrs. O. H. Middleton Sr., May 24, 1864, Oliver Hering
Middleton Family Correspondence, SCHS.

35. Gabriel Edward Manigault Autobiography, SCL, 359; Wells, *Sketch of the
Charleston Light Dragoons,* 38.

36. McPherson, *Battle Cry of Freedom,* 724.

37. Gordon C. Rhea, "'The Hottest Place I Was Ever In': The Battle of Haw's Shop,
May 28, 1864," *North and South* 4, no. 4 (2001): 43–44.

38. Ibid., 45.

39. Ibid., 44–45.

40. Ibid., 46–49.

41. Wells, *Sketch of the Charleston Light Dragoons,* 42.

42. Gabriel Edward Manigault Autobiography, SCL, 360.

43. Rhea, "Hottest Place I Was Ever In," 48–49.

44. Ibid., 49.

45. Wells, *Sketch of the Charleston Light Dragoons,* 39–40.

46. Ibid., 43; National Archives, Compiled Service Records, microcopy 267, 4th
South Carolina Cavalry, rolls 24–30.

47. Rhea, "Hottest Place I Was Ever In," 51–52.

48. Wells, *Sketch of the Charleston Light Dragoons,* 42; National Archives, Compiled Service Records, microcopy 267, 4th South Carolina Cavalry, rolls 28–29.

49. Rhea, "Hottest Place I Was Ever In," 51.

50. B. H. Rutledge to M. C. Butler, undated, B. H. Rutledge Letterbook, 307, SCHS;
Gabriel Edward Manigault Autobiography, SCL, 361; Rhea, "Hottest Place I Was Ever
In," 55.

51. Pinckney, "Reminiscences of the War," p. 22, 34/0594, SCHS.

52. Wells, *Sketch of the Charleston Light Dragoons,* 43.

53. Ibid. After the battle witnesses claimed that the dragoons' high casualties stemmed from their needless exposure to enemy fire and their failure to take advantage of the available cover. In a postwar defense of their behavior, Wells claimed that Lt. Nowell had moved along the dragoons' line cautioning his men against disregarding their personal safety.

54. Wells, *Sketch of the Charleston Light Dragoons,* 44; Rhea, "Hottest Place I Was Ever In," 53; B. H. Rutledge to M. C. Butler, undated, B. H. Rutledge Letterbook, 309, SCHS.

55. B. H. Rutledge to M. C. Butler, undated, B. H. Rutledge Letterbook, 309–10, SCHS; Edward L. Wells, *Hampton and His Cavalry in '64* (1899; repr., Richmond, Va.: Owens Publishing Company, 1991), 159–60.

56. Pinckney, "Reminiscences of the War," pp. 22–23, 34/0594, SCHS.

57. Wells, *Sketch of the Charleston Light Dragoons,* 44–45; Rhea, "Hottest Place I Was Ever In," 53–54.

58. Pinckney, "Reminiscences of the War," p. 23, 34/0594, SCHS.

59. Ibid.; National Archives, Compiled Service Records, microcopy 267, 4th South Carolina Cavalry, roll 28; Wells, *Sketch of the Charleston Light Dragoons,* 46.

60. National Archives, Compiled Service Records, microcopy 267, 4th South Carolina Cavalry, roll 27; Gabriel Edward Manigault Autobiography, SCL, 362; Wells, *Sketch of the Charleston Light Dragoons,* 46. A Confederate surgeon removed the leg two days later.

61. National Archives, Compiled Service Records, microcopy 267, 4th South Carolina Cavalry, roll 27; Gabriel Edward Manigault Autobiography, SCL, 362; Wells, *Sketch of the Charleston Light Dragoons,* 46. The following month, a captured Union soldier found carrying O'Hear's pistol related how the lieutenant had died. Gabriel Edward Manigault Autobiography, SCL, 362.

62. Wells, *Sketch of the Charleston Light Dragoons,* 44–45.

63. Ibid., 45; Gabriel Edward Manigault Autobiography, SCL, 406; Rhea, "Hottest Place I Was Ever In," 54; Wells, *Hampton and His Cavalry,* 160–61; McPherson, *For Cause and Comrades,* 40–43. Wells claimed that the dragoons retreated "coolly, fighting their way through at close quarters in good order" (*Hampton and His Cavalry,* 160–61). This account conflicts with evidence found in the Compiled Service Records and other accounts of the panic that seized the second squadron.

64. William Bell Alumni Undergraduate Records, Seeley G. Mudd Manuscript Library.

65. Jno. Gallader to Thos. R. Waring, September 4, 1864, Allen Miles Correspondence, Confederate Museum, Charleston, S.C.

66. Wells, *Sketch of the Charleston Light Dragoons,* 44–45; Gabriel Edward Manigault Autobiography, SCL, 406.

67. Wells, *Sketch of the Charleston Light Dragoons,* 45; Gabriel Edward Manigault Autobiography, SCL, 406; Rhea, "Hottest Place I Was Ever In," 54; Wells, *Hampton and His Cavalry,* 160–61. There is some confusion regarding other details of the

engagement, including the nature of B. F. Huger's wound. Wells claims that he was shot in the arm, while the Compiled Service Records report that he was shot in the right thigh.

68. Gabriel Edward Manigault Autobiography, SCL, 363–64.

69. Ibid., 55; Wells, *Sketch of the Charleston Light Dragoons,* 46; National Archives, Compiled Service Records, microcopy 267, 4th South Carolina Cavalry, rolls 24–30.

70. National Archives, Compiled Service Records, microcopy 267, 4th South Carolina Cavalry, roll 26; Wells, *Sketch of the Charleston Light Dragoons,* 46.

71. National Archives, Compiled Service Records, microcopy 267, 4th South Carolina Cavalry, roll 26; Wells, *Sketch of the Charleston Light Dragoons,* 46; *Confederate Military History,* 6:912.

72. Lucy P. Anderson to Harriott Middleton, June 9, 1864, Harriott K. Middleton Family Correspondence, SCHS; Mrs. W. Brewton to Harriott Middleton, July 27, 1864, Harriott K. Middleton Family Correspondence, SCHS; Maria Dabney to Alicia Middleton, August 2, 1864, Harriott Middleton Family Papers, SCHS.

73. National Archives, Compiled Service Records, microcopy 267, 4th South Carolina Cavalry, roll 27; Henry Edmund Ravenel, *Ravenel Records: A History and Genealogy of the Huguenot Family of Ravenel. . . .* (Atlanta: Franklin Printing and Publishing, 1898), 67.

74. Gabriel Edward Manigault Autobiography, SCL, 405.

75. Ibid., 407; Wells, *Sketch of the Charleston Light Dragoons,* 48.

76. Gabriel Edward Manigault Autobiography, SCL, 405.

77. Ibid., 404.

78. National Archives, Compiled Service Records, microcopy 267, 4th South Carolina Cavalry, roll 28; Wells, *Sketch of the Charleston Light Dragoons,* 46.

79. Earl J. Hess, *The Union Soldier in Battle: Enduring the Ordeal of Combat* (Lawrence: University Press of Kansas, 1997), 151–52.

80. Wells, *Sketch of the Charleston Light Dragoons,* 46.

81. Ibid.; McPherson, *For Cause and Comrades,* 85.

82. Gabriel Edward Manigault Autobiography, SCL, 407; Wells, *Sketch of the Charleston Light Dragoons,* 46; B. H. Rutledge to M. C. Butler, undated, B. H. Rutledge Letterbook, 312, SCHS.

83. Samuel J. Martin, *Southern Hero: Matthew Calbraith Butler, Confederate General, Hampton Red Shirt, and U.S. Senator* (Mechanicsburg, Pa.: Stackpole Books, 2001), 88.

84. Gordon C. Rhea, *Cold Harbor: Grant and Lee, May 26–June 3, 1864* (Baton Rouge: Louisiana State University Press, 2002), 134.

85. Gabriel Edward Manigault Autobiography, SCL, 409.

86. Rhea, *Cold Harbor,* 133–34.

87. U. R. Brooks, *Butler and His Cavalry in the War of Secession, 1861–1865* (Columbia, S.C.: State Company, 1909), 205–6.

88. Gabriel Edward Manigault Autobiography, SCL, 409.

89. Martin, *Southern Hero,* 1–12; Edgar, *South Carolina: A History,* 254–64. Butler was a prewar state legislator, and was the nephew of U.S. Senator Andrew P. Butler and son-in-law of South Carolina Governor Francis W. Pickens.

90. Rhea, *Cold Harbor,* 134.

91. Wells, *Sketch of the Charleston Light Dragoons,* 50.

92. Rhea, *Cold Harbor,* 134, 135.

93. Wells, *Sketch of the Charleston Light Dragoons,* 50.

94. Rhea, *Cold Harbor,* 135.

95. Ibid., 136.

96. National Archives, Compiled Service Records, microcopy 267, 4th South Carolina Cavalry, rolls 24–30; Wells, *Sketch of the Charleston Light Dragoons,* 52–53.

97. Paul Gervais Bell, "The Battles of Hawes Shop and Cold Harbor and William Bell's Involvement in Them," 7, Paul Gervais Bell Papers, 0140, SCHS.

98. National Archives, Compiled Service Records, microcopy 267, 4th South Carolina Cavalry, rolls 24–30; Wells, *Sketch of the Charleston Light Dragoons,* 52–53. Wells's tabulation of casualties conflicts with the numbers listed in the Compiled Service Records.

99. Albert Rhett Elmore, "Incidents of Service with the Charleston Light Dragoons," *Confederate Veteran* 24, no. 12 (December 1916): 541.

100. *South Carolina Genealogies,* 4:312.

101. National Archives, Compiled Service Records, microcopy 267, 4th South Carolina Cavalry, rolls 24–30; Wells, *Sketch of the Charleston Light Dragoons,* 53; Gabriel Edward Manigault Autobiography, SCL, 411.

102. Hopkins, *Lower Richland Planters,* 264; National Archives, Compiled Service Records, microcopy 267, 4th South Carolina Cavalry, roll 24.

103. Wells, *Sketch of the Charleston Light Dragoons,* 53.

104. Gabriel Edward Manigault Autobiography, SCL, 412; Wells, *Sketch of the Charleston Light Dragoons,* 54.

105. Gabriel Edward Manigault Autobiography, SCL, 412; B. H. Rutledge to M. C. Butler, undated, B. H. Rutledge Letterbook, 313, SCHS; Wells, *Sketch of the Charleston Light Dragoons,* 54–56; Elmore, "Incidents of Service," 542.

106. Gabriel Edward Manigault Autobiography, SCL, 412; Wells, *Sketch of the Charleston Light Dragoons,* 55–56; Elmore, "Incidents of Service," 542.

107. Gabriel Edward Manigault Autobiography, SCL, 368–69.

108. B. H. Rutledge to M. C. Butler, undated, B. H. Rutledge Letterbook, 314, SCHS.

109. Gabriel Edward Manigault Autobiography, SCL, 368.

110. Peter Watson, *War on the Mind: The Military Uses and Abuses of Psychology* (New York: Basic Books, 1978), 231.

111. Wells, *Sketch of the Charleston Light Dragoons,* 46, 53; National Archives, Compiled Service Records, microcopy 267, 4th South Carolina Cavalry, rolls 24–30.

112. B. H. Rutledge to M. C. Butler, undated, B. H. Rutledge Letterbook, 314, SCHS.

113. McPherson, *For Cause and Comrades,* 81; Richard Holmes, *Acts of War: The Behavior of Men in Battle* (New York: Free Press, 1985), 141.

114. McPherson, *For Cause and Comrades,* 44–45; Paddy Griffith, *Battle Tactics of the Civil War* (New Haven, Conn.: Yale University Press, 1989), 50; Holmes, *Acts of War,* 214–18.

115. Gabriel Edward Manigault Autobiography, SCL, 373.

5. Transformation

1. Wells, *Sketch of the Charleston Light Dragoons,* 56–57; Gabriel Edward Manigault Autobiography, SCL, 371.

2. Gabriel Edward Manigault Autobiography, SCL, 373.

3. Ibid., 374; Wells, *Sketch of the Charleston Light Dragoons,* 59.

4. Gabriel Edward Manigault Autobiography, SCL, 377; Wells, *Sketch of the Charleston Light Dragoons,* 59–60.

5. Eric J. Wittemberg, *Glory Enough for All: Sheridan's Second Raid and the Battle of Trevilian Station* (Washington, D.C.: Brassey's, 2001), 22–23.

6. Ibid., 25, 37, 44, 60–61, 71.

7. Wells, *Sketch of the Charleston Light Dragoons,* 63.

8. Gabriel Edward Manigault Autobiography, SCL, 377.

9. B. H. Rutledge to M. C. Butler, undated, B. H. Rutledge Letterbook, 315, SCHS.

10. Wittemberg, *Glory Enough for All,* 75.

11. B. H. Rutledge to M. C. Butler, undated, B. H. Rutledge Letterbook, 316, SCHS.

12. Gabriel Edward Manigault Autobiography, SCL, 377–78; National Archives, Compiled Service Records, microcopy 267, 4th South Carolina Cavalry, roll 24.

13. Brooks, *Butler and His Cavalry,* 243; Wittemberg, *Glory Enough for All,* 79.

14. Wittemberg, *Glory Enough for All,* 79–81.

15. Smith, Smith, and Childs, *Mason Smith Family Letters,* 123, 124. Wells, *Sketch of the Charleston Light Dragoons,* 64.

16. B. H. Rutledge to M. C. Butler, undated, B. H. Rutledge Letterbook, 316–17, SCHS. In his description Rutledge writes of himself using the third person.

17. Ibid., 317.

18. Smith, Smith, and Childs, *Mason Smith Family Letters,* 123–24.

19. Gabriel Edward Manigault Autobiography, SCL, 369.

20. B. H. Rutledge to M. C. Butler, undated, B. H. Rutledge Letterbook, 317, SCHS; National Archives, Compiled Service Records, microcopy 267, 4th South Carolina Cavalry, rolls 24, 27; Wells, *Sketch of Charleston Light Dragoons,* 64–65. Rutledge's account of when Boone and Fairly were killed differs from Wells's, but since Wells had been captured by the time of their deaths, I have relied on Rutledge's account.

21. Wittemberg, *Glory Enough for All,* 97–101; Wells, *Sketch of the Charleston Light Dragoons,* 65; National Archives, Compiled Service Records, microcopy 267, 4th South Carolina Cavalry, roll 26.

22. B. H. Rutledge to M. C. Butler, undated, B. H. Rutledge Letterbook, 320–22, SCHS. The remaining dragoons were probably with Rutledge during his movement and were therefore with Barber on his detour.

23. Wittemberg, *Glory Enough for All,* 176.

24. Brooks, *Butler and His Cavalry,* 265.

25. Wells, *Sketch of the Charleston Light Dragoons,* 67–68.

26. Ibid., 71; Smith, Smith, and Childs, *Mason Smith Family Letters,* 123–24.

27. Wittemberg, *Glory Enough for All,* 292.

28. Ibid.

29. National Archives, Compiled Service Records, microcopy 267, 4th South Carolina Cavalry, rolls 24–30; B. H. Rutledge to M. C. Butler, undated, B. H. Rutledge Letterbook, 320–22, SCHS.

30. National Archives, Compiled Service Records, microcopy 267, 4th South Carolina Cavalry, rolls 24–30; B. H. Rutledge to M. C. Butler, undated, B. H. Rutledge Letterbook, 320–22, SCHS.

31. Brooks, *Butler and His Cavalry,* 212. During the June 11 engagement, Confederate cavalrymen recaptured Dragoon Lt. James W. O'Hear's ring and pistols from a member of the 7th Michigan Cavalry who had taken them from O'Hear's body during the fight at Haw's Shop. Wittemberg, *Glory Enough for All,* 118.

32. Rhea, "Hottest Spot I Was Ever In," 55; Wells, *Sketch of the Charleston Light Dragoons,* 46; National Archives, Compiled Service Records, microcopy 267, 4th South Carolina Cavalry, rolls 24–30.

33. Brooks, *Butler and His Cavalry,* 380; Elmore, "Incidents of Service," 542.

34. O. H. Middleton to William Porcher Miles, July 23, 1864, box 4, file 52, William Porcher Miles Papers, SHC.

35. Ravenel, *Ravenel Records,* 67–68.

36. Jno. Gallader to Thos. R. Waring, Sept. 4, 1864, Allen Miles Correspondence, Confederate Museum; newspaper clipping titled "To the Family of J. Allen Miles," Allen Miles Correspondence, Confederate Museum.

37. E. M. Rutledge to Alfred Huger, undated, Vanderhorst Family Papers, SCHS; Alfred Huger to Arnoldus Vanderhorst, August 20, 1864, Vanderhorst Family Papers, 12/200/18, SCHS.

38. Marszalek, *Diary of Miss Emma Holmes,* 353.

39. Woodward, *Mary Chesnut's Civil War,* 766.

40. Ibid., 618; Randolph Kirkland, interview, October 31, 1999.

41. Marszalek, *Diary of Miss Emma Holmes,* 356.

42. Woodward, *Mary Chesnut's Civil War,* 618, 766.

43. Taylor, Matthews, and Power, *Leverett Letters,* 315, 321–22.

44. *Charleston Mercury,* June 22, 1864.

45. See the Harriot Middleton Family Papers, especially the correspondence of Susan M. Middleton, SCHS; B. H. Rutledge to Barnwell Rhett, December 3, 1863, Benjamin Huger Rutledge Papers, 1863, Rare Book, Manuscript, and Special Collections Library.

46. Hopkins, *Lower Richland Planters,* 35.

47. William Bell Alumni Undergraduate Records, 3–4, Seeley G. Mudd Manuscript Library.

48. Ibid., 4.

49. National Archives, Compiled Service Records, microcopy 267, 4th South Carolina Cavalry, rolls 24–30.

50. Smith, Smith, and Childs, *Mason Smith Family Letters,* 131, 133, 147.

51. Gabriel Edward Manigault Autobiography, SCL, 393, 396.

52. Ibid., 400.

53. National Archives, Compiled Service Records, microcopy 267, 4th South Carolina Cavalry, rolls 24–30.

54. Wells, *Sketch of the Charleston Light Dragoons,* 76; Elmore, "Incidents of Service," 543; National Archives, Compiled Service Records, microcopy 267, 4th South Carolina Cavalry, roll 27.

55. *Confederate Military History,* 5:715–16; National Archives, Compiled Service Records, microcopy 267, 4th South Carolina Cavalry, roll 29.

56. National Archives, Compiled Service Records, microcopy 267, 4th South Carolina Cavalry, rolls 24–25; Wells, *Sketch of the Charleston Light Dragoons,* 76; Martin, *Southern Hero,* 114–22.

57. National Archives, War Department Collection of Confederate Records, RG 109, Inspection Reports and Related Records Received by the Inspection Branch in the Confederate Adjutant and Inspector General's Office (hereafter Inspection Reports), microcopy 935 3-P-24, roll 10; R. H. Colcock to B. H. Rutledge, 12 November 1864, Colcock Family Papers, Special Collections, Tulane University Library, New Orleans, La.

58. John C. Bickley, Charleston Light Dragoon Roll Book, Private Collection, Elizabeth Settle, Charleston, S.C. This volume is the roll book of the dragoons' 1st sergeant, who kept it for most of the war. It also contains lists of lost and replaced equipment and clothing issues.

59. National Archives, Compiled Service Records, microcopy 267, 4th South Carolina Cavalry, roll 28.

60. Ibid.; Wells, *Sketch of the Charleston Light Dragoons,* 78. Burgess Mill marked the last dragoon casualty until December 1864. On October 12, 1864, Dragoon J. J. Miles was sent to Stoney Creek with the remainder of the brigade's dismounted men. He was captured there on December 1, 1864, and sent to Point Lookout in Maryland, where he spent the remainder of the war. Elmore, "Incidents of Service," 543; National Archives, Compiled Service Records, microcopy 267, 4th South Carolina Cavalry, roll 28.

61. Smith, Smith, and Childs, *Mason Smith Family Letters,* 146–47.

62. National Archives, Inspection Reports, microcopy 935, 36-P-33, roll 11; 1-P-37, roll 12; and 6-P-43, roll 13. The 4th probably lost its regimental and company books when Custer's Michigan brigade captured Hampton's wagons at Trevilian Station. Wittenberg, *Glory Enough for All,* 97–132.

63. National Archives, Compiled Service Records, microcopy 267, 4th South Carolina Cavalry, roll 27; Wells, *Sketch of the Charleston Light Dragoons,* 78.

64. Wells, *Hampton and His Cavalry,* 389.

65. Martin, *Southern Hero,* 133–36; Brooks, *Butler and his Cavalry,* 403.

66. Martin, *Southern Hero,* 133–36; Brooks, *Butler and his Cavalry,* 403.

67. Wells, *Sketch of the Charleston Light Dragoons,* 79.

68. Massey, *Refugee Life in the Confederacy,* 81–82.

69. Martin, *Southern Hero,* 136, 139.

70. Note attributed to Langdon Cheves on newspaper clipping, December 27, 1931, Charleston Light Dragoons, Vertical File, 30-14-73, SCHS.

71. Edward Laight Wells, "Who Burnt Columbia?" *Southern Historical Society Papers* 10 (March 1882): 109–19.

72. Wells, *Sketch of the Charleston Light Dragoons,* 81–83.

73. Louis Manigault Scrapbook, box 1, 303, Louis Manigault Papers, 0177, SCHS; Wells, *Sketch of the Charleston Light Dragoons,* 83.

74. Ibid.; McPherson, *For Cause and Comrades,* 79.

75. Wells, *Sketch of the Charleston Light Dragoons,* 83; Gabriel Edward Manigault Autobiography, SCL, 340.

76. Martin, *Southern Hero,* 144–45, 147.

77. McPherson, *For Cause and Comrades,* 148–49.

78. Wells, *Sketch of the Charleston Light Dragoons,* 83–85.

79. Martin, *Southern Hero,* 143, 147.

80. Smith, Smith, and Childs, *Mason Smith Family Letters,* 172; Wells, *Sketch of the Charleston Light Dragoons,* 87–88; Martin, *Southern Hero,* 147.

81. Wells, *Sketch of the Charleston Light Dragoons,* 89–91.

82. M. C. Butler to Edward L. Wells, March 27, 1900, Edward L. Wells Correspondence, Charleston Library Society, Charleston, S.C. (hereafter CLS); Mark L. Bradley, *Last Stand in the Carolinas: The Battle of Bentonville* (Campbell, Calif.: Savas Woodbury Publishers, 1996), 96.

83. Edward Laight Wells, "A Morning Call on Kilpatrick," *Southern Historical Society Papers* 12 (March 1884): 127–28; Wells, *Sketch of the Charleston Light Dragoons,* 90.

84. M. C. Butler to Edward L. Wells, March 27, 1900, Wells Correspondence, CLS; Zimmerman Davis to Edward L. Wells, June 10, 1898, Wells Correspondence, CLS.

85. Wells, *Sketch of the Charleston Light Dragoons,* 100.

86. Ibid., 105–8; Wade Hampton to Edward L. Wells, December 20, 1897, and Edward L. Wells to Wade Hampton, February 8, 1899, Wells Correspondence, CLS; Smith, Smith, and Childs, *Mason Smith Family Letters,* 172, 274; Wells, *Hampton and His Cavalry,* 33; John G. Barrett, *Sherman's March through the Carolinas* (Chapel Hill: University of North Carolina Press, 1956), 133. Some Confederates were incredulous about accounts of the fight. General Lafayette McLaws believed that the South Carolinians were inclined to embellish tales of their exploits for their own benefit.

87. Wells, *Sketch of the Charleston Light Dragoons,* 93.

88. Halliburton, *Saddle Soldiers,* 195, 197.

89. Smith, Smith, and Childs, *Mason Smith Family Letters,* 196.

90. Wells, *Sketch of the Charleston Light Dragoons,* 93; Bradley, *Last Stand in the Carolinas,* 408.

91. Wells, *Sketch of the Charleston Light Dragoons,* 94; Halliburton, *Saddle Soldiers,* 199. Stokes claimed that he marched the 4th South Carolina Cavalry to Asheboro, North Carolina, and disbanded the regiment at 8:30 P.M. on April 27. Edward Wells claimed that the dragoons were present when Johnston surrendered.

92. Smith, Smith, and Childs, *Mason Smith Family Letters,* 196.

93. Gabriel Edward Manigault Autobiography, SCL, 416, 427.

6. Beginning Again

1. James L. Roark, *Masters without Slaves: Southern Planters in the Civil War and Reconstruction* (New York: W. W. Norton, 1977), 160.

2. Charleston Light Dragoons Records, 11/511, miscellaneous, "Dragoon Saber," No. 1, 1887, SCHS; Stephen Meats and Edwin Arnold, eds. *The Writings of Benjamin F. Perry,* 2 vols. (Spartanburg, S.C.: Reprint Company, 1980), 1:204.

3. Richard Zuczek, *State of Rebellion: Reconstruction in South Carolina* (Columbia: University of South Carolina Press, 1996), 74.

4. Linderman, *Embattled Courage,* 268–69; Hess, *Union Soldier in Battle,* 160–61.

5. Wells, *A Sketch of the Charleston Light Dragoons,* 96.

6. Robert Adams, "Remarks at the Meeting of the Survivors of the Charleston Light Dragoons, held in Charleston, South Carolina, on November 1, 1870," Robert Adams Papers, collection of Weston Adams, Columbia, S.C.

7. At least eleven thousand and perhaps as many as twenty-two thousand Union shells had fallen on it during the war. W. Chris Phelps, *The Bombardment of Charleston 1863–1865* (Gretna, La.: Pelican Publishing, 2002), 167.

8. John T. Trowbridge, *The Desolate South 1865–1866: A Picture of the Battlefields and of the Devastated Confederacy* (New York: Duell, Sloan, and Pearce, 1956), 275.

9. Doyle, *New Men, New Cities, New South,* 58.

10. Ibid., 60, 71–76. Even after Reconstruction many Charlestonians proved reluctant to enter new business and clung to agriculture as the bedrock of the local economy.

11. Smith, Smith, and Childs, *Mason Smith Family Letters,* 228.

12. *Charleston City Directory for 1867–68.* . . . (Charleston, S.C.: Jno. Orwin Lea, 1868). Wells lists C. T. Lowndes and Company, Cotton Merchants, as his employer.

13. Hopkins, *Lower Richland Planters,* 36–37.

14. Ibid., 37, 41, 264.

15. "The Battles of Hawes Shop . . . ," Paul Gervais Bell Papers, 10–11, 0140, SCHS.

16. Alexia Jones Helsley, *South Carolina's African American Confederate Pensioners, 1923–1925* (Columbia: South Carolina Department of Archives and History, 1998), 73–74.

17. Arnoldus Vanderhorst Papers, 1896–1902, 12/213/16, SCHS.

18. Wells, *Sketch of the Charleston Light Dragoons,* 95.

19. Zuczek, *State of Rebellion,* 138–39.

20. Ibid.

21. Meeting Minutes, 1875–1891, August 4, 1876, Charleston Light Dragoons Records, SCHS.

22. Zuczek, *State of Rebellion,* 174–75.

23. Melinda Meeks Hennessey, "Racial Violence during Reconstruction: The 1876 Riots in Charleston and Cainhoy," *South Carolina Historical Magazine* 86 (April 1985): 100–12; Meeting Minutes, 1875–1891, September 7, 1876, Charleston Light Dragoons Records, SCHS.

24. Zuczek, *State of Rebellion,* 175.

25. Meeting Minutes, 1875–1891, October 4, 1876, Charleston Light Dragoons Records, SCHS. Ironically, the unit's finances were just as much a concern following the war, although unit members had far fewer resources. In the midst of the election crisis unit members debated how best to convince members who were in arrears to pay their dues to the organization.

26. Zuczek, *State of Rebellion,* 167.

27. "Proclamation re Military Clubs," October 7, 1876, box 15, folder 4, Governor Chamberlain Papers, SCDAH.

28. Zuczek, *State of Rebellion,* 178.

29. Hennessey, "Racial Violence during Reconstruction," 100–12.

30. Edgar, *South Carolina: A History,* 424.

31. Doyle, *New Men, New Cities, New South,* 58.

32. Meeting Minutes, 1875–1891, April 4, 1877, Charleston Light Dragoons Records, SCHS.

33. Ibid., April 16, 1877.

34. *Acts and Joint Resolutions of the General Assembly of the State of South Carolina Passed at the Regular Session of 1875–76* (Columbia, S.C.: Republican Printing, State Printers, 1876), 527–30.

35. David W. Blight, *Race and Reunion: The Civil War in the American Memory* (Cambridge, Mass.: Belknap Press of Harvard University Press, 2001), 77.

36. *Charleston Mercury,* June 22, 1864.

37. *Proceedings at the Unveiling of the Monument to the Charleston Light Dragoons,* . . . (Charleston, SC: Walker, Evans, and Cogswell, 1889), 10.

38. Ibid.; Gaines Foster, *Ghosts of the Confederacy: Defeat, the Lost Cause, and the Emergence of the New South, 1865 to 1913* (New York: Oxford University Press, 1987), 88–103.

39. "Proceedings at the Unveiling," 10–28. Shortly after the dedication the Survivors Association turned the maintenance of their monument over to the company with their best wishes. In turn, the unit made each member of the Survivors Association an honorary member. Wells, *Sketch of the Charleston Light Dragoons,* 96.

40. Blight, *Race and Reunion,* 74–76.

41. Wells, *Sketch of the Charleston Light Dragoons,* 3.

BIBLIOGRAPHY

Manuscripts

Charleston Library Society, Charleston, S.C.
    Edward L. Wells Correspondence
Confederate Museum, Charleston, S.C.
    Allen Miles Correspondence
Private collections
    Weston Adams, Columbia, S.C.
        Robert Adams Papers
    William H.Chandler, Hemingway, S.C.
        John C. Wilson Papers
    Elizabeth Settle, Charleston, S.C.
        John C. Bickley Charleston Light Dragoon Roll Book
Rare Book, Manuscript, and Special Collections Library, Duke University, Durham, N.C.
    Benjamin Huger Rutledge Papers
Seeley G. Mudd Mansucript Library, Princeton University, Princeton, N.J.
    William Bell Alumni Undergraduate Records
South Carolina Department of Archives and History, Columbia, S.C. (SCDAH)
    Governor Chamberlain Papers
    Records of the General Assembly, Petitions, 1831
    Report from the Adjutant General, 1849
South Carolina Historical Society, Charleston, S.C. (SCHS)
    Allston Family Papers
    Elias Ball Bull Research Papers
    Bee-Chisholm Family Papers
    Paul Gervais Bell Papers
    Charleston Light Dragoons Records
    Charleston Light Dragoons Vertical File
    Charles Izard Manigault Family Papers
    Louis Manigault Papers
        Louis Maingault Scrapbooks
    Harriott Middleton Family Papers
    Harriott K. Middleton Family Correspondence
    Henry A. Middleton Papers
    Oliver Hering Middleton Family Correspondence
    Thomas Pinckney Reminiscences
    Elizabeth W. Allston Pringle Family Papers
        Elizabeth W. Allston Pringle Diary
    Benjamin Huger Rutledge Letterbook
    St. Cecilia Society Records

Vanderhorst Family Papers
  Arnoldus Vanderhorst Dueling Papers
  Arnoldus Vanderhorst Papers
  Lewis Morris Vanderhorst Travel Journal
  Morton N. Waring Travel Diary
  Edward L. Wells Papers
South Caroliniana Library, University of South Carolina, Columbia, S.C. (SCL)
  John Caldwell Calhoun Order Book
  Gabriel Edward Manigault Autobiography
Southern Historical Collection, University of North Carolina, Chapel Hill, S.C. (SCH)
  Elliott-Gonzalez Family Papers
  William Porcher Miles Papers
Special Collections, Tulane University Library, New Orleans, La.
  Colcock Family Papers

Newspapers

Charleston City Gazette
Charleston Daily Courier
Charleston Mercury
Charleston News and Courier
Columbia Daily Southern Guardian

Printed Primary Sources, Public Documents, and Reminiscences

Acts and Joint Resolutions of the General Assembly of the State of South Carolina Passed at the Regular Session of 1875–76. Columbia, S.C.: Republican Printing, State Printers, 1876.

Charleston City Directory for 1867–68. . . . Charleston, S.C.: Jno. Orwin Lea Publishers, 1868.

Charleston City Directory, 1875–6. Compiled by T. M. Haddock and J. E. Baker. Charleston, S.C.: Walker, Evans, and Cogswell, 1875.

The Charleston Club, Chartered 1852. Miscellaneous. South Carolina Historical Society.

Charleston Directory and Stranger's Guide for 1840 and 1841. . . . Charleston, S.C.: T. C. Fay, 1840.

Confederate Military History: Extended Edition. 17 vols. Reprint, Wilmington, N.C.: Broadfoot Publishing, 1987.

Cooper, Thomas, and David J. McCord, eds. *The Statutes at Large of South Carolina.* 26 vols. Columbia, S.C.: A. S. Johnston, 1836–76.

Cyclopedia of Eminent and Representative Men of the Carolinas, Vol. 1, *South Carolina.* Madison, Wis.: Brant and Fuller, 1892.

De Saussure, N. B. *Old Plantation Days: Being Recollections of Southern Life before the Civil War.* New York: Duffield, 1909.

Directory of the City of Charleston . . . 1860. Vol. 1. Charleston, S.C.: W. Eugene Ferslew, 1860; microfilm, SCHS.

Easterby, J. H., ed. *The South Carolina Rice Plantation as Revealed in the Papers of Robert F. W. Allston.* Chicago: University of Chicago Press, 1945.

Halliburton, Lloyd. *Saddle Soldiers: The Civil War Correspondence of General William Stokes of the 4th South Carolina Cavalry.* Orangeburg, S.C.: Sandlapper Publishing, 1993.

Helsley, Alexia Jones. *South Carolina's African American Confederate Pensioners, 1923–1925.* Columbia: South Carolina Department of Archives and History, 1998.

Hewett, Janet B. *South Carolina Confederate Soldiers, 1861–1865.* Vol. 2, *Unit Roster.* Wilmington, N.C.: Broadfoot Publishing, 1998.

Hyde, Joseph Bell. *Union Kilwinning Lodge No. 4, Ancient Freemasons of South Carolina.* Charleston, S.C.: n.p., 1930.

Jowits Charleston City Directory and Business Register, 1869–70. . . . Charleston, S.C.: Walker, Evans, and Cogswell, 1869.

Kirkland, Randolph W., Jr. Interview regarding William Lennox Kirkland. October 31, 1999.

———. *South Carolina Soldiers, Sailors, and Citizens Who Died in the Service of Their Country and State in the War for Southern Independence, 1861–1865.* Charleston: South Carolina Historical Society, 1995.

Lord, Walter, ed. *The Fremantle Diary. Being the Journal of Lieutenant Colonel James Arthur Lyon Fremantle, Coldstream Guards, on His Three Months in the Southern States.* Boston: Little, Brown, 1954.

Marszalek, John F., ed. *The Diary of Miss Emma Holmes, 1861–1866.* Baton Rouge: Louisiana State University Press, 1979.

Matthews, James W., ed. *The Statutes at Large of the Confederate States of America . . . First Session . . . First Congress.* Richmond, Va.: R. M. Smith, 1862.

Meats, Stephen, and Edwin Arnold, eds. *The Writings of Benjamin F. Perry.* 2 vols. Spartanburg, S.C.: Reprint Company, 1980.

Proceedings at the Unveiling of the Monument to the Charleston Light Dragoons, Magnolia Cemetery, Charleston, S.C., May 10th, 1886, Orations of Generals M. C. Butler and B. H. Rutledge. Charleston, S.C.: Walker, Evans, and Cogswell, 1889.

Proceedings of the Most Worshipful Grand Lodge of Ancient Freemasons of South Carolina at the Annual Communication, November 5859. Charleston, S.C.: A. J. Burke, 1859.

Ravenel, Henry Edmund. *Ravenel Records: A History and Genealogy of the Huguenot Family of Ravenel.* . . . Atlanta: Franklin Printing and Publishing, 1898.

Smith, Daniel E. Huger, Alice R. Huger Smith, and Arney R. Childs. *Mason Smith Family Letters.* Columbia: University of South Carolina Press, 1950.

South Carolina Genealogies: Articles from the South Carolina Historical (and Genealogical) Magazine. 5 vols. Spartanburg, S.C.: Reprint Company, 1983.

State Papers on Nullification. . . . Boston: Dutton and Wentworth, 1834.

Taylor, Frances Wallace, Catherine Taylor Matthews, and J. Tracy Power, eds. *The Leverett Letters: Correspondence of a South Carolina Family, 1851–1868.* Columbia: University of South Carolina Press, 2000.

Trowbridge, John T. *The Desolate South, 1865–1866: A Picture of the Battlefields and of the Devastated Confederacy.* New York: Duell, Sloan, and Pearce, 1956.

War of the Rebellion: The Official Records of the Union and Confederate Armies. Washington, D.C.: Government Printing Office, 1880–1909.

War of the Rebellion: The Official Records of the Union and Confederate Navies. Washington, D.C.: Government Printing Office, 1894–1914.

Wells, Edward L. *Hampton and His Cavalry in '64.* Richmond, Va.: B. F. Johnson, 1899.

———. *A Sketch of the Charleston Light Dragoons, from the Earliest Formation of the Corps.* Charleston, S.C.: Lucas, Richardson, 1888.

Woodward, C. Vann. *Mary Chesnut's Civil War.* New Haven, Conn.: Yale University Press, 1981.

Year Book—1891. City of Charleston, So. Ca. Charleston, S.C.: Walker, Evans, and Cogswell, 1891.

"Your Servant, Quash": Letters of a South Carolina Freedman. Columbia, S.C.: Chicora Foundation, 1994.

Articles

Easterby, J. H. "The South Carolina Rice Factor as Revealed in the Papers of Robert F. W. Allston." *Journal of Southern History* 7 (May 1941): 160–72.

Elmore, Albert Rhett. "Incidents of Service with the Charleston Light Dragoons." *Confederate Veteran* 24, no. 12 (December 1916): 538–43.

Harleston, John. "Battery Wagner on Morris Island." *South Carolina Historical Magazine* 57 (January 1956): 8–13.

Wells, Edward Laight. "A Morning Call on Kilpatrick." *Southern Historical Society Papers* 12 (March 1884): 123–30.

———. "Who Burnt Columbia?" *Southern Historical Society Papers* 10 (March 1882): 109–19.

Government Records

National Archives. War Department Collection of Confederate Records. RG 109. Compiled Service Records of Confederate Soldiers Who Served in Organizations from the State of South Carolina. Microcopy 267, Capt. Rutledge's Company, Cavalry Militia, roll 55; 4th South Carolina Cavalry, rolls 24–30.

———. RG 109. Inspection Reports and Related Records Received by the Inspection Branch in the Confederate Adjutant and Inspector General's Office. Microcopy 935, roll 10.

———. RG 109. Letters Received by the Confederate Secretary of War. Microcopy 437, rolls 6 and 93.

United States Bureau of the Census. *Fifth Census of the United States (South Carolina), 1830.* Washington, D.C.: Government Printing Office, 1835.

———. *Eighth Census of the United States (South Carolina), 1860.* Washington, D.C.: Government Printing Office, 1865.

Secondary Sources

Banner, James M., Jr. "The Problem of South Carolina." In *The Hofstadter Aegis: A Memorial,* edited by Stanley Elkins and Eric McKitrick, 60–93. New York: Alfred A. Knopf, 1974.

Barrett, John G. *Sherman's March through the Carolinas*. Chapel Hill: University of North Carolina Press, 1956.

Blight, David W. *Race and Reunion: The Civil War in the American Memory*. Cambridge, Mass.: Belknap Press of Harvard University Press, 2001.

Bradley, Mark L. *Last Stand in the Carolinas: The Battle of Bentonville*. Campbell, Calif.: Savas Woodbury Publishers, 1996.

Brooks, U. R. *Butler and His Cavalry in the War of Secession, 1861–1865*. Columbia, S.C.: State Company, 1909.

Bryan, Evelyn McDaniel Frazier. *Colleton County, S.C.: A History of the First 160 Years, 1670–1830*. Jacksonville, Fla.: Florentine Press, 1993.

Burton, E. Milby. *The Siege of Charleston, 1861–1865*. Columbia: University of South Carolina Press, 1970.

Channing, Steven. *Crisis of Fear: Secession in South Carolina*. New York: Simon and Schuster, 1970.

Coclanis, Peter A. *The Shadow of a Dream: Economic Life and Death in the South Carolina Low Country, 1670–1920*. New York: Oxford University Press, 1989.

Cote, Richard N. *Mary's World: Love, War, and Family Ties in Nineteenth-Century Charleston*. Charleston, S.C.: Corinthian Books, 2000.

Davidson, Chalmers Gaston. *The Last Foray; The South Carolina Planters of 1860: A Sociological Study*. Columbia: Published for the South Carolina Tricentennial Commission by the University of South Carolina Press.

Donald, David, ed. *Why the North Won the Civil War*. Baton Rouge: Louisiana State University Press, 1960.

Doyle, Don H. *New Men, New Cities, New South: Atlanta, Nashville, Charleston, Mobile, 1860–1910*. Chapel Hill: University of North Carolina Press, 1990.

Dusinberre, William. *Them Dark Days: Slavery in the American Rice Swamps*. New York: Oxford University Press, 1996.

Edgar, Walter. *South Carolina: A History*. Columbia: University of South Carolina Press, 1998.

Egerton, Douglas R. *He Shall Go Out Free: The Lives of Denmark Vesey*. Madison, Wis.: Madison House, 1999.

Eliot, Elsworth, Jr. *Yale in the Civil War*. New Haven, Conn.: Yale University Press, 1932.

Faust, Drew Gilpin. *Mothers of Invention: Women of the Slaveholding South in the American Civil War*. Chapel Hill: University of North Carolina Press, 1996.

Flynn, Jean Martin. *The Militia in Antebellum South Carolina Society*. Spartanburg, S.C.: Reprint Company, 1991.

Foster, Gaines. *Ghosts of the Confederacy: Defeat, the Lost Cause, and the Emergence of the New South, 1865 to 1913*. New York: Oxford University Press, 1987.

Frank, Joseph Allen, and George A. Reaves. *"Seeing the Elephant": The Experience of Combat in the American Civil War*. New York: Greenwood Press, 1989.

Franklin, John Hope. *The Militant South, 1800–1861*. Cambridge, Mass.: Harvard University Press, 1956.

Freehling, William W. *Prelude to Civil War: The Nullification Controversy in South Carolina, 1816–1836*. New York: Harper & Row, 1965.

————. *The Road to Disunion.* Vol. 1, *Secessionists at Bay.* Oxford: Oxford University Press, 1990.

Green, Jack P., Rosemary Brana-Shute, and Randy J. Sparks, eds. *Money, Trade, and Power: The Evolution of Colonial South Carolina's Plantation Society.* Columbia: University of South Carolina Press, 2001.

Griffith, Paddy. *Battle Tactics of the Civil War.* New Haven, Conn.: Yale University Press, 1989.

Grimsley, Mark. *The Hard Hand of War: Union Military Policy toward Southern Civilians, 1861–1865.* Cambridge: Cambridge University Press, 1995.

Hadden, Sally E. *Slave Patrols: Law and Violence in Virginia and the Carolinas.* Cambridge, Mass.: Harvard University Press, 2001.

Hess, Earl J. *The Union Soldier in Battle: Enduring the Ordeal of Combat.* Lawrence: University Press of Kansas, 1997.

Holmes, Richard. *Acts of War: The Behavior of Men in Battle.* New York: Free Press, 1985.

Hopkins, Laura Jervey. *Lower Richland Planters: Hopkins, Adams, Weston and Related Families of South Carolina.* Columbia, S.C.: R. L. Bryan, 1976.

Irving, John B. *A Day on Cooper River.* Columbia, S.C.: R. L. Bryan, 1969.

Jimerson, Randall C. *The Private Civil War: Popular Thought during the Sectional Conflict.* Baton Rouge: Louisiana State University Press, 1988.

Jordan, Ervin L., Jr. *Black Confederates and Afro-Yankees in Civil War Virginia.* Charlottesville: University Press of Virginia, 1995.

Junior League of Charleston. *Charleston Receipts.* Charleston, S.C.: Wimmer Brothers, 1950.

Klein, Maury. *Days of Defiance: Sumter, Secession, and the Coming of the Civil War.* New York: Alfred A. Knopf, 1997.

Lesser, Charles H. *Relic of the Lost Cause: The Story of South Carolina's Ordinance of Secession.* Columbia: South Carolina Department of Archives and History, 1990.

Linder, Suzanne Cameron. *Historical Atlas of the Rice Plantations of the ACE River Basin—1860.* Columbia: South Carolina Department of Archives and History Foundation, Ducks Unlimited, and the Nature Conservancy, 1995.

Linderman, Gerald F. *Embattled Courage: The Experience of Combat in the American Civil War.* New York: Free Press, 1987.

Littlefield, Daniel C. *Rice and Slaves: Ethnicity and the Slave Trade in Colonial South Carolina.* Baton Rouge: Louisiana State University Press, 1981.

Martin, Samuel J. *Southern Hero: Matthew Calbraith Butler, Confederate General, Hampton Red Shirt, and U.S. Senator.* Mechanicsburg, Pa.: Stackpole Books, 2001.

Massey, Mary Elizabeth. *Refugee Life in the Confederacy.* Baton Rouge: Louisiana State University Press, 1964.

McCaslin, Richard B. *Portraits of Conflict: A Photographic History of South Carolina in the Civil War.* Fayetteville: University of Arkansas Press, 1994.

McCusker, John J. *How Much Is That in Real Money? A Historical Commodity Price Index for Use as a Deflator of Money Values in the Economy of the United States.* Worcester, Mass.: American Antiquarian Society, 2001

McInnis, Maurie D. *In Pursuit of Refinement: Charlestonians Abroad, 1740–1860.* Columbia: University of South Carolina Press, 1999.

McPherson, James M. *Battle Cry of Freedom: The Civil War Era.* New York: Oxford University Press, 1988.

———. *For Cause and Comrades: Why Men Fought in the Civil War.* New York: Oxford University Press, 1997.

———. *What They Fought For, 1861–1865.* Baton Rouge: Louisiana State University Press, 1994.

Mitchell, Reid. *Civil War Soldiers.* New York: Viking, 1988.

———. *The Vacant Chair: The Northern Soldier Leaves Home.* New York: Oxford University Press, 1993.

Morgan, Edmund. *Inventing the People: The Rise of Popular Sovereignty in England and America.* New York: W. W. Norton, 1988.

Morgan, Philip D. *Slave Counterpoint: Black Culture in the Eighteenth Century Chesapeake and Lowcountry.* Chapel Hill: Published for the Omohundro Institute of Early American History and Culture, Williamsburg, Va., by the University of North Carolina Press, 1998.

Oates, Stephen B. *The Fires of Jubilee: Nat Turner's Fierce Rebellion.* New York: Harper & Row, 1975; New York: HarperPerennial, 1990.

Olwell, Robert. *Masters, Slaves and Subjects: The Culture of Power in the South Carolina Low Country, 1740–1790.* Ithaca: Cornell University Press, 1998.

Pease, William H., and Jane H. Pease. *The Web of Progress: Private Values and Public Styles in Boston and Charleston, 1828–1843.* New York: Oxford University Press, 1985.

Phelps, W. Chris. *The Bombardment of Charleston 1863–1865.* Gretna, La.: Pelican Publishing, 2002.

Power, J. Tracy. *Lee's Miserables: Life in the Army of Northern Virginia from the Wilderness to Appomattox.* Chapel Hill: University of North Carolina Press, 1998.

Rable, George C. *Civil Wars: Women and the Crisis of Southern Nationalism.* Urbana: University of Illinois Press, 1989.

Rhea, Gordon C. *Cold Harbor: Grant and Lee, May 26–June 3, 1864.* Baton Rouge: Louisiana State University Press, 2002.

Roark, James L. *Masters without Slaves: Southern Planters in the Civil War and Reconstruction.* New York: W. W. Norton, 1977.

Robertson, James I., Jr. *Soldiers Blue and Gray.* Columbia: University of South Carolina Press, 1988.

Rogers, George C., Jr. *Charleston in the Age of the Pinckneys.* Norman: University of Oklahoma Press, 1969.

———. *The History of Georgetown County, South Carolina.* Columbia: University of South Carolina Press, 1970.

Rosen, Robert. *The Jewish Confederates.* Columbia: University of South Carolina Press, 2000.

Rowland, Lawrence S., Alexander Moore, and George C. Rogers Jr. *The History of Beaufort County, South Carolina.* Vol. 1, *1514–1861.* Columbia: University of South Carolina Press, 1996.

Scarborough, William Kauffman. *Masters of the Big House: Elite Slaveholders of the Mid-Nineteenth-Century South.* Baton Rouge: Louisiana State University Press, 2003.

Sears, Stephen W. *Landscape Turned Red: The Battle of Antietam.* New York: Ticknor and Fields, 1983.

———. *To the Gates of Richmond: The Peninsula Campaign.* New York: Ticknor and Fields, 1992.

Starr, Stephen Z. *The Union Cavalry in the Civil War.* Vol. 1, *From Fort Sumter to Gettysburg, 1861–1863.* Baton Rouge: Louisiana State University Press, 1979.

Thornton, J. Mills, III. *Politics and Power in a Slave Society: Alabama, 1800–1860.* Baton Rouge: Louisiana State University Press, 1978.

Walther, Eric H. *The Fire-Eaters.* Baton Rouge: Louisiana State University Press, 1992.

Watson, Peter. *War on the Mind: The Military Uses and Abuses of Psychology.* New York: Basic Books, 1978.

Wellman, Manly Wade. *Giant in Gray: A Biography of Wade Hampton of South Carolina.* New York: Charles Scribner's Sons, 1949.

Wiley, Bell Irvin. *The Life of Johnny Reb: The Common Soldier of the Confederacy.* New York: Bobbs Merrill, 1943.

Williams, David. *Rich Man's War: Class, Caste, and Confederate Defeat in the Lower Chattahoochee Valley.* Athens: University of Georgia Press, 1998.

Wittemburg, Eric J. *Glory Enough for All: Sheridan's Second Raid and the Battle of Trevilian Station.* Washington, D.C.: Brassey's, 2001.

Wood, Gordon S. *The Radicalism of the American Revolution.* New York: Alfred A. Knopf, 1992.

Woodman, Harold D. *King Cotton and His Retainers: Financing and Marketing the Cotton Crop of the South, 1800–1825.* Columbia: University of South Carolina Press, 1968.

Woods, Peter H. *Black Majority: Negroes in Colonial South Carolina from 1670 through the Stono Rebellion.* New York: Alfred A. Knopf, 1974.

Wyatt-Brown, Bertram. *Southern Honor: Ethics and Behavior in the Old South.* New York: Oxford University Press, 1982.

Zuczek, Richard. *State of Rebellion: Reconstruction in South Carolina.* Columbia: University of South Carolina Press, 1996.

Articles

Flynn, Jean Martin. "South Carolina's Compliance with the Militia Act of 1792." *South Carolina Historical Magazine* 69 (January 1968): 26–43.

Hennessey, Melinda Meeks. "Racial Violence during Reconstruction: The 1876 Riots in Charleston and Cainhoy." *South Carolina Historical Magazine* 86 (April 1985): 110–12.

Reimer, Terry. "Poisonous Techniques and Dressing." *North and South* 5, no. 1 (2001): 72–73.

Rhea, Gordon C. "'The Hottest Place I Was Ever In': The Battle of Haw's Shop, May 28, 1864." *North and South* 4, no. 4 (2001): 42–57.

Stauffer, Michael. "Volunteer or Uniformed Companies in the Antebellum Militia: A Checklist of Identified Companies, 1790–1859." *South Carolina Historical Magazine* 88 (April 1987): 108–16.

INDEX